**University of Hertfordshire**

D1614477

College Lane, Hatfield, Herts. AL10 9/

Learning and Information Services
de Havilland Campus Learning Resources Centre, Hatfield

For renewal of Standard and One Week Loans,
please visit the web site **http://www.voyager.herts.ac.uk**

This item must be returned or the loan renewed by the due date.
The University reserves the right to recall items from loan at any time.
A fine will be charged for the late return of items.

Excess Cash Flow

Excess Cash Flow

A Signal for Institutional and Corporate Governance

Rahul Dhumale

First published 2003 by
PALGRAVE MACMILLAN
Houndmills, Basingstoke, Hampshire RG21 6XS and
175 Fifth Avenue, New York, N.Y. 10010
Companies and representatives throughout the world.

PALGRAVE MACMILLAN is the global academic imprint of the Palgrave Macmillan division of St Martin's Press, LLC and of Palgrave Macmillan Ltd. Macmillan® is a registered trademark in the United States, United Kingdom and other countries. Palgrave is a registered trademark in the European Union and other countries.

ISBN 1–4039–0039–6

This book is printed on paper suitable for recycling and made from fully managed and sustained forest sources.

A catalogue record for this book is available from the British Library.

Library of Congress Cataloging-in-Publication Data

Dhumale, Rahul.
  Excess cash flow: a signal for institutional and corporate governance / by Rahul Dhumale
    p. cm.
Includes bibliographical references and index.
ISBN 1–4039–0039–6 (cloth)
  1. Corporations – India – Finance. 2. Cash flow – India. 3. Cash management – India. 4. Corporations – Finance. 5. Cash flow. 6. Cash management. I. Title.
HG4241 .D48 2002
658.15'244–dc21   2002072116

10 9 8 7 6 5 4 3 2 1
12 11 10 09 08 07 06 05 04 03

Printed and bound in Great Britain by
Antony Rowe Ltd, Chippenham and Eastbourne

To Ana

Contents

List of Tables

List of Figures

Acknowledgements

This book has benefited from comments, assistance and insights from many people who have helped in one way or another. I would like to begin by thanking Ajit Singh for discussing many of the ideas developed in this study. Our 'talks' have been a constant source of inspiration to me. I thank him most of all for being a great listener and friend during the past few years. I would also like to thank Alister McFarquhar and Robert Cassen who encouraged me to undertake this study from the start. I am equally grateful for the continuous support I received from my colleagues while working in Washington, DC, including Judith Brandsma, Nemat Shafik (World Bank) and Susan Fennell (International Monetary Fund).

Special thanks are due to Boyle, Achilles, P, Gere, Daphne, Brenty, the 'Tailors', Tom, Ms Slattery, Noha, Bryan, Craig, Al, and Tony, whose support throughout this study have meant a lot to me. I would also like thank all of my family and friends who believed in me throughout the years. Their encouragement has and always will be very important to me. Lastly, I would like to thank the Policy and Analysis Group at the Federal Reserve Bank of New York for encouraging me to complete this book.

The views expressed in this book are entirely those of the author and should not be attributed in any manner to the Federal Reserve Bank of New York or the Federal Reserve System.

Every effort has been made to contact all copyright-holder for material used in this book, but if any have been inadvertently omitted the publishers will be pleased to make the necessary arrangement at the first opportunity.

RAHUL DHUMALE

1
Introduction

1.1 Introduction

Economic studies which examine the financing patterns of firms, especially in emerging economies, seldom consider the market environment in which they operate. The most recent Asian financial crisis and its exposure of institutional failures in the context of financial sector liberalisation shows that these market conditions are vital. At a microeconomic level, free market economies function through institutions and corporate governance mechanisms including but not limited to well-defined bankruptcy procedures, disclosure norms, an effective market for corporate control, etc. – all of which reduce information imperfections and facilitate transparency and accountability. When these institutional conditions fail, market problems arise including adverse selection and moral hazard behaviour. Furthermore, the lack of a sound institutional and legal framework compounds these problems, with important implications for the corporate governance structures of firms. An examination of the financing choices of these firms can help to reveal the source of some of these institutional failures.

In trying to decipher the effects of the institutional environment on a firm's financing choices, it might be useful to briefly consider some of the existing research on both corporate financing patterns and the importance of the institutional environment. In a path-breaking paper more than forty years ago, Modigliani and Miller illustrated that in a perfect market with zero taxes and no transaction costs, a firm's value depends solely on the level of risk and its future cash flows and not on its choice of financing (Modigliani and Miller, 1958). Since the publication of this seminal article, a vast theoretical literature has emerged to identify the conditions under which this irrelevance hypothesis does not hold. Harris and Raviv surveyed the theoretical literature that explains differences in observed capital structures in developed economies (Harris and Raviv, 1990). However, empirical evidence on the determinants of a firm's capital structure remains scarce. Some of the more important empirical work in this area for US firms includes Titman and Wessels (1988), Smith and Watts (1992), McConell and Servaes (1995), Lang, Otek and Stultz (1996). Another approach to capital structure choices by firms was developed by Myers and Majluf who postulated the so-called 'pecking order' hypothesis (Myers and Majluf, 1984). In their work, Myers and Majluf hypothesise that firms face a hierarchy in choosing their sources of funds so that they first draw from their internal resources and only then turn to external funds. Here again, they first prefer to raise money through debt and then issue equity as a last resort. As for the institutional and legal approach, La Porta *et al.* show how legal traditions and specific creditors and minority shareholders' rights shape the access to external finance and the corporate ownership structures around the world (La Porta *et al.*, 1998). Rajan and Zingales document cross-country regularities in the correlation between corporate financial structures and various firms' characteristics (Rajan and Zingales, 1995). Demirguc-Kunt and Maksimovic explore the impact of stock market development on firms' leverage (Demirguc-Kunt and Maksimovic, 1999). They find that how much the firm can grow by relying on external finance does depend on the legal environment. Rajan and Zingales and Carlin and Mayer disentangle the financial, legal, and technological factors that determine firms' access to external finance (Rajan and Zingales, 1998; Carlin and Mayer, 1999). Others highlight the impact of particular institutional arrangements on firms' external financing possibilities (see, for instance, Hoshi, Kashyap and Scharfstein, 1990). Evidence showing how informational asymmetries affect the choice of security when seeking external finance is presented in Barclay and Smith (1995), Stoh and Mauer (1996), Myers and Majluf (1984), Rajan (1992), Petersen and Rajan (1994), Diamond (1991), Jensen and Meckling (1976), Myers (1977). Overall, the existing literature for developed economies certainly suggests that the institutional environment has some role in determining the capital structures of firms.

Mayer's seminal investigation of corporate financing patterns in developed markets including the US, UK, Japan, Germany, France, Italy, Canada and Finland between 1970 and 1985 is mainly concerned with the long-standing view that there is a fundamental difference between the financial systems of the Anglo-Saxon countries and those of Japan and Germany, reflecting the contrast between market-based and bank-based systems (Mayer, 1988, 1990). The main findings of Mayer suggested that firms in developed countries depend more on internal sources of finance and have minimal dependence on equity. Specifically, their study revealed the following: (a) corporations do not raise a substantial amount of finance from the stock market in any one country; (b) banks are the dominant source of external finance in all countries except Japan, France and Italy; (c) retention is the dominant source of finance in all countries; (d) internal finance is more important in the Anglo-Saxon countries than in Japan, France and Italy.

With regard to developing countries – including India – Singh and Hamid conducted one of the first studies which examined the capital structure of large firms in nine countries using the 100 largest manufacturing firms listed on stock exchanges (Singh and Hamid, 1992). It is interesting to note that India, after the US, has the second largest number of listed firms on its stock exchanges but is much smaller in market capitalisation. Given these characteristics, several interesting issues can be raised regarding the sources and uses of investment funds within the Indian market. In fact, Singh and Hamid, in their cross-country analysis, revealed that external sources in general, and equity in particular, were much more important in developing than in developed countries. These results were surprising not only because they were unexpected, but also because they suggested a 'reverse pecking order' for developing countries (Bhaduri, 1999). However, more recent studies which focus on the Indian corporate sector have not been able to confirm Singh and Hamid's results, for several reasons. Cherian indicates that Singh and Hamid's findings of a 'reverse pecking order' are mostly the result of their definition of internal finance; Singh and Hamid exclude depreciation as an internal source of finance (Cherian, 1996). He also finds that internal sources of finance play a less important role for Indian than for US firms. Cobham and Subramaniam also disagree with Singh and Hamid and found internal sources to be relatively important – more important for larger than for smaller firms (Cobham and Subramaniam, 1995). Studies also indicate that debt plays a much bigger role in India. Therefore, given this mixed empirical evidence, the existence of the 'pecking order' in India remains controversial and unresolved at best.

The two main sources of information on corporate finance in different countries are, first, the national flow-of-funds statements which record capital flow between different sectors of the economy and between domestic and overseas residents, and second, company accounts which are constructed on an individual firm basis but are often aggregated to an industry or economy level (Mayer, 1988). The flow-of-funds statistics record transactions between sectors; however, company accounts, not always available, are more reliable. In particular, flow-of-funds statistics often constructed from a variety of different sources are rarely consistent.[1] This study is based on individual firm accounts with analyses conducted by examining changes in balance sheets over time. The balance sheet approach assumes the firm's sources of funds flow from decreases in assets and increases in liabilities while the uses of funds increase assets and decrease liabilities. Internal finance is measured here – similar to Cherian (1996) – as reserves, surplus (retained earnings) plus depreciation. Other approaches compare internal finance as retained earnings net of depreciation with net capital expenditures (Prais, 1976). The Prais approach may be useful to study the financing of growth of a firm in terms of net capital expenditures, but this study concentrates on the broader issue of all sources and uses of funds for the firm and therefore depreciation is treated as a source of funds for the firm.

1.2   India's capital markets

Countries differ widely in their relative reliance on bank vs. market finance. Germany and Japan, for instance, are regarded as bank based since their volume of bank lending relative to the stock market is rather large. At the same time, the United States and the United Kingdom are considered to be more market based. Recent studies have measured the relative importance of bank vs. market finance by the relative size of stock aggregates, by relative trading or transaction volumes, and by indicators of relative efficiency. Developing countries are shown to have less developed banks and stock markets in general. The financial sector – banks, other financial intermediaries, and stock markets – becomes larger, more active and more efficient, as countries become richer. Given these basic characteristics, in developing countries like India, financial systems tend to be more bank based.[2] To some extent this may be the result of the common perception that agency costs and information problems are lower in bank than stock market oriented systems. However, in considering some differences between bank vs. market based systems especially as they apply to a market like India, it is equally as important to note that information is significantly more imperfect in developing countries in both quantity and availability. Specifically, accounting and auditing procedures are less comprehensive and rigorous and there is less pressure from regulatory authorities and the press for the disclosure of information. In India, market capitalisation and market turnover are relatively low so that capital markets benefit less greatly from any economies of scale which might exist. Spreads between bid and ask prices are typically higher and liquidity is low with a large amount of 'noise' in price movements. These factors suggest that stock market finance is a relatively expensive source of finance for Indian firms and that the stock market may not be an efficient mechanism for the allocation of capital between firms.

India is a bank oriented system similar to the universal banks in Germany and the main bank system in Japan. In the late 1960s, India devised three types of lead banks for raising the rate of financial savings, allocating financial resources to the most productive uses, and improving the investment and productive efficiency of public enterprises. The three types of banks were: (a) lead development banks for investment financing; (b) lead commercial banks for working capital finance; (c) commercial and cooperative banks in districts for providing bank finance to small enterprises.[3] Commercial banks and cooperative banks generally cater to the working capital needs of the corporate sector. Since 1992–3, commercial banks have diversified into several new areas of business like merchant banking, mutual funds, leasing, venture capital, and other financial services. Commercial and cooperative banks hold around two-thirds of total assets of the Indian banks and other financial institutions taken together. Medium and long-term finance is provided in part by development financial institutions (DFIs), investment institutions like Life Insurance Corporation (LIC) and General Insurance Corporation (GIC) mutual funds, and state-level financial institutions. In addition there are around 12,500 non-banking financial companies in the private sector which cater to the financing needs of the corporate sector. Stock exchanges also serve as an important source of funds for the corporate sector.

However, the lead development bank system in India has not succeeded in promoting the efficient mobilisation and allocation of capital as a result of deficiencies in project appraisal, monitoring and supervision, and mechanisms which anticipate problems. One of the main reasons for the lack of adequate monitoring has been the failure of the lead development banks to coordinate efficiently with commercial banks which usually provide capital finance. Similarly, the lead commercial bank system has not fulfilled its objectives due to the lack of an institutional framework for coordinating decisions among banks leading to the classic free rider problem which affects the monitoring of borrowers' activities. The institutional framework in India has been significantly different from that of Japan and Germany, making the lead bank system very different, to a point where commercial banks in India may hold significant equity stakes in firms. Also, term finance provided by these banks can be converted to equity, further exacerbating the asymmetric information problem.

1.3 Overview of Indian financial sector reforms

In mid-1991, India responded to a foreign exchange crisis with a gradualist structural liberalisation programme. A sharp increase in India's import bill and declining wages associated with the Gulf war in 1990 and 1991 precipitated an external crisis. International reserves fell to the cost of two weeks of imports. It was clear that India would have to change fundamental aspects of its economic system to achieve long-term growth without unnecessary balance of payments or inflationary pressures. The programme included a gradual reform of trade, industrial, and financial policies. Financial sector reform was the core of the liberalisation process. During the 1980s, India's financial system had been subject to pervasive government control, regulation, and direct intervention. Its economy had become decapitalised, repressed, segmented, and technologically backward. With the liberalisation programme, the government and the Reserve Bank of India embarked on a programme of gradual but steady changes involving monetary and credit control instruments, commercial banking, money and government securities markets, capital markets, and foreign exchange rules. They replaced most of the controls and the long-standing market interventions with prudential regulation and recapitalised financial institutions. An overriding objective was the gradual transition from direct to indirect market-based forms of monetary control.

In the 1980s, the government began to allow public enterprises to borrow directly in overseas financial markets. The authorities also began to permit firms to authorise selectively and restrictively private firms to carry out corporate issues through global depository receipts (GDRs) and foreign currency convertible bonds (FCCBs). During the period 1991–2 to 1996–7 funds collected by such means amounted to $6.2 billion. At the start of the reforms, capital began to flow slowly into India through such instruments, and Indian firms even introduced Euro-issues. However, more significant changes came in 1992 and 1993 when the government allowed Foreign Institutional Investors

(FIIs) to enter Indian equity markets. The net cumulative investment made by the foreign institutional investors (FIIs) in the Indian stock markets between 1993 and 1997 amounted to \$7.1 billion (RBI, Report on Currency and Finance 1998–99). The government also issued comprehensive guidelines to Indian firms for access to international capital markets through equity and equity related GDRs and FCCBs. This removed some of the intense bureaucratic restrictions. Authorities also relaxed restrictions on foreign direct investment and licensing requirements allowing India to benefit from globalised capital markets.[4]

The authorities were also determined to modernise India's capital markets which they believed already possessed a relatively well-developed institutional framework. Stock markets existed in India well before Independence in 1947 – the Mumbai Stock Exchange dates to 1875 – and by the late 1980s there were about twenty other stock exchanges in other Indian cities.

As Table 1.1 indicates, through the years thousands of companies have been listed and market capitalisation has been relatively high. Share ownership was widespread and had been effectively widened further through the various mutual funds operated by the government-owned Unit Trust of India. Prior to the reforms, the underlying problem was that the effectiveness and the efficiency of the capital markets had been limited by excessive regulation and intervention. A Controller of Capital Issues regulated initial share offerings, even fixing the prices at which they took place. Moreover, other foreign exchange, securities, and stock exchange laws and regulations sharply restricted foreign participation in the capital markets. Although the Mumbai and other stock exchanges based their practices on British markets, many years of isolation, limited growth, and a lack of quality control left the Indian market behind its immediate competitors. In the late 1980s, the authorities realised that it was essential to transform India's capital markets by developing and adopting modern regulatory and enforcement systems to guarantee that financial market operations took place on a fair and transparent basis. After the crisis of 1991, the pace of reforms within capital markets quickened and included the abolishment of the Controller of Capital Issues. The Securities and Exchange Board of India (SEBI),which had been established in 1988, was given the authority to oversee India's capital markets. Given the long-standing history of India's stock exchanges, many of the reforms introduced by the SEBI to modernise the function of the stock markets often met resistance; however, in recent years, the SEBI's capabilities have become increasingly credible and effective.

Table 1.1   Mumbai stock exchange indicators

Indicator	1988	1991	1992	1993	1995	1996	1997
Number of listed companies	2240	2556	2781	3263	5398	5999	5843
Market capitalisation/GDP (%)	8.6	36.2	39	50.3	45.4	50.2	52.6
Turnover ratio (%)	59.5	59.2	37	27.5	10.5	17	42

Source: International Finance Corporation, Mumbai Stock Exchange, Reserve Bank of India.
Note: All figures correspond to the financial year ending March 31.

1.4   Inflows into India's capital markets

The new guidelines governing India's capital markets attracted significant capital into India's equity markets especially from foreign investors. In early 1993, the inflow surge began and India ran an extraordinarily large capital account surplus. Risk capital flows increased from $92 million in 1990s to $3.65 billion in 1992/93 and $4.8 billion in 1997/98. Moreover, the easing of restrictions on foreign investment allowed the number of FIIs to increase from 1 in 1989 to 752 in 1997, as indicated in Table 1.2.

Risk capital found India particularly attractive during the post-reform period. Stabilisation had been achieved and there had been clear progress with the reform programme. Since India's financial markets had been closed for so long, they were particularly attractive to financial newcomers. These foreign observers reasoned it prudent to penetrate a market as large as India's. International fund managers viewed India's stock exchanges as a source of diversification.

The FIIs used the local foreign exchange markets to convert funds into local currency to purchase equities. India's equities markets responded vigorously to the significant inflow of funds. The availability of funds in the stock markets meant that firms could issue equity and even debentures, including convertible bonds, on relatively

Table 1.2   Foreign investment inflows (US$ million)

Category	1989/90	1992/93	1994/95	1997/98
FIIs	1	1665	1746	752
GDRs	86	1602	1839	3842
Offshore funds and others	5	382	239	204
Total	92	3649	3824	4798

Source: Reserve Bank of India.

favourable terms. Some large public offerings during this period included the large publicly owned State Bank of India, which accounts for more than 25% of India's commercial bank assets, and the Industrial Development Bank of India. India's stock markets found themselves undergoing significant modernisation during this period of capital inflow. The Mumbai Stock Exchange was overwhelmed by the sharply increased transaction volumes and had to improve and update its back office operations. A national electronic stock market, the National Stock Exchange, was introduced, as was an electronic Over-the-Counter Exchange (OTCEI). In the foreign exchange markets, liquidity improved greatly and the market acquired greater flexibility. The forward market for foreign exchange deepened significantly, allowing operations such as forward cover on capital transactions, foreign currency options, and foreign currency on lending. Indian firms were not only using new methods to finance their investments, but they were also using new techniques to hedge their exposure in foreign currency.

1.5 Purpose of study

Although there is evidence of a positive relationship between investment and internal finance, the analytical basis for the underlying cash flow theory remains unresolved. The dominant view, beginning with Fazzari *et al.*, was that a firm's observed reliance on internal finance for capital expenditures was due mainly to asymmetric information considerations (AIA) with little or no role for the managerial/principal agent approach (MPAA) (Fazzari *et al.*, 1988). The approach of this study marks a fundamental departure from most of the evidence in the literature so far. To date, only Blanchard *et al.*, have found similar results for firms in developed countries which distinguish alternative theories of corporate financing (Blanchard *et al.*, 1994). Their study confirmed at least the existence of the MPAA and questioned the validity of the asymmetric information model for all capital markets.

Little research distinguishes between the MPAA and AIA which underpin the cash flow theory of investment especially for developing countries. Evidence suggests that internal finance is more important for large rather than small firms and firms which produce luxury rather than essential goods in India (Singh and Hamid, 1992; Athey and Laumas, 1994).[5] Existing firms are likely to be bigger than new firms – this supports the case for the MPAA explanation of investment behaviour in the Indian context. Further, Athey and Laumas found internal finance to be more important for firms which produce luxury rather than essential goods. Since it is assumed that R&D expenditures for firms producing luxury goods are likely to be lower than for firms producing essential goods and given that agency costs are likely to be higher as well, this evidence again seems to support the MPAA theory of investment for some firms in India.

The results from this study may influence the efficiency of resource allocation in the economy. Clearly, if the assumptions made by Modigliani and Miller held true, different mixes of internal and external finance would yield similar returns on investment due to their substitutability. However, under the MPAA and the AIA, the return on investment by firms with varying levels of internal and external finance are not equal, so that firms realise different returns with different mixes of internal and external finance. Along these lines, Jensen argues that when firms use external finance, they face constant scrutiny by the capital market – capital market pressure hypothesis – which acts as an efficiency-enhancing device, keeping managerial discretion to a minimum, as illustrated by leveraged buy-outs (Jensen, 1986). Friedman and Laibson study the relationship between return on investment and the capital mix of firms (Friedman and Laibson, 1989). The evidence from their regressions supports the predictions of the cash flow theories in that firms more dependent on external finance attain higher rates of return on investments than firms more dependent on internal finance. This supports the 'capital market pressure' hypothesis and implies that the overall resource allocation process is likely to be at least partly efficient. In a country like India, this suggests that even though the stock market – with its inherent ability to reflect the aforementioned capital market pressure through share price – plays a limited role as a source of finance, policy initiatives to reform the financial sector and develop capital markets can enhance the overall efficiency of the resource use in the economy.

The AIA assumes managers maximise shareholder value, but the MPAA assumes that managers are more interested in objectives like sales maximisation, size of the firm, and perquisites rather than the market value of the firm. Some evidence supports the MPAA rather than the AIA, and it could well be that overinvestment by old, more mature firms could be displacing or 'crowding out' investment by young, dynamic firms at or above the market discount rate. Consequently, the use of resources in the economy implied by the MPAA theory of investment can be considered inefficient from a welfare point of view. This study begins by developing a basic model based on firm characteristics to reveal the best policy for shareholders. The succeeding chapters consider benefits and disadvantages accruing to shareholders in different situations including the level of leveraging, bankruptcy, and mergers and acquisitions. An underlying theme runs throughout each of the these topics – namely, the informational consequences of source of finance choices on shareholder value.

1.6 Plan of study

Chapter 2 introduces and describes the two approaches to the cash flow theories of investment: namely, the managerial/principal agent and the asymmetric information approach. The latter approach suggests that managers maximise shareholder value while the former believes that managers are primarily interested in the growth rate of the firm. These differences remain crucial in this study, for differing behaviour of managers in their approach to internal finance alters firm behaviour. Consequently, the efficient use of resources by firms is often determined by the approach the manager chooses. Evidence suggests – especially in the Indian case – that managers prefer the managerial/principal agent rather than the asymmetric information approach.

Chapter 3 considers the empirical evidence. Earnings retention is often criticised because agency costs permit managerial objectives to diverge from the interests of shareholders. Managers can easily misuse retained earnings for perquisites or other non-value-adding investments; however, retained earnings provide internal finance which can be less costly than external finance. This trade-off between the cost of excess cash, i.e., retained earnings, and the benefits of internal finance is the central focus of this chapter. Jensen's Free Cash Flow Theory (FCFT) model compares the use of these retained earnings against the external finance premium predicted by asymmetric information theories. The Jensen model may apply to a firm with poor investment opportunities whereas a strategy of cash retention could benefit certain firms under given uncertainty. A model explores firm characteristics which affect the choice of best policy for shareholders. A dynamic model version explores the conditions under which earnings re-investment might seem preferable. The objective is to compare both the benefits and costs of investing earnings. The optimal strategy depends on the firm's cost of borrowing which in turn depends on asymmetric information costs. These ultimately follow from the private information held by the firm. The model is tested in varying economic conditions, i.e., recessions and booms.

Chapter 4 examines the relationship between the debt/equity ratio, earnings retention and performance in a large sample of firms. The FCFT suggests that there is a positive relationship between leverage and economic performance in developed markets. It is hypothesised that the relationship is negative for Indian firms because in India government-owned institutions dominate the short and long-term lending markets.

Chapter 5 extends the analysis by considering the role of a firm's capital structure and its probability of bankruptcy. One aim is to see whether retained earnings influence bankruptcy in firms with fewer investment opportunities (i.e., low q vs. high q firms). Bankruptcy theory provides a useful framework by combining the corporate financial structure of a firm, including the relationship between debt and equity, the composition and source of corporate debt, and the structure of share ownership. Leveraging becomes very important as it can shift the balance of bargaining power during bankruptcy. Such imbalances not only exacerbate asymmetric information between debtors, creditors, and equity holders, but they also allow low-quality firms to continue to overinvest.

Chapter 6 examines the informational value of a firm's financial structure. The first part analyses the relationship between bidder, target, and total abnormal returns in different types of firms. If q is used as a measure of firm quality, the results indicate that target, bidder, and total returns are greater if the target is a low-quality firm being taken over by a high-quality firm. Furthermore, the results confirmed Jensen's FCFT by showing the effectiveness of classifying firms into High Free Cash Flow and Low Financial Slack firms. The results demonstrated that low-quality and high-quality firms which do not abide by the FCFT's recommendations for retaining cash suffer from less than average returns. The study also indicates that returns are greater in all firms involved in an acquisition or takeover involving related lines of business. Diversifying through acquisitions into unrelated lines of business yields lower returns. Lastly, this chapter tries to show the benefits of analysing abnormal returns of firms during acquisitive activities through an FCFT approach. The inclusion of firm quality and the type of acquisitive activity in the regressions enhances the results and the explanatory power of the model. In the second part, the *Long Purse* theory of predation is used to show how a firm's financial structure – including its retained earnings – can lead to an inefficient allocation of resources in the economy as a whole. Small and medium-sized firms can easily fall prey to larger counterparts and therefore the chapter concludes by reviewing some of the negative policy implications in encouraging such an active market for corporate control.

2
Internal Finance as a Source of Investment: Managerial/Principal Agent or Asymmetric Information Approach?

2.1 Introduction

Although there is evidence of a strong relationship between investment and internal finance, the reasons behind this relationship remain subject to controversy. So far, the literature has identified at least two approaches to the underlying cash flow theory of investment which influence this relationship: specifically, the managerial/principal agent framework and the asymmetric information approach. A dominant theory in corporate financing patterns for many years has been a firm's preference for internal over external finance to fund investments. Baumol clearly articulated this idea which would be called a 'financing hierarchy' by later researchers, stating:

> [i]t would appear that the bulk of business enterprise should finance its investment insofar as possible entirely out of retained earnings because that is, characteristically, the cheapest way to raise additional funds. Only when it becomes impossible to provide enough money from internal sources should the firm turn to the stock market or to borrowing for resources. (Baumol, 1965)

Although many researchers agree that the information asymmetries which are the root cause of the preference for internal finance have an important impact on investment, there is substantially less agreement about their cause. Thus, there still remains the question of whether information asymmetries between borrowers and lenders lead to firms that face 'financing constraints', where profitable investment projects are not exploited, or whether agency costs lead managers to waste the firm's resources.

Before both the neoclassical theory of investment and the Modigliani–Miller theorems, the dominant explanations of investment decisions of firms were the liquidity theory of investment preceded by the accelerator theory.[1] Significant aspects of the neoclassical theory of investment are based on the Modigliani–Miller theorems. The neoclassical theory assumes that a firm can always obtain necessary funds to undertake investments as long as it provides a return above the cost of capital. Consequently, internal and external finance are viewed as substitutes; firms use external finance to smooth investment when internal finance is scarce. The neoclassical view also implies a complete separation of real and financial decisions faced by the firm. On the contrary, cash flow theories of investment emphasise financing hierarchies faced by the firm and therefore the crucial role of cash flow in determining the capital expenditures. For instance, the asymmetric information approach to investment explicitly considers capital market imperfections which raise the cost of external finance, whereas the managerial/principal agent approach allows managers to use their discretion when considering similar decisions.[2] Thus, cash flow seems irrelevant for all other models of investment including the accelerator, modified neoclassical, and Q models of investment as they say nothing about the source of finance. Based on these differences, it is useful from the outset to distinguish between the managerial/principal agent (MPAA) and asymmetric information approaches (AIA).

2.2 Asymmetric information approach to investment

Asymmetric information intensifies financing constraints. In asymmetric information models, firm managers or insiders are assumed to possess private information about the characteristics of the firm's investment opportunities. According to Myers and Majluf, the theoretical underpinning of this empirical regularity is underinvestment. Financing constraints due to asymmetric information problems in the issuance of equity cause the cash flow investment dependence (Myers and Majluf, 1984). They also showed that, if outside suppliers of capital are less well informed than insiders about the value of the firm's assets, equity may be mispriced by the market. In particular, the market may associate new equity issues with low-quality firms. Due to the information asymmetry in comparison with insiders, providers of capital expect insiders to raise capital when this new capital is overvalued. The implication of this adverse selection is that managers and firms face a premium on external financing. Therefore, firms will initially fund investments from internal sources. In this case, the project will be rejected even if its Net Present Value (NPV) is positive. Thus, asymmetric information results in imperfect substitutability between internal and external finance. However, this resulting underinvestment can be avoided if the firm can finance the new project using a security which is not so severely undervalued by the market. For example, internal funds and/or riskless debt involve no undervaluation, and therefore will be preferred to equity. Myers refers to this as a 'pecking order' theory of financing, i.e., that capital structure will be driven by firms' desire to finance new investments, first internally, then with low-risk debt, and lastly with equity only as a last resort (Myers, 1984).

Asymmetric information in debt financing may increase the cost of new debt or even restrict firms from borrowing due to credit rationing (Stiglitz and Weiss, 1981; Greenwald, Stiglitz and Weiss, 1984). The reason is that lenders do not know how the money they lend is being invested. For instance, increasing the interest rate may induce firms with valuable projects to drop out (adverse selection). Thus asymmetric information may hinder firms with growth opportunities. Firms then only invest when internally generated funds are available stemming from equilibrium credit rationing by providers of external funds. This results in a positive dependence between cash flow and investment. In fact, this positive relationship is also seen as evidence of liquidity constraints faced by firms. Consequently, external finance and internal finance are not perfect substitutes for the firm as assumed by Modigliani–Miller and the neoclassical theory of investment. In a world of heterogeneous firms, finance constraints influence the investment decisions of firms. In particular, investment may depend on financial factors such as the availability of internal finance, access to new debt or equity finance, liquidity, or the functioning of particular credit markets.

Firm heterogeneity can be explored further by classifying firms on the basis of earnings retention practices reflecting capital market constraints due to informational problems (Fazzari *et al.*, 1988). External funds should constrain investment if and only if the firm has to pay a premium for new debt or equity finance. Fazzari *et al.* indicate a substantially greater sensitivity of investment to cash flows in firms which retain nearly all of their income (Fazzari *et al.*, 1988). This statistical and economic difference was also found to be significant while using several models and estimation techniques. Banks may reduce the impact of asymmetric information in debt markets. Diamond and Fama, among others, argue that banks enjoy an advantage in producing private information about firms. Therefore, banks reduce the agency costs of debt and may insure borrowers against credit rationing (Fama, 1985; Diamond, 1991; Dellariccia and Marquez, 2000). This should relax the cash flow constraint. Bank–firm relationships, however, may also impose costs. Rajan shows that the production of private information gives the bank bargaining power over the firm's profits. This may increase the dependence of investment on internal funds (Rajan, 1992). Hoshi *et al.* (1990) utilised a similar procedure by dividing a sample of Japanese firms into two groups according to whether the firm had a close institutional relationship with a bank or not. The authors believed that liquidity constraints arising from asymmetric information may be less important where the bank maintains a close relationship with the firm. They found that the q ratio – the ratio of market value of the firm to the replacement cost of capital – was more significant and cash flow less significant for the firms which were closely related to the banks.

It is important to point out that this evidence is also consistent with the predictions of the managerial/principal agent theory. Firms which maintain a close relationship with banks are likely to face lower agency costs because of closer monitoring by banks. In these firms with low agency costs, net cash flow is likely to be less significant; in other words, reliance on internal finance is likely to be less in firms with close relationships with banks. Therefore, the finding that cash flow is less significant in firms with a close relationship with banks is consistent with the asymmetric information as well as managerial/principal agent approaches to investment.

2.3   Managerial/principal agent theory of investment

The MPAA inherently assumes maximisation by the firm of objectives such as sales, staff, emoluments, market share, etc., rather than profits . In some sense, the MPAA theory of investment constitutes two different ideas – managerial capitalism and agency theory.[3] The recognition of the divergence of the incentives of managers and the owners of a public corporation dates back at least to Berle and Means (Berle and Means, 1932). Donaldson suggests that managers prefer internal funds because 'internal financing is the line of least resistance' and 'are funds over which management has complete control'. Using internal finance 'avoids the glare of publicity ... which accompanies the decisions and actions of management if [investment is] externally financed' (Donaldson, 1961). Jensen and Meckling show that incomplete monitoring provides managers with incentives to expand the scale of the firm faster than optimal (Jensen and Meckling, 1976).

Managers would not overinvest if they were monitored perfectly, or if their interests were perfectly aligned with shareholders' interests. Corporate governance therefore is critical for the managerial discretion problem. Under the MPAA firms aim for greater output and faster growth than is consistent with maximising the current stock market value of the firm, assumed here as a proxy for shareholder value. The ability of managerial discretion to maximise factors other than profits depends upon a minimum constraint imposed by the capital market or upon sustaining a market value high enough to forestall a disciplinary takeover bid in the market for corporate control. In the MPAA theory of the firm, the fundamental determinant of investment is the availability of internal finance. Managers are seen to push investment to a point where its marginal rate of return does not coincide with maximum shareholder, welfare resulting in overinvestment. Consequently, internal finance is preferred as the most accessible capital rather than external finance which subjects managers to the discipline of the external capital market. Therefore, under MPAA – unlike neoclassical theory where what matters is only the cost and not the source of capital – cash flow becomes relevant for the firm's investment decisions.

Several specific corporate governance mechanisms like the board of directors, market for corporate control, and large shareholders are expected to align the interests of mangers to those of shareholders. Managers who can be replaced by the board, through hostile takeovers, or by pressure from large outside shareholders, should protect shareholder concerns. In some firms, however, these control mechanisms may be ineffective. If insider shareholdings align the interests of managers with those of other shareholders, then insiders should internalise more of the financial consequences of their overinvestment decisions (Jensen and Meckling, 1976). Managerial entrenchment resulting from high insider stakes, however, implies that the relation between managers' interest and shareholders is non-monotonic, so that at higher levels of insider shareholdings managerial entrenchment outweighs incentive effects and increases the cash flow investment sensitivity (Morck, Shleifer and Vishny, 1988; Hadlock, 1998). Furthermore, Grossman and Hart point out that if bankruptcy is costly for managers because they lose control or reputation, then debt can create an incentive for managers to work harder, consume fewer perquisites and make better investment decisions, because this behaviour reduces the probability of bankruptcy (Grossman and Hart, 1982).

2.4   Managerial/principal agent vs. asymmetric information: some empirical facts

Under the MPAA, a financing hierarchy exists because managers utilise internal funds at their discretion and thus implicitly face a low opportunity cost. The central issue in the MPAA theory of investment is the prevalence of managerial discretion; internal finance is important for investment decisions precisely because of this since managers are averse to the dictates of the external capital market. However, under the asymmetric information approaches (AIA), a financing hierarchy exists because of incomplete information between managers and suppliers of external finance. As discussed earlier, Myers and Majluf show that firms are faced with a capital market which pays less for new equity than its true value since the market cannot fully learn the expected return on the firm's investment. Furthermore, the AIA to investment emphasises the role of asymmetries in information and essentially views managerial discretion as an aspect of asymmetric information; internal finance is important for investment because of the prevalence of asymmetric information. The unifying factor between the two approaches is the separation of ownership and control which generates asymmetries in the AIA and engenders discretionary managerial behaviour in the MPAA.[4]

For present purposes, it is important to distinguish between the AIA and MPAA at the firm level. Beginning with Fazzari *et al.*, most empirical work in this area identified asymmetries of information as the principal force behind the observed positive relationship between internal finance and investment. However, this study distinguishes itself from previous work by also identifying managerial considerations as equally important drivers of the cash flow theory of investment. Thus, throughout this study an attempt is made to differentiate between the two approaches on the basis of observed firm characteristics. To date, there have been similar studies (see below) which use firm characteristics to classify firms as either following the MPAA or the AIA. However, this study tries to build on these former analyses by not only further exploring specific firm characteristics which can help to distinguish between MPAA and AIA but also by considering the implications each approach has on firm behaviour under different corporate scenarios.

Several studies have considered different firm characteristics including age, size, dividend payout behaviour, exchange listing, R&D expenditures, bank relationships, stock trades by insiders, etc. to see whether firms follow the MPAA or the AIA. To begin, Fazzari, Hubbard and

Petersen divide a sample of US firms into subsamples based on the dividend payout behaviour (Fazzari, Hubbard and Petersen, 1988). Dividends are assumed to relate to financial constraints. The hypothesis under the MPAA is that managers are primarily interested in maximising the growth of the firm rather than shareholder value and would invest without considering the cost of capital. Grabowski and Mueller show that this is especially true for internal finance since the scope for managerial discretion is maximum (Grabowski and Mueller, 1972). Reliance on internal finance also helps managers to build *financial slack* and escape capital market constraints.[5] One way to maximise internal finance is by distributing as small a dividend as possible. In other words, MPAA also predicts that firms with low dividend ratios are likely to be more dependent on internal finance and less dependent on external finance. Likewise, the agency cost explanation for dividends suggested by Rozeff and Easterbrook predicts a negative relationship between dividend practices and internal finance (Rozeff, 1982 and Easterbrook, 1984). In their view, high dividends lower agency costs by minimising the amount of excess discretionary cash flow available to the managers; low dividends increase the agency costs associated with excess cash flow. Under the AIA, dividend payout ratios are one way to identify firms which are likely to face relatively high costs of external finance. The results of Fazzari *et al.* show that the impact of cash flow on investment is larger for firms with low dividends. If the cost disadvantage is only slight, then divided payout ratios should reveal little about financing practice. Therefore, firms which pay out the least dividends are the ones that are likely to face the greatest information problems and liquidity constraints and so are likely to be more dependent on internal finance and less dependent on external finance.

Oliner and Rudebusch use the cash flow coefficient in an investment regression model with proxies for information asymmetry (firm age, listing at exchange, and stock trades by insiders), agency costs (insider shareholdings and ownership concentration) and transaction costs (firm size) (Oliner and Rudebusch, 1993). The authors also include the dividend yield for comparison with Fazzari, Hubbard and Petersen (1988). Exchange listing shows whether a firm's common shares are traded over the counter (OTC) or on other stock exchanges. The authors use the exchange as a proxy for maturity (Oliner and Rudebusch, 1993). When firms go public, stock is issued over the counter (OTC) as they usually cannot meet the listing requirements of the major exchanges. The AIA suggests that OTC firms are more likely to face greater asymmetries of information between managers and external suppliers of finance. Consequently, OTC firms should be more dependent on internal than on external finance. Research finds that OTC firms experience more asymmetric information than Fortune 500 firms because they are smaller, have more value in intangible assets, and receive less attention from investment analysts (Chari and Jaganathan, 1988, Howe, 1990). For Canadian firms, Chirinko and Schaller define subsamples based on age (years of inclusion in a financial database), concentration of ownership, industry (manufacturing and other), and group or independent (Chirinko and Schaller, 1995). The cash flow constraints are most relevant for young firms, firms with dispersed ownership, independent firms and manufacturers. The MPAA suggests that OTC firms are more likely to be younger, smaller, and fast growing so agency costs are likely to be lower compared with non-OTC firms. Consequently, OTC firms should be less dependent on internal finance and more dependent on external finance (Mueller, 1972). Mueller uses the life-cycle theory of the firm to show that young dynamic firms with attractive investment opportunities are more likely to use external finance, while older, more mature firms with limited growth opportunities are largely dependent on internal finance. Again, these positions can be reversed for the case of non-OTC firms.

Expenditures on R&D is another type of investment which raises several issues between the MPAA and AIA. Himmelberg and Petersen's study of R&D spending of small firms in high-tech industries indicates that cash flow is an extremely important source of their financing probably because of liquidity constraints created by asymmetric information (Himmelberg and Petersen, 1994). One explanation, however, as Vogt suggests, is that the intangible nature of R&D spending makes it difficult to monitor, which raises the potential for overinvestment under the MPAA when cash flow is available. Jensen presents evidence that this may be the case for the largest firms in the US while Chauvin and Hirschey find that R&D spending creates large and positive increases in market value (Jensen, 1993; Chauvin and Hirschey, 1993; Vogt, 1994). The AIA suggests that asymmetries of information between insiders and outsiders are likely to be the greatest in the case of firms with high R&D expenditures. These firms should therefore be most dependent on internal finance and least dependent on external finance. Arrow argues that moral hazard problems hinder the external financing of highly risky business activities involving innovation (Arrow, 1962). More recently, Stiglitz and Weiss and Myers and Majluf developed formal models of moral hazard and adverse selection in the context of external finance, i.e., debt and equity, which is especially relevant for R&D investments (Stiglitz and Weiss, 1981; Myers and Majluf, 1984). The MPAA suggests that conflicts between shareholders and managers are likely to be fewer in technologically progressive, dynamic firms with high R&D to sales ratio and attractive growth opportunities (Mueller, 1972). These firms should be less dependent on internal finance and more dependent on external finance.

Other relevant contributions have included Hoshi, Kashyap and Scharfstein, and Hadlock (Hoshi, Kashyap and Scharfstein, 1991; Hadlock, 1998). Hoshi, Kashyap and Scharfstein investigate the cash flow sensitivities for a sample of Japanese firms, which is divided into group and non-group firms. The latter ones, characterised by relatively weak ties with banks, have a higher cash flow coefficient. Hadlock studies the impact of insider ownership on the cash flow sensitivity of investment based on both MPAA and AI problems (Hadlock, 1998). Hadlock concludes that his findings are inconsistent with the MPAA and consistent with AIA problems. Finally, research based on size shows that under the MPAA, cash flow investment sensitivity is highest in the sample of large firms, whereas the opposite holds true under the AIA. Gertler argues that information-based financial constraints are likely to have a greater impact on small firms than large firms partly because large firms tend to be mature and have more credible relations with providers of finance (Gertler, 1988). The AIA therefore hypothesises that small firms are likely to be more dependent on internal finance and less dependent on external finance. However, under the MPAA, the ownership of small firms is likely to be more concentrated, with managers holding significant blocks of shares which could mitigate agency problems and align shareholder and managerial incentives better. Therefore, MPAA implies that small firms are likely to be less dependent on internal finance and more dependent on external finance.

2.5 Further issues

In principle, the Indian system had hoped to stem agency costs and information problems by relying on a bank oriented system, and indeed it switched to a more bank oriented system in the 1960s. However, the actual mechanisms or the lack thereof which monitor and coordinate the operations of capital markets have led to an inefficient allocation of capital from a welfare point of view. In many cases, firms had to rely on internal sources of finance when the external sources, i.e., banks and the stock market, have not been able to meet their needs. The remainder of this study will consider the behaviour of these firms and whether the interests of the owners of these firms, i.e., the shareholders, always took precedence during financing and investment decisions. At a firm level, it is interesting to note a general trend in dividend yield and stock prices for Indian firms overall. Figure 2.1 shows a general rise in stock prices with a simultaneous decline in dividend yields of listed firms on the Mumbai Stock Exchange between 1987 and 1993: i.e., 1987 – 4% dividend yield; 1993 – 1% dividend yield. One interpretation of the evidence from this period suggests that investors were willing to forgo dividend payments in return for future possible capital gains. Perhaps this is a result of the substantial liberalisation programme undertaken by the Indian government in 1991 which has provided firms with greater freedom to investigate more investment opportunities.

That shareholders allow firms to retain greater cash suggests lower agency costs; shareholders trust managers to not abuse excess cash flows. Given this new condition, it is even more important to analyse the use or misuse of excess cash flows in Indian firms.

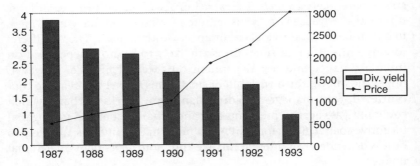

Source: Based on data from IFC EMDB
Figure 2.1   Dividend yield vs. stock price in India, 1987–93

3
Cash Retention Strategies: Test of Free Cash Flow Theory

3.1 Introduction

This chapter examines financing decisions by firms listed on the Mumbai Stock Exchange. A study by Singh and Hamid of stock market data for the top 100 manufacturing firms in several industrialising countries showed how these firms use internal and external resources to finance investment (Singh and Hamid, 1992). They concluded that variations in corporate financing in developing countries have some common characteristics. They show that although firms in these countries maintain significant retention ratios, they quite often use external funds and shares to finance their investment. This differs from the more commonly accepted *pecking order* pattern of finance in most industrialised countries where profits and debt are more commonly used than equity as a source of capital. Singh and Hamid focus on large indigenous firms, but many collaborative ventures involving multinationals and smaller local firms also use similar financing measures as evident by their presence in emerging equity markets. Cherian (1996), Cobham and Subramaniam (1995), and Bhaduri (1999) are sceptical of the evidence regarding the level dependence on external finance as presented by Singh and Hamid. This chapter tries to extend this work by considering one of the basic determinants underlying the choice between internal and external finance: cash retention policy.

When firms disburse cash and use equity markets and external resources to finance their investment, there can be no single optimal solution for selecting appropriate financing options for all firms given firm heterogeneity. This chapter considers the benefits and disadvantages of earnings retention within the context of the imperfect capital market in which they operate. Furthermore, varying macroeconomic conditions, i.e., recessions and booms, at their most extreme levels will be used to test the viability of this approach.

3.2 Purpose

A dynamic model explores the conditions for a dominant strategy of earnings retention using different views regarding excess cash flow. An optimal earnings strategy, balancing the benefits and costs of retained earnings, is one of the goals. Section 3.1 to 3.6 present the case for the Free Cash Flow Theory (FCFT) (Jensen, 1986), the consequences of imperfect capital markets (Fazzari, Hubbard and Petersen, 1988; Bernanke and Gertler 1990), and the financial accelerator (Bernanke, Gertler and Gilchrist, 1993). It will be emphasised that the appropriate use of excess cash should vary according to individual characteristics given firm heterogeneity. A further hypothesis that optimal earnings strategies are more important in firms with higher asymmetric information costs is analysed with the understanding that asymmetric information costs are greater for firms with private information. Small, high Tobin's q firms should retain earnings; moreover, the economic cycle, i.e., boom or recession, should influence the level of investment.

In sections 3.7 and 3.8 a model of earnings strategies which examines a sample of firms determines how cash flow influences their investment decisions. The model will attempt to capture the essential tradeoff between the two extreme cash strategies: earnings disbursement and earnings retention. Instances where a high external finance premium makes an earnings retention strategy superior to a earnings disbursement strategy will be demonstrated. Since the model is highly stylised, the chapter turns to an empirical investigation of investment and earnings retention, using a select sample of public firms listed on the Mumbai Stock Exchange. It finds that firms do not follow either extreme strategy as hypothesised, but rather they follow a mix of both strategies. To test for dynamic treatment of excess cash flow, tests will be conducted during times of monetary contraction to see how individual firms behaved and how their treatment of cash flow and dividend policies changed. A formula for calculating the optimal earnings retention level for firms will be devised.

When firms raise capital in the equity market, the object is greater future cash flow for shareholders. When this cash flow is not paid out as dividends, it is retained by firm managers for further investment. In a world without asymmetric information, shareholders would trust managers. With asymmetric information the abuse of earnings by firm managers is possible. So, dividend policy plays a crucial role as a signal which might alleviate some asymmetric information costs. The interpretation or even misinterpretation of this signal – good, bad, no effect – in India is addressed below.

3.3 Theories on excess cash flow

3.3.1 Basic assumptions

Cash retention has often been criticised by proponents of agency costs which arise when managerial interests diverge from the interests of shareholders. When shareholders allow firms to retain cash, managers have the opportunity to misuse cash, i.e., to invest in perquisites and other unprofitable investments. However, retained earnings as a means of internal finance, under certain conditions, can be cheaper than external finance. This tradeoff between cheaper 'free' or 'excess' cash and the cost of its misuse is the central focus of the FCFT.

Jensen's FCFT is an extension into principal–agent costs, since managers' incentives are not always aligned with the interests of the shareholders. In Jensen's view, increased leverage or increased dividends can assure manager efficiency and lower the cost of asymmetric information between managers and shareholders; therefore, free cash flow, the after-tax cash flow in excess of the amount needed to fund positive NPV projects, should be disbursed as dividends in order to maximise the firm's value. This is difficult to refute given perfect capital markets, because only positive NPV projects are expected to increase firm value. Other possible excess cash policies, such as excess cash flow for acquisitions or non-value-enhancing investments, can only maintain or decrease a firm's value. It is the uncertainty inherent in project evaluation which makes excess cash flow retention advantageous to a firm.

The FCFT suggests an increase in dividends or debt even for high growth firms which have excess cash flow. Although some 'Genetech' fast-growing firms would have many positive NPV projects to absorb cash flow, it is possible that a firm could have excess cash flow. In light of future time periods, research could reveal new positive NPV projects to which the excess cash flow could be applied. To finance these projects, the firm might have to reduce its dividend or forgo other good investments. Evidence generally shows that a fall in dividend payments reduces firm value both in theory and in share price (Pettit, 1972). Capital markets are not perfect, according to theories of asymmetric information. These asymmetries predict that credit rationing could occur in the capital market where firms are heterogeneous. Asymmetries make an excess cash retention policy a superior strategy.

With imperfect capital markets and heterogeneous firms seeking capital, certain firms will suffer disproportionately more in the event of an economic downturn. If these firms suffer because of asymmetric information, they should consider dynamic investment policies. These firms must look towards future growth possibilities; therefore, excess cash flow policy can be important if it helps offset future difficulty in obtaining capital . In light of empirical evidence that certain firms' investment is more sensitive to cash flow than others, it appears that excess cash flow can be used as a buffer against both the reduced net worth and reduced cash flow which is the typical consequence of an economic downturn. Excess cash flow can essentially dampen the 'financial accelerator' effects which predict that financial problems often caused by some macroeconomic policy, e.g., monetary contraction/expansion.

The typical analysis of a firm's investment decision implicitly assumes that capital markets are perfect and efficient. Perfect capital markets will provide the necessary funds for all firms which have potential positive NPV projects. Under perfect capital markets, a firm's financing decision is a matter of evaluating possible projects and investing in those which will provide a net value increase – the financing method and the financial structure are not relevant. Much financial decision-making strategy is based on the work of Miller and Modigliani who verified that under perfect capital markets both capital structure (albeit ignoring tax-created advantages) and dividend policy were irrelevant to a firm's market value. Agency costs became a matter of merely balancing the expected costs of bankruptcy against the benefits of debt. The monitoring of managers, as agents of shareholders for public firms, was noted as a problematic agency cost if the manager's incentives differed from those of a firm's shareholders.

3.3.2 Free cash flow theory: dividend recommendation

In its basic form, Jensen's FCFT states that a firm's free or excess cash flow should be distributed as dividends to shareholders if a firm's management acts in the best interest of its shareholders – maximising the net worth of a firm. According to Jensen, management could misinvest any excess cash by selecting negative NPV projects which may increase the firm's physical assets, such as fixed capital, but will cause a decline in financial value. This prediction is not surprising, considering that any negative NPV investment will never recover the initial investment costs. Free cash flow proponents argue that a misalignment of interests between managers and shareholders motivates misinvestment. A declining profit margin throughout the economy coupled with a stable level of investment at a rising cost of capital are often cited as clear signs of such negative NPV investments (Downe and Pan, 1992). In assuming managers choose to finance negative NPV projects, the FCFT assumes that investment projects can be clearly evaluated as either positive or negative NPV. Although it may be that capital markets cannot evaluate all projects *efficiently*, i.e., including opportunity costs, agency costs, etc., the FCFT says that managers do not always act as perfect agents for shareholders.

Agency costs vary across firms since the conflict between management and shareholders is firm specific. Jensen argues that the agency cost – balancing the costs of managerial monitoring against loss caused by misinvestment – is positively correlated to a firm's excess cash flow (Jensen, 1987). High excess cash flow increases managerial freedom which according to Jensen cannot enhance value since all positive NPV projects are already financed. An example of cash abuse could be the use of excess cash to finance an investment whose expected probability of success and subsequent high returns is very low. Expected NPV might even be negative, but since success has high managerial rewards and failure results in minute costs dispersed to all shareholders, it is more costly to attempt to prevent such managerial abuses. The FCFT implies that managers, because of agency costs, are allowed to maximise their utility which includes excess cash flow as well as firm value. According to Jensen, maximum firm value is not the utility maximising choice for a manager.

Excess cash flow is valuable for management not only because it provides financial freedom but also because investments in physical assets including operations increase managerial control. Incumbent managers can control physical assets whereas excess cash disbursed as dividends escape managerial control. With difficulty monitoring management, asymmetric information allows managers to control greater resources and increase perquisites. If managerial compensation is linked to firm value, agency costs are mitigated, but as long as managers value perquisites and control, they will choose to retain some excess cash. According to organisational theory, larger firms have greater incentives, due to bureaucratic control of resources, to maximise perquisites with a non-value-adding investment. Although negative NPV projects reduce a firm's value, managers increase control over the physical resources. Moreover, negative NPV projects, if undertaken to diversify real investments, provide managerial security although at a cost to shareholders.

Dividend policy is pivotal because without remaining positive NPV projects, dividend payments will remove excess cash from managerial discretion. Empirical evidence reveals that announcements of dividend changes of listed firms are positively correlated to changes in the firm's stock prices (Pettit, 1972). According to the efficient markets hypothesis, a stock's value equals the present value of its future dividend stream; therefore, an increase in dividends should raise the firm's value. Jensen argues that this correlation helps substantiate his theory – stock prices increase because firms release cash flow from managerial discretion.

3.3.3   The dividend signalling model

To subscribe to Jensen's view, dividends must not provide additional information to the public; rather, they signal that a firm has unproductive excess cash. A rise in firm value is simply the result of approaching the optimal arrangement – keeping excess cash had kept this firm's value below its potential. However, in a world of asymmetric information, the possibility that dividends convey valuable private information is important. Moreover, not all firms that announce dividends have excess cash flow. If a firm does not have excess cash flow, a dividend payment announces that it might not be financing all its value-enhancing projects. As long as firms face an external finance premium, they will never release funds which can be profitably invested. According to the FCFT, firms are already biased towards retaining earnings. With the addition of an external finance premium, there is even greater incentive to retain earnings.

Through a signal mechanism, a dividend reduces the uncertainty regarding a firm's financial status. If a firm is able to obtain external finance at nearly the same costs as internal finance, the benefits of dividend signalling may be greater than the cost of having to use the external finance for its positive NPV investments. The value of information suggests that dividends are not solely a release of unproductive excess cash. Since dividend changes are positively correlated with firm values contrary to the Miller–Modigliani propositions, dividend signalling could be the reason (Pettit, 1972). The signalling model suggests a dividend increase is a signal that future cash flow will be higher rather than reflecting a reduction in the current cash flow. Signalling effects imply that managers have private information concerning future cash flow. With the signalling model, the FCFT is weakened since managers have an incentive to announce dividends, particularly if their compensation is correlated to firm value, i.e., stock options are part of their salaries. Moreover, if their job security improves with firm performance, they might actually favour dividends.

An empirical study by Lang and Litzenberger compared the FCFT and the dividend signalling theory (Lang and Litzenberger, 1989). They examined the average return to a dividend announcement for two distinct categories of firms: those with positive NPV projects and those without. They compared the average daily return with a dividend increase of 10% and decrease of 10% for firms with Tobin's $q < 1$ and Tobin's $q > 1$. Tobin's q, the ratio of market value to replacement costs of assets, was used as the proxy for investment opportunities. Typical of investment studies, the division was made at unity: where less than unity implied no profitable opportunities for investment and more than unity implied profitable opportunities. Intuitively, if market value is greater than the replacement cost of assets, the market valuation must include prospective growth. Increase in stock value of firms with Tobin's q's < 1 associated with an announcement of a dividend increase was three times greater than the increase in stock value of a firm with a Tobin's $q > 1$ that also announced an increase in dividends at the 1% significance level. This supported the FCFT (Lang and Litzenberger, 1989). This study provides evidence that firms benefit by paying dividends if they do not foresee profitable investment opportunities – unless the low q firms' dividends had large informational content, the dividend signalling model does not explain the abnormally high return for low Tobin's q firms.

3.3.4 Free cash flow theory: debt recommendation

The second prediction of the FCFT is that if a firm does not release excess cash as dividends, the second best solution is to increase leverage in a firm's capital structure. Excess cash could finance a debt–equity exchange. Debt creates a bond by creating a prior claim on a firm's cash flow; this bond encourages efficiency and is guaranteed legally by bankruptcy courts (Jensen, 1987). By increasing leverage, firms must operate more efficiently to meet interest payments to debt holders. Contrary to Miller–Modigliani propositions, in a tax-free world there is an optimal debt–equity structure where the marginal benefit of debt equals the marginal cost of bankruptcy. In firms with excess cash flow, debt could eliminate the excess cash where the excess cash flow exactly equals the interest payments on additional debt. Jensen supports this *control hypothesis* for debt creation by noting that transactions which increase leverage typically result in positive increases in common stock prices for a firm (Jensen, 1986). Increased debt benefits firms which have higher than average agency costs, particularly those with few investment opportunities and large cash flow.

3.3.5   Empirical evidence for the free cash flow theory

Since FCFT is particularly aimed at mature industries which have fewer profitable investment opportunities (Tobin's q is less than unity) but large cash flow, much empirical work has focused on investment in declining industries. A study of managers' corporate investment decisions by McConnell and Muscarella investigates whether a manager maximises firm value or firm size (McConell and Muscarella, 1985). Maximisation of size occurs when investment exceeds the profitable level. Firms suffering from excess cash flow abuse are trading off firm value for firm size. This study indicates that some industrial firms do invest to maximise value, whereas public utilities, whose profits are regulated, have less incentive to invest in value-enhancing projects. The key evidence revealing value maximisation for industrial firms is the positive correlation between announcements of research and development or increased capital expenditures with stock prices (McConnell and Muscarella, 1985). If the market upgrades firm value with each project announcement, then managers must be investing (or people believe managers are investing) in positive NPV projects. An interesting finding in this study is that the announcement of development and exploration in oil and gas industries had negative effects on stock value throughout the late 1970s and early 1980s. These firms are identified as possible size maximisers.

The oil shocks in the 1970s left oil companies with extremely large cash flow but with drastically reduced demand. Another similar high cash industry which faced a declining demand was the tobacco industry in the late 1970s. The excess capacity in both industries was a sign that these industries should release excess cash as dividends rather than continue to invest in an industry with declining demand. However, the large quantity of excess cash allowed such firms to avoid capital market pressures and stock market evaluations to reduce production and investment (Jensen, 1987). Announcements of exploration reduced firm values because investors realised that such capital expenditures were intended for negative NPV projects. As pressure mounted on these excess cash flow firms to stop intra-industry investment, managers used excess cash to fund acquisitions in other industries to diversify. Such strategies reduced firm value and were spotted as management attempted to retain control of excess cash.

3.3.6 Free cash flow theory and takeovers

Another possible way to investigate excess cash flow effects is to measure the consequential effect of a takeover given the bidder's current cash flow. Acquisitions should be more profitable for a bidder with many investment opportunities identified by a high Tobin's q. Lang, Stulz and Walkling (1989) posit the view that cash flow effects on low Tobin's q target firms should negatively influence overall returns, while these cash flow effects on profitable target firms should be negligible. Their findings strongly support the FCFT: for every cash surplus equal to 1% of a bidder firm's assets, the bidding firm's gain is reduced by 1% of stock value if target firms have low Tobin's q. The correlation between bidder returns and cash flow for low Tobin's q target firms clearly suggests that firms are acquiring loss-making investments.

Financial economists tend to think takeovers improve management – inefficient firms will be taken over and run more efficiently. In this case, if firms are misinvesting excess cash flow, they become good targets for acquisition. By acquiring a high excess cash flow firm, the bidder can use the newly obtained cash to finance the buyout; moreover, by increasing leverage, the value of the firm should increase due to the debt benefits implied in the FCFT (Browne and Rosengren, 1987). Leveraged buyouts serve as effective control devices for capital markets which cannot effectively govern firms with large excess cash holdings. The bidding firm's management acquires a larger stake of equity after the merger, thereby reducing agency costs. A merger creates value reflected in stock price as excess cash from the acquired firm can fund better available investments selected by the bidding firm. If managers value job security, they should always maximise firm value rather than risk the chance of being acquired (Frydl, 1987). High excess cash firms tend to be mature; therefore, it may be difficult to obtain funds to finance a hostile takeover. Managers of these firms will hold excess cash if the probability of being acquired is low.

3.4 Asymmetric information, imperfect capital markets, and the 'flight to quality'

FCFT implies that managerial control over excess cash flow is never value maximising. This is true only in perfect capital markets. A general statement concerning excess cash flow cannot apply to every firm, particularly when each is treated differently in the capital market. However, the FCFT applies in an imperfect market – declining or mature firms which lack valuable investment opportunities should restrict managerial control over excess cash. Other firms may benefit from excess cash retention if the cost of internal finance differs from external. To complete the analysis, it is necessary to consider the effects of imperfect capital markets which are likely to complement rather than contradict the FCFT.

3.4.1 Imperfect capital markets: the lemons problem

A typical assumption in investment project evaluation is that funds are always readily available for all firms; moreover, the supply of capital will be elastic for each firm, so that as long as a project is confirmed as having a positive NPV it will be able to obtain the necessary finance, given no preference between external and internal finance. A perfect capital market also requires that heterogeneous firms are treated as equals, but mature firms with longer and better credit histories have better access to credit markets than young firms (Gertler, 1988). A perfect market is concerned only with the investment rather than the financing decision. However, literature on asymmetric information emphasises the difference between sources of finance. Investment depends upon financial conditions including asymmetries in obtaining credit and not just upon a NPV criterion. The cost of capital differs between sources and projects.

Asymmetric information is reflected in Akerlof's *Lemons Problem*, in which buyers and sellers in a used car market cannot clear the market because of asymmetric information (Akerlof, 1970). Sellers of low-quality used cars have an incentive to advertise their cars falsely as good-quality (and thus demand a higher price, although their marginal cost is below that of a good quality car's marginal cost). Buyers cannot know whether cars are of good or bad quality because of asymmetric information. The owners of good cars have a higher marginal cost and ask for a higher price; however, buyers' fear of purchasing a high-priced poor-quality car ensures that they will only pay a price less than the marginal cost of a good-quality used car. Both sellers and buyers lose, since buyers would pay more for a better car and good car owners are unable to sell their cars at a price which would be mutually accept-able in the presence of complete information. For the sellers of a good car there exists a lemons premium. They must sell at a price below its true marginal cost. The difference between the sale price and the mar-ginal costs is the lemons premium created by asymmetric information.

In a capital market, the lemons problem means possible investors, or lenders, are afraid to buy securities from a firm or lend to a firm because they feel managers are distorting published information. Firms with poor investments or risky investments distort information much like the owners of Akerlof's poor-quality used cars. Presenting risky firms as reliable reduces the amount investors are willing to lend. This is inefficient from a resource allocation perspective since managers are presented with positive NPV projects but cannot invest because a lemons premium (arising as investment funds are under-supplied) makes the investment unprofitable; thus, the positive NPV investment is bypassed. Like the seller of a good car, the firm may have to obtain funds at a higher cost.

Since dividends have informational content about future cash flow, firms which do not pay dividends are likely to face a greater lemons premium (MacKie-Mason, 1990). Initially, it appears that the FCFT is again supported, since paying dividends reduces the lemons premium and increases firm value. But a reduction of the lemons premium is valuable only to firms which need to invest. The mature, high excess cash firms in Jensen's theory are predicted to have only negative NPV projects. Moreover, these high-profile, mature firms would face a nearly symmetric credit market anyhow (Calomiris and Hubbard, 1990). Younger firms with less net worth and private information are likely to face a greater lemons premium. These firms could benefit from retaining excess cash flow by allowing avoidance of the external capital markets and, consequently, also the lemons premium.

3.4.2 Imperfect capital markets: credit rationing

Asymmetric information fosters a higher lemons premium, and it can also create a situation of credit rationing at the macroeconomic level. Given fixed aggregate credit, there is not a perfectly elastic supply curve; therefore, credit goes to *safe* firms first – there is essentially a credit hierarchy. If information costs are greater for smaller, or younger firms, they will be excluded from the capital market with limited funds. Credit rationing also occurs on the microeconomic level when similar firms with near similar net worth seek credit in scarce capital markets and not all can receive credit (Calomiris and Hubbard, 1990). If these firms have similar investment opportunities, credit rationing causes a net aggregate loss in welfare. Firms thus excluded lose a competitive edge, particularly if they are rationed out in an economic downturn. These are significant costs to a firm that cannot receive necessary investment funding.

Credit rationing is most likely to occur in the event of a downturn, especially during a monetary contraction. The scarcity of funds during a contraction due to a rise in interest rates causes the good borrowers (those with higher net worth) to seek funds elsewhere. Lenders in the loan market expect these remaining loan applicants to be riskier and have lower expected profits and thus ration credit to an even greater degree (Fazzari, Hubbard and Petersen, 1988). Those firms lower in credit hierarchies need an alternate strategy to deal with such dynamic fluctuations in credit conditions. The smaller, growing firms which tend to be the first to be rationed out of the credit market are also those most likely to need the investment funds. These firms are often financing high-return, high-technology projects and are fighting to mature and capture a market share in their industry.

3.4.3   Internal vs. external finance: asymmetric information costs and intermediation

Imperfect markets are the reason for differing costs between internal and external finance. After internal finance is exhausted, firms turn to external capital markets. The cost of external capital is increased by a lemons premium, particularly for firms lacking a strong reputation or financial record. External debt requires a premium because of the risk involved in guaranteeing that cash flow will meet interest payments; external equity requires a premium because new shareholders are worried about the future cash flow from the new investment. It has been noted that the premium on external finance is inversely related to a borrower's net worth which is the total value of all physical assets and present value of future cash flow (Bernanke, Gertler and Gilchrist, 1993). Intuitively, a higher net worth, primarily through physical assets (because future cash flow is unpredictable given asymmetric information), provides higher collateral for external debt. Legally, external debt has more security if firms have more valuable physical assets. The same security is not true for new equity holders. FCFT predicts that firms which maximise physical assets should disburse their excess cash to shareholders. These firms, given their high net worth, do not pay a very high external finance premium, *ceteris paribus*. On the other hand, low net worth firms who pay the high external finance premium favour internal finance. These small firms also seek short-term debt primarily from banks, an indication that perhaps bank intermediation can help mitigate asymmetric information and minimise the difference between external and internal finance costs (Fazzari, Hubbard and Petersen, 1988).

3.4.4 Banking relationships and the asymmetric information problem

Banks monitor their borrowers and provide information about a firm's financial condition thus reducing the costs of external finance, particularly debt financing. Such functions help match a borrowing firm's needs with diverse investors by intermediating both risk and liquidity preferences and information asymmetries. During an economic contraction, distressed firms have a better chance of receiving credit through banks since they serve as *extended internal capital markets* because they have more information about a firm's net worth and investment opportunities than disparate investors (Kashyap, Stein and Wilcox, 1993). When credit is rationed, firms vulnerable to being locked out of capital markets will benefit the most from banking relationships. Studies into banking relationships have revealed that a smaller firm's available credit depends upon its banking relationship – more credit is available as the length of the relationship increases (Kashyap and Stein, 1992). In a dynamic, long-term banking relationship, information costs decline and credit lines can be established. Although intermediation reduces the costs of external finance, many firms will still have much lower finance costs if earnings are retained and internal finance is utilised.

The benefits of a banking relationship imply that firms with strong banking ties should not be as liquidity constrained in their investment decisions; therefore, their investment to cash flow fluctuations should be smaller. Hoshi, Scharfstein and Kashyap study how banking relationships influenced investment in the post-World War II Japanese economy (Hoshi, Kashyap and Scharfstein, 1990). Japanese regulations typically enforced firms to raise funds through debt; therefore, strong banking ties were established. Banks had equity stakes in many of the firms they provided capital to, and firms were attached to particular banks for credit. The Japanese economy's strong *keiretsu* – banking and industrial groups – provide good evidence on bank relationship effects on investment because financial deregulation in the early 1980s freed many firms from bank debt finance. Previously, the Japanese government required the following: domestic corporate debt issued had to be secured, debt issued to foreigners had to gain government permission, and debt interest rates had to stay below an uncompetitive ceiling. Therefore, it was easier for firms to simply turn to banks to get external finance. After deregulation, many firms eschewed their banking relationships and sought alternative means of external finance.

Hoshi, Kashyap and Scharfstein discovered that firms which reduced their ties to banks were those with higher growth and Tobin's q's than those which remained in strong banking relationships, and that these same firms' investment became more strongly influenced by their liquidity (Hoshi, Kashyap and Scharfstein, 1990). That investment is more sensitive to a firm's liquidity is straightforward when one considers that internal finance becomes more essential to firms not in banking relationships. The finding that firms with reduced banking relationships had greater growth is puzzling, since growth firms gain the most from banking relations under asymmetric information. Hoshi, Kashyap and Scharfstein address this issue by noting that higher Tobin's q firms are valued higher in the public capital market; therefore, they could easily gain investment finance (Hoshi, Kashyap and Scharfstein, 1990). Information costs do not seem too high in the Japanese context since the market efficiently values these firms. However, during an economic contraction, the capital market becomes less efficient and even high q firms might not gain credit.

3.5 Free cash flow theory effects vs. benefits of free cash flow retention

3.5.1 Asymmetric information in the free cash flow theory framework

FCFT predicts that inefficiencies arise if managers are able to escape the scrutiny of the capital market. However, imperfect capital markets undermine Jensen's recommendation that all excess cash be disbursed as dividends. If a firm's growth prospects are perfectly valued by the market, then it may be that credit is available for firms with positive NPV projects and unavailable for firms without such projects. However, if not all firms have equal access to credit markets, then some firms will be unable to fund all positive NPV projects.

Consider a quick-growing firm close to a technological breakthrough which cannot reveal information without losing its competitive advantage. Assume also that its past cash flow exceeded its investments in prior years (before the new technology was considered). An imperfect capital market could evaluate this firm as having no positive NPV projects without any further information. If a similar firm in the industry obtained and invested funds in a positive NPV project with a lower NPV than the former firm, capital markets have been inefficient. If the former firm had retained excess cash flow in liquid assets, it would have more internal finance to invest in the secret research. But if it had released its excess cash as dividends, it would be short of investment funds. Given imperfect capital markets, excess cash holdings can serve as a buffer of liquidity for investment funding when capital markets do not or cannot accurately value projects with publicly available information.

3.5.2 Financial flexibility and its benefits

Myers and Majluf investigate the idea of financial flexibility, i.e., unused leverage capacity and retained earnings (Myers and Majluf, 1984). They hypothesise that since managers have better knowledge of a firm's investment opportunities than outsiders, financial flexibility allows managers to finance these investments. Jensen criticises this work by noting that agency costs of excess cash flow offset the benefits of financial flexibility (Jensen, 1987). In his view, any managerial discretion over excess cash has negative effects on balance. He does not consider the costs of asymmetric information to shareholders by curtailing positive NPV investment. Myers and Majluf argue that with asymmetric information, managers must offer a premium to raise financing for a firm unless it has internal finance or unused low-cost debt capacity. If it issues equity at a lower value (which the market would require in this case as a premium), its old shareholders would lose unless they revalued their equity positions (Myers and Majluf, 1984). They reveal that given a positive NPV project, a firm without financial flexibility might not issue equity to finance a project, thereby causing firm value to fall. So, the capital market is imperfect and capital is inefficiently allocated. The importance of financial flexibility increases as capital markets become more imperfect.

Since financial flexibility includes unused debt capacity, a firm following the FCFT increases leverage and reduces its set of feasible investment opportunities. Therefore, firm value will again fall short of its potential value. Just as dividends reduce internal finance, increased leverage reduces access to external debt finance as bankruptcy risk rises. Once the optimal debt–equity structure is reached, debt capacity is exhausted. In both cases, some financial flexibility is lost. A firm can theoretically still increase its debt–equity level as long as an investment's return justifies such an increase. But, in order to justify a higher level of debt–equity, the project must have an adequately positive NPV. Therefore, if the quality of available projects remains constant, the debt capacity for marginally productive investments is eroded.

Under credit-rationing, the external finance problem is exacerbated. Myers and Majluf define *financial slack* as the sum of cash, marketable securities, and risk-free debt (similar to financial flexibility). Their predictions contradict Jensen's in that restricting dividends is a means of accumulating financial slack. This increases managerial discretion, and allows managers to avoid the lemon premium when a firm has to seek external finance. Traditional Modigliani–Miller theory fails here since the assumption that finance for every project is readily available does not hold true (Myers and Majluf, 1984). A criticism of their results is their assumption that firms never undertake negative NPV projects even with internal funding because it could invest instead in liquid securities with a minimum of zero return (Myers and Majluf, 1984). Their work provides an example of inefficiency due to asymmetric capital markets. They do not directly confront the FCFT since they implicitly and incorrectly assume managers will never accept negative NPV projects.

3.5.3   Excess cash strategies

The FCFT can be reconciled with Myers and Majluf's findings as large and more mature firms misuse excess cash. In Jensen's theory, large firms face a more symmetrical capital market and may have massive financial slack since capital market asymmetries affect them to a lesser degree. On the other hand, smaller, dynamic firms have more growth options; therefore, the use of financial slack as a substitute for credit insufficiencies or an underpriced equity issue is a tenable financial strategy. Private information, such as in technologically advanced industries, justifies financial slack due to asymmetric information. This allows firms to maximise the value of inside information without the cost of disseminating confidential technology (Myers and Majluf, 1984).

Firms could invest excess cash in securities which could be easily liquidated during a credit crunch. Although this reduces shareholders' influence on investment, which dividends increase, it maximises a firm's discounted value. Jensen says managers would sometimes misuse funds rather than 'park' them in liquid assets, so there must be some reason for such behaviour. One way to avoid this is a compensation package for managers. In Jensen's framework, managers' utility depends upon firm value and excess cash which can be divided into reinvested cash and liquid assets. For example, managerial compensation could depend on the value of such liquidity. Managers could be given a percentage of shares of a liquid mutual fund providing them with the incentive to maintain liquidity; both shareholders and managers can benefit. This might be coupled with another incentive related to the firm's value or managers would reduce investment in positive NPV projects for the personally lucrative mutual funds. The incentives must reconcile the manager's priority to maximise firm value subject to the constraint of putting more surplus cash into mutual funds. In the end, the direct compensation of liquid assets should offset the desire to misinvest.

Another possible strategy contradicting the FCFT is to use excess cash to retire debt. Although this action increases the flow of cash available to management in later periods, in high-growth firms it is likely that cash flow will be invested productively anyhow. This enhances a firm's credit status and increases the available financial slack. It would also reduce the premium imposed on the firm when it seeks external funds, since the debt–equity ratio would be reduced. If there were truly no preference for finance sources, then both strategies would be equal. However, capital market imperfections create preferences among alternatives – a finance hierarchy or *pecking-order*, which is discussed below.

3.5.4   Finance hierarchies

The finance hierarchy ranks costs of differing sources of finance. External finance is either debt or equity financing; internal finance is mostly retained earnings. Internal finance is cheaper because it avoids the lemons premium of asymmetric information, lowers financial distress (bankruptcy) costs, and avoids transactions cost of debt seeking and equity issuing (Fazzari, Hubbard and Petersen, 1988).

Firm studies of financial hierarchy in industrialised countries reveal that most firms prefer internal over external finance and debt over equity. Myers and Majluf's study noted that managerial capitalism – the belief that managers seek to avoid market discipline by using internal finance – can be explained by the cost of different sources of finance (Myers and Majluf, 1984). MacKie-Mason's study reveals that debt-equity finance choice is important and that the source – whether public or private – matters (MacKie-Mason, 1990). MacKie-Mason find that different industries in different time periods favoured different methods of finance. This makes sense since different firms are treated differently by the capital market; therefore, some firms rely more upon internal funding than others.

Fazzari, Hubbard and Petersen study cash retention policies and investment. If there is a cost disadvantage in external funds, firms' investments should be sensitive to cash flow variation; moreover, if the cost differential was not substantial, then external finance should be used and investment should not be as sensitive to cash flow variation (Fazzari, Hubbard and Petersen, 1988). It is implicit that internal finance is less costly while new equity is the most. Their findings are consistent with the idea that asymmetric information effects are greatest with new equity; when issuing debt, information effects can be reduced by intermediation or collateral values. Since the supply of debt available will depend upon the firm's Tobin's q value, a firm with low investment opportunities and high asymmetric information may secure less investment finance than it desires and so investment responses will be highly correlated with the level of internal finance (Fazzari, Hubbard and Petersen, 1988).

Fazzari, Hubbard and Petersen use dividends payout policy as a proxy for reliance upon internal funds. Low dividend firms should have more profitable investment if they act optimally. Firms with the lowest dividend payments use their cash flow for investment which are more volatile; high dividend firms use less internal cash flow for investment; correlation between excess cash and investment is higher for low dividend firms (Fazzari, Hubbard and Petersen, 1988). They prove empirically that internal finance, reflected in internal cash/investment correlations, is important particularly for low dividend firms. These low dividend firms tend to be growth firms; this complements the idea that such firms should retain excess cash as insurance against less cash in future periods. All firms do not fit into a finance hierarchy, which is especially important for smaller growing firms.

3.5.5 Tax and the finance hierarchy

Some debt finance is beneficial for all firms since interest on debt is tax deductible. This serves to increase the optimal debt level in the finance hierarchy. When firms seek the optimal debt–equity ratio, they include the benefits of tax deduction against the costs of bankruptcy. But debt financing increases cash flow, and tax structures tend to favour internal finance, at least from the shareholders' perspective. Internal finance avoids the double taxation which earnings would face if paid as dividends; moreover, higher capital gains tax encourages re-investment. Even considering the influence of corporate tax, debt finance is still a more costly means of funding investment than internal finance if managers truly seek to maximise shareholders' returns.

3.5.6 Using excess cash as collateral

Imperfect information in credit markets affects firms differently according to their net worth; a firm's net worth and available collateral become more significant. If credit is related to a firm's collateral, the financing and investment decision become interdependent (Calomiris and Hubbard, 1990). By increasing the net worth of a firm, the cost of asymmetric information is reduced in credit markets. Moreover, throughout the economy, more loans are provided by the banks as firms' net worth increases (Calomiris and Hubbard, 1990). Increasing net worth implies that borrowers improve in quality; therefore, the riskiness of making loans decreases, i.e., the lemons problem is partially offset. In an economic upturn, it becomes easier to obtain credit, as banks' net values increase (and therefore their available funds increase) and the probability of borrower default decreases. If enough individual firms increase in firm value, and therefore collateral, macroeconomic credit effects can at least be partially offset.

Hubbard notes that firms can be divided into categories of constrained – cannot use non-collateralised debt – or unconstrained; therefore, collateral is valuable (Hubbard, 1990). Net worth is the closest proxy for collateral, since net worth is related to a firm's physical asset value. Higher-valued firms are much more likely to be unconstrained, and unconstrained firms have investment policies which can be more independent from general aggregate economic conditions. Freedom from the discipline of capital markets in a downturn is beneficial to a firm with good investment opportunities and small present cash flow. Low-value firms could design excess cash flow policies which accommodate for a lack of collateral. Instead of signalling a dearth of profitable investments, excess cash accumulation can signal a firm which is projecting and saving for future profitable investment. The investment of excess cash in liquid assets can serve as a form of collateral for extended credit.

The importance of net collateral to the lending activity of banks is critical when the possibility of a widespread credit crisis is considered. If a firm's net worth or balance sheet is important to a bank, certain firms will suffer more than others in an economic downturn. These differential impacts can lead to a general inefficient aggregate investment level if banks contract loans and aggregate demand is rationed. Moreover, since economic shocks strike both banks and firms, lending contraction can continue in a vicious cycle – as banks decrease lending, their external benefits of information intermediation services decline and asymmetric information costs mount. The agency cost increases even exceed those suggested by the lost intermediation benefits, since a decline in firm net worth also increases agency costs. Since agency costs rise as net worth declines, there is a minimum level of net worth which cannot be exceeded by firms or else the mere evaluation of investment projects becomes unprofitable for banks and investment collapses (Bernanke and Gertler, 1990). The collapse of investment will have macroeconomic consequences.

Firm net worth is apparent since investment reduction could occur even as market interest rates decline. Traditional economic analysis considers that investment declines as market interest rates increase since the opportunity cost of borrowing increases. However, if a negative productivity shock struck the goods market, market interest rate would decline. Although the interest rate declines, the amount of investment could simultaneously decrease due to the decline in net worth caused by the recession. Balance sheet problems affect the economy by reducing aggregate investment. To make investment less dependent on macroeconomic conditions, firms must consider the strength of their balance sheets.

3.5.7   An example of financial fragility and the use of debt

Bernanke and Gertler characterise a *financially fragile* situation when potential borrowers who have access to productive investments have little wealth relative to project costs (Bernanke and Gertler, 1990). The consequences of this situation might lead to economic inefficiencies. Stability occurs when borrowers have higher net values, since these borrowers lower agency costs by being able to finance more of their projects internally and obtain external finance at a lower cost (Bernanke and Gertler, 1990). Bernanke and Gertler model the situation where individuals with the same endowment are randomly chosen as investors or entrepreneurs. They reveal that in a situation of asymmetric information, investment can collapse if investors have to turn to capital markets for investment funds. They note that the optimal contract involves the establishment of a credit line with an intermediary so that the probabilities of success and loss are arranged to benefit both parties – i.e., in a successful state, firms receive less (and banks receive more) and in a bad state firms lose less (and banks more) (Bernanke and Gertler, 1990). Excess cash helps to provide financial stability since excess cash can enhance a firm's net worth and thus increase the probability of establishing such a credit line.

In considering the question of financial fragility, it is informative to re-examine the debate over the benefits and costs of debt financing. Whereas the FCFT predicts that debt has beneficial effects by limiting managerial discretion over cash flow, debt also increases the financial fragility of a firm. Debt limits managerial discretion but often in a negative way. Debt finance still faces agency costs since creditors have different interests from these of shareholders. Debt holders realise that ideally managers must maximise shareholder wealth; therefore, they often demand protective covenants on debt issuance. These covenants, often tied to working capital, effectively limit managerial attempts to invest in projects even if they have a positive NPV (Fazzari, Hubbard and Petersen, 1988). Debt holders gain nothing from positive NPV projects except increased collateral values for their debt, since they are not residual claimants on a firm's value. By increasing financial fragility, increased leverage can be dangerous to the aggregate national economy. Evidence cited for the dangers of debt includes the crash of the US stock market in 1987. On the whole, increased debt can help accelerate or sensitise the mechanism by which financial factors transmit themselves into real economic effects. If cash retention can buffer against this transmission mechanism, a policy of cash retention could be extremely beneficial on a microeconomic and, subsequently, a macroeconomic scale.

3.6   Financial transmission to real economic activity

3.6.1   Mechanisms with real economic consequences: the lending channel

Many studies assume that monetary policy has no real effect on aggregate demand because they ignore the possibility that loan interest rates and bond interest rates can differ. In this view, there are only money effects of monetary policy. During a monetary contraction the supply of money decreases, and the market bond interest rate increases. These effects hurt firms only when they face higher interest rates as determined by the money effect. There is no reason for the bond interest rate to equal a bank's interest rate on loans. During a monetary contraction, the decline in net worth reduces lending by banks. According to this *lending view*, bank loans are not equal to securities since they will have differing interest rates. A curtailment of money supply is no longer the only effect of the central bank's contractionary policy (Kashyap and Stein, 1992). This lending view has more relevance in a market with asymmetric information, for differing financial characteristics imply different impacts on firms. If the available supply of funds is altered by monetary policy, there will be an additional effect on aggregate demand. A decline in investment will force some marginal borrowers to suffer. Monetary policy exacerbates an economic downturn through two distinct channels: the money channel and the lending channel. The traditional money channel is best revealed in the simple IS-LM framework where both the goods and money markets share a common interest rate. As shown in Figure 3.1, during a monetary contraction, the LM curve shifts to the left as money supply is reduced.

The rise in the interest rate causes a decline in GNP, as investment declines to create an equilibrium in the goods market (point B in Figure 3.1). The omission of the lending channel is evident in the failure of the IS curve to shift. The money channel effect suggests that interest rates will rise and some firms will be rationed out of the credit market, but it does not consider any additional shock that would occur as banks' net values decline. Banks act like firms where their output is loanable funds (Stiglitz, 1992); therefore, an economic contraction will reduce banks' willingness to lend as a result of their reduced monetary base. These ripple effects are proportional to the lending multiplier.

The *lending view* is often depicted in models as a contraction in aggregate demand which follows the contraction in the money market. In the IS-LM framework, this could be represented as a leftward shift in both the LM and IS curves (point C in Figure 3.1). The basic premise of the lending view is that a monetary contraction may cause additional effects characterised generally by a credit crunch where banks refuse to issue credit.[1] A credit crunch may also occur as the money supply is expanded. In this case, credit does not increase even though interest rates decline. Credit crunches either worsen or make monetary policy futile. During a credit crunch, asymmetric information exacerbates the

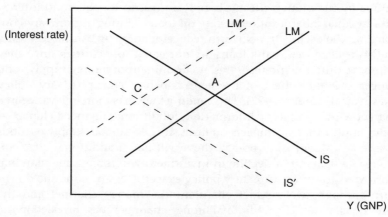

Figure 3.1   IS-LM depiction of the lending channel

adverse selection problem and generally less optimistic and concerned banks are unwilling to make loans which are perceived as even slightly risky. Although credit rationing does not explicitly result from the lending channel, it intensifies the reduction in available credit. The money channel reduces the banking system's reserves and the lending channel reduces the asset side of the bank's balance sheet (Kashyap, Stein and Wilcox, 1993).

Kashyap, Stein and Wilcox note that for the lending channel to have any economic effect, the following two conditions must be met: (i) banks must not find security and loan holding as perfect substitutes for assets – banks must offset a decline in net worth by reducing some loans instead of meeting the reduction entirely with a change in security holdings; (ii) individual firms cannot simply issue commercial paper or other securities to meet a decline in loans (Kashyap, Stein and Wilcox, 1993). Although banks reduce lending during monetary contractions, a criticism of the lending channel is that the decline in loan demand is the prime cause of the reduction – i.e., during a monetary contraction, firms need less funds; therefore, they simply enter the demand side of the loan market less frequently. It has been demonstrated empirically that a reduction in loan demand is not the cause of declining bank loans, as the demand for other nonbank assets such as commercial paper does not decline (Kashyap, Stein and Wilcox, 1993). Loans and nonbank assets are not perfect substitutes; moreover, loans are typically less expensive for firms since banks reduce information costs. Bank loans should therefore increase before commercial paper increases, unless the loan market is affected from the supply side as is posited. More intuitively, if loan demand decreases, the banking loan interest rate should decline if banks are willing to supply more loans than loan demand. Over-supply typically induces a decline in price (measured by loan interest rate). Since a decline in loans does not usually occur concurrently with a decline in loan rates, it seems unlikely that the reduction in loans is a demand effect.

If the lending channel exists, it makes the task of finding cash flow effects on different firms clearer. The lending view suggests that aggregate investment will decline by more than what the money channel alone would cause in the event of a monetary contraction. Monetary policy can therefore be used as a critical measure of the economic environment faced by firms. The lending channel also implicitly introduces the financial accelerator mechanism, as the accelerator highlights that during a downturn an economic contraction will have different contractionary impacts on individual firms' investment. By aggregating these contractionary effects, the additional aggregate economic decline predicted by the lending view becomes clearer. Bank dependent firms will suffer disproportionately more in an economic downturn. Furthermore, these *bank dependent* firms are likely to share characteristics such as size, maturity, and growth potential.

3.6.2 The financial investment accelerator

If the lending view is correct, the financial accelerator becomes important since lending effects increase the accelerator mechanism's speed. In its basic form, the accelerator principle suggests that a firm's investment will vary according to its output or sales; therefore, in an economic downturn, a firm's investment will typically decline as aggregate income declines. The lending channel implies that certain firms become cash strapped, for they can no longer obtain risk-free debt; therefore, cash flow becomes more important to firms which seek to invest. Since cash flow also contracts, excess cash retention could serve as a buffer during an economic downturn, particularly since external finance is curtailed by the decline in collateral values. It is this contraction due to decreased investment which via the accelerator mechanism is propagated cyclically over several time periods (Bernanke, Gertler and Gilchrist 1993).

Since cash flow and net worth are related to macroeconomic fluctuations, it is reasonable to assume that in an economic downturn firm responses regarding investment will vary. With the apparent difference between the cost of internal and external finance, some firms' investment decisions will be strongly influenced by their present cash flow. Since future output and sales will depend upon a firm's present investment, firms should seek to break free of the accelerator mechanism. Retaining excess cash to mediate the vagaries of the accelerator is reasonable as excess cash is basically internal finance to be used in future periods. Cash-strapped and cash-flush firms are treated differently in imperfect capital markets; thus, for cash-strapped firms, the marginal cost of external finance is higher than the marginal cost of internal finance due to a higher premium. If the difference between the costs of finance is greater than the opportunity cost of holding excess cash – even if it is not invested in liquid assets – an excess cash policy makes sense.

3.6.3 Inventory response and firm size

Since a decline in credit availability increases the accelerator, smaller firms must react differently to economic shocks than larger and more mature firms. An examination of inventory policy indeed reveals that smaller firms which are cash strapped and have been injured by the lending channel must shed their inventories even at low values to obtain the necessary cash. Gertler and Gilchrist find that after a monetary contraction large firms increase their inventories by 5% and smaller firms decrease their inventories by 11% (Kashyap and Stein, 1992). These small firms rely heavily on cash flow because they are unable to obtain credit and have declining collateral values during a contraction. Since inventories are considered investment, clearly the accelerator mechanism hurts those firms unable to finance the costs of inventory holdings. Large firms are able to hold inventories and sell them when aggregate income eventually increases, whereas smaller firms, exposed to greater risk because of low cash, must quickly shed inventories during a contraction, even at a cost to themselves. By applying the accelerator principle, the initial decision to curtail investment and inventories continues over several periods.

3.6.4   Investment effects on the macroeconomic level

By aggregating the net effects of investment contraction, there will be suboptimal investment. The accelerator mechanism causes a market failure which hurts firms to differing degrees in a cyclical nature. The rising market and loan interest rates during monetary contraction increases the accelerator effects as fewer investments have positive NPVs when evaluated, and creditors – even those in a banking relationship – discount a firm's expected profits to a greater extent. Consequently, such behaviour by banks leads to even less external finance, even for larger firms. The credit crunch and accelerator mechanism lead the economy into a prolonged recession due to the economy-wide suboptimal investment. If firms adopt excess cash policies to offset accelerator effects, they might help reduce suboptimal investment on a macroeconomic level. By not adopting the excess cash policies, firms face accelerator effects and all firms suffer as the economy settles at a lower net aggregate income.

Since a critical component of the accelerator mechanism is the viability of the lending channel, the accelerator mechanism predicts that smaller, credit constrained firms will be those who suffer disproportionately during investment contraction. Larger firms will be less exposed to accelerator influences due to their lower asymmetric information qualities. The retention of excess cash by small firms can be a good strategy from a microeconomic and macroeconomic viewpoint. Moreover, the accumulation of excess cash allows small firms to finance inventory holding similar to their larger counterparts. The accelerator principle simply makes asymmetric information problems more costly to firms during a recession. Even if the accelerator influences cannot be totally offset, excess cash will help increase a small firm's value by allowing inventory retention while prices and value remain low throughout the economy.

3.7   A firm model comparing earnings retention, re-investment, and external borrowing

Earnings retention has been criticised because of agency costs which permit managerial objectives to diverge from the interests of share-holders. Managers can misuse cash for perquisites or other non-value-adding investments; however, retained earnings provide internal finance which can be less costly than external finance. This tradeoff between the cost of retained earnings' misuse and retained earnings' internal finance benefits is the central focus of this part of the study. The Jensen model compares the use of retained earnings with the external finance premium predicted by asymmetric information. The Jensen model may apply for the firm with poor investment opportunities, whereas a strategy of earnings retention could benefit certain firms under conditions of uncertainty. This model explores firm characteristics which affect the choice of best policy for shareholders. A dynamic model explores the conditions under which earnings re-investment might be preferable. The objective is to balance both the benefits and costs of investing earnings. The optimal strategy should vary according to individual firms' cost of borrowing which in turn depends on asymmetric information and private information held by the firm.

A critical question concerning the treatment of retained earnings is whether there exists an optimal level of retained earnings for each firm which maximises its firm value. Given the different costs between external and internal finance, investment will depend upon a firm's strategy for dividends paid out of earnings and/or any remaining cash surplus. Two extreme cash policies are either retaining or disbursing all cash as dividends. A model compares the returns to the shareholder of the two strategies.

In the model, the manager first chooses the firm's dividend strategy and then decides whether to invest in the projects or hold the cash. The key tradeoff balances the cost of externally financing good invest-ments against the possibility that the manager will use the retained earnings for a poor investment. Earnings retention typically returns more to shareholders if only better investments exist, i.e., return to shareholders exceeds dividends allowing for risk and shareholder preference for cash, and earnings disbursement is generally better for shareholders if only bad investments exist.

The model has three time periods for cash strategy when the firm decides whether to invest in the projects or not (T = 1, 2, 3), i.e., to hold cash or to pay dividends. At t = 1 a firm must decide its cash strategy, at t = 2 the manager must make an investment decision, and at t = 3 returns to the shareholders are evaluated (see Figure 3.2). A model firm has cash flow x (resulting from activities at t = 0) at t = 1 which it can disburse or retain. This firm has a cash flow proportional to its size; thus, $x = \alpha s$ (let α = .10 and s = size of firm). Cash flow is 10% of the firm's net worth. This model only depicts the extreme strategies – earnings are either fully distributed or fully retained – but one could imagine different intermediate strategies given a firm's retention policy. At t = 2, the manager decides whether to invest in the available projects or not. If a firm disburses all of its cash, it will finance all of its investment externally. However, external finance is not costless; therefore, firms which disburse all of their earnings as dividends pay a premium, ϕ, on borrowed capital. ϕ will vary according to firm specific characteristics and asymmetric information effects.[2] To simplify, the external finance premium is assumed to depend only on firm size: f, $(\partial \phi / \partial s) = \beta$, where $\beta < 0$, i.e., $\phi = \phi_0 + \beta_s$ (Figure 3.3).

At period t = 3, returns to shareholders show the difference between the two strategies. In Figure 3.2, P represents the probability of a good investment. Since three possible investment types are considered, the probability of a good investment (P) is assigned a value of 2/3 – this makes each branch of the shareholders' return equally likely (1/3).

Using Tobin's q as a measure of investment quality simplifies the model, for one can use q as a measure of return assuming that the average q equals the marginal q.[3] Tobin's q measures a firm's investment opportunities, with q greater than unity indicating good investments opportunities. Other measures of investment quality exist with a common basis to compare the relative quality of the investment opportunities. A firm's marginal q will generally be the return on the firm's available investment; thus, if a firm has a $q < 1$, only non-profitable investments exist. If a firm's q is zero (or below unity) then the shareholders' return is higher in an earnings disbursement policy. If a firm's q is greater than unity, the shareholders' return will be maximised under an earnings retention strategy. In the model, various conditions and asymmetric information cause q values to fluctuate. By allowing a firm's q value to be uncertain, the expected returns to each strategy can be compared.

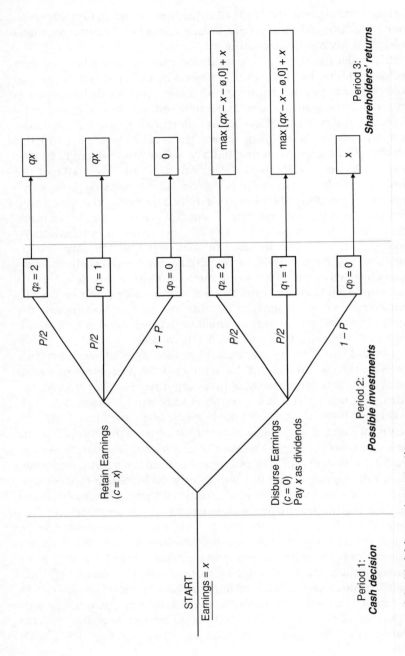

Figure 3.2 Model for earnings retention

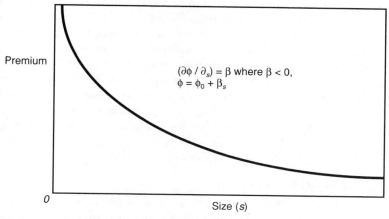

Figure 3.3   Firm size and external finance premium (ϕ)

3.7.1   Expected return of the earnings retention strategy

In the branches of the earnings retention strategy where the invest-ment is good, or $q > 1$, the shareholders' return should equal to qx. Since the model assumes that q measures the marginal quality of investment and x is the initial cash flow at $t = 0$, the value of the investment is simply qx. Any $q > 1$ yields a return greater than the initial cash flow. In the model, q_1 and q_2 represent good investments. In the case where the investment was poor, or $q < 1$, the return to the shareholders would be less than x. In the extreme situation shown, where $q_0 = 0$, the return would be 0. The zero return in the q_0 branch is the key to the FCFT. The FCFT argues that at $t = 2$ managers recognise that $q_0 = 0$ (or $q_0 < 1$) and continue to invest since maximising share-holders' return is not their main priority.

3.7.2   Expected return of the earnings disbursement strategy

If a firm disburses all of its earnings as dividends at $t = 1$, investment must be financed externally. In this case, shareholders will receive x in dividends plus the net return of its investment projects. In the q_0 case, the shareholders receive only x since the investment itself returns nothing. If the investment is profitable, the investment's return to the shareholder will be $qx - x$ without the external finance premium since a firm must return the x borrowed to finance the investment. With the finance premium ϕ, the net return will be $qx - x - \phi$. If the return were $qx - x - \phi < 0$, this would be an unprofitable investment. The firm basically borrows to finance loss-making investments; therefore, it would avoid such cases and only borrow when $q > 1$ and the return = max $\{qx - x - \phi\} + x$. A manager will not borrow and knowingly finance bad investments because external finance places a legal bond of repayment. The direct cost of external finance exceeds cost of using retained earnings. It is crucial to note that under this strategy, when $q_0 < 1$, or $q_0 = 0$ as in Figure 3.2, the manager does not invest in non-profitable projects. The return to the shareholder is the dividend payout.

3.7.3   A comparison of returns

This model incorporates the tradeoff between Jensen's FCFT and the use of internal finance. The premium ϕ is assumed to describe the difference between the cost of internal and external finance; therefore, the model considers these additional costs to firms which choose external finance. By employing variations in the possible investments captured by q_0, q_1, and q_2, the model incorporates probability to reflect both imperfect knowledge in the evaluation of projects and the possibility that managers will knowingly misuse funds.[4]

By calculating the expected values of the two extreme strategies – earnings retention and earnings disbursement – the model reflects the main tradeoff between external and internal finance. In the earnings retention branches, the q_0 branch is critical for the calculation of the strategy's expected value because it returns nothing to the shareholder. Since this is equally weighted with the other two outcomes in the branch, this is the outcome which shareholders fear since the expected value of the overall strategy declines.

In the earnings disbursement branch, the q_0 outcome returns a guarantee of x to the shareholders because of the dividend payment. However, the extra cost of borrowing is distributed between the remaining branches (q_1 and q_2). When the returns in these branches are compared with their counterparts in the earnings retention strategy, one realises that the cost of external financing makes the returns to the earnings disbursement branches $qx - \phi$ the best case for shareholders. This is less than the return in the earnings retention branches (qx) if $\phi > 0$. The q_1 and q_2 branches favour an earnings retention policy and the q_0 branch favours the earnings disbursement strategy. This is the central tradeoff between the two alternatives. When external finance premia are large, the earnings retention strategy becomes dominant and when the probability of a q_0 investment increases, the earnings disbursement strategy becomes dominant.

To compare expected returns, reconsider Tobin's q as a measure of return. Since the breakeven value of Tobin's q is 1, an investment has positive return only if the following condition is met: $qx \geq 1x$ – i.e., with internal finance. With external finance, the profitability criterion becomes more strict $qx - \phi \geq 1x$. This highlights the more stringent investment criterion which small, cash-strapped firms will face if they have to rely upon external finance, for $q \geq 1 + (\phi/x)$. Since ϕ decreases as size of the firm increases, and vice versa, smaller firms can only profitably undertake projects where q is extremely high. Cash flow x remains fixed because of the assumption that cash flow is proportional to firm size. Adding arguments to the function ϕ, such as banking relationships, net worth, dividends, and financial slack, allows the model to handle heterogeneous firms.

In calculating the expected return to the shareholders, the model assumes that the two profitable projects have $q_1 = 1.1$ and $q_2 = 2$. The model also assumes that each investment will occur with equal probability; therefore, the probability of a good investment $P = 2/3$. Table 3.1 compares expected returns from each of the branches. The returns in branches 1 and 2 are greater for the earnings retention – due to the external finance premium ϕ required under earnings disbursement. The return in branch 3 is greater in earnings disbursement – since in the earnings disbursement strategy managers have no funds to misinvest when there are no profitable projects. In this particular example, the expected return to the earnings retention strategy is higher if $x - 2\phi < 0$, or $x < 2\phi$.

Comparing the expected values of the two strategies in the model reflects the tradeoff between external finance premium ϕ and managerial use of funds ending up with a zero return. To compare the expected values of more general strategies, consider three different cases. In Table 3.2 these particular cases are summarised.

Table 3.1 Comparison of strategy: expected returns

	Earnings retention strategy	Earnings disbursement strategy
Branch 1 return	$2x$	$2x - x - \phi + x$, or $2x - \phi$
Branch 2 return	$1.1x$	$1.1x - \phi$
Branch 3 return	0	x
Total Expected Return	$(3.1x)/3$	$(4.1x - 2\phi)/3$

Table 3.2 Model's three cases

	Case 1	Case 2	Case 3
Assumption	$q_2 > q_1$	$q_2 > q_1$	$q_2 > q_1$
Constraint A – (1A, 2A, 3A)	$x(q_1 - 1) > \phi$	$x(q_1 - 1) < \phi$ and $x(q_2 - 1) > \phi$	$x(q_2 - 1) < \phi$ thus $x(q_1 - 1) < \phi$
Constraint B – (1B, 2B, 3B)	$\phi > x(1 - q_0)/2$	$\phi > -x(q_1 + q_0 - 2)$	$q_2 + q_1 + q_0 > 3$
Expected return – earnings retention	$(q_2 x + q_1 x + q_0 x)/3$	$(q_2 x + q_1 x + q_0 x)/3$	$(q_2 x + q_1 x + q_0 x)/3$
Expected return – earnings disbursement	$[q_2 x - \phi]/3 + [q_1 x - \phi]/3 + x/3$	$[q_2 x - \phi]/3 + x/3 + x/3$	$x/3 + x/3 + x/3 = x$

As the cases progress, the assumed value of the premium ϕ is increased (constraint A). In Case 1, $x(q_1 - 1) > \phi$ (constraint 1A); moreover, because $q_2 > q_1$, the expected value for a strategy of earnings disbursement equals $\frac{1}{3}[q_2x - x - \phi + x] + \frac{1}{3}[q_1x - x - \phi + x] + \frac{1}{3}x$. Since the expected value of an earnings retention strategy always equals $\frac{1}{3}q_2x + \frac{1}{3}q_1x + \frac{1}{3}q_0x$, one finds that the expected value of an earnings retention strategy is greater than the expected value of a cash disbursing strategy when $\phi \geq \dfrac{x\,(1-q_0)}{2}$ (constraint 1B; see Appendix 2 for details). After assumptions are made for the external finance premium ϕ and the quality of investments q_0, q_1, q_2 one can determine precisely when an earnings retention strategy is better. Moreover the set of solutions for earnings retention strategies can be depicted visually.[5] For a strategy of earnings retention to have a higher expected value, both constraints must be satisfied.

Examining Cases 2 and 3 is simpler, for the conditions favouring a strategy of earnings retention are less stringent when $x(q_1 - 1) < \phi$ and $x(q_2 - 1) < \phi$ respectively. In each case, some terms in the expected value of an earnings disbursement policy are reduced as the max $\{.....\}$ expression collapses to a zero value. Given a probability of good investment equal to 2/3 and holding f and x constant, the probability of a dominant earnings retention strategy increases. In Case 2, $x(q_1 - 1) < \phi$ and $x(q_2 - 1) > \phi$ (2A); therefore, the expected value of cash disbursement is

$$\tfrac{1}{3}[q_2x - x - \phi + x] + \tfrac{1}{3}[0 + x] + \tfrac{1}{3}x \tag{3.1}$$

With the given assumptions, this is a lower value than the expected return in Case 1. As shown above, the second condition required for an earnings retention policy is $f \geq -x(q_1 + q_0 - 2)$ (constraint 2B; see Appendix). Case 3 is a straightforward comparison between expected values:

$$\tfrac{1}{3}q_2x + \tfrac{1}{3}q_1x + \tfrac{1}{3}q_0x \geq \tfrac{1}{3}x + \tfrac{1}{3}x + \tfrac{1}{3}x. \tag{3.2}$$

Thus, the two requirements for an earnings retention policy are

$x(q_2 - 1) < \phi$ (constraint 3A)
$q_2 + q_1 + q_0 \geq 3$ (3B); (see Appendix 2). $\tag{3.3}$

So there exist certain conditions in which holding cash is beneficial. Comparing alternate situations is essential to demonstrate how ϕ, x, q values, and probabilities of investment (P) interact.

As ϕ increases, earnings retention becomes better while expected return to earnings disbursement declines. The model also suggests that there is a counterbalancing effect in favour of earnings disbursement inherent in the disbursement decision's third branch returns. A poor investment q_0, as defined above, significantly lowers the return of earnings retention relative to earnings disbursement. Releasing dividends prevents managerial misinvestment in this particular model. Table 3.3 summarises the model's predictions as variables are increased:

As investment quality or q values increase, earnings retention gains a relative advantage over earnings disbursement. When all variables increase, the relative advantage column in Table 3.3 indicates which strategy's returns are more sensitive to the increase; likewise, in the case of a decrease, the relative advantage indicates a relative loss in advantage, i.e., a decline in ϕ worsens the earnings retention strategy's return relative to earnings disbursement. As P declines, the shareholders' expected return under earnings retention declines by a greater proportion than return under earnings disbursement. A key to the model is that the strategy of retention is independent from changes in ϕ, but more sensitive to changes in P. Thus when ϕ is high, *ceteris paribus*, retention is likely to be dominant, and when P is low, *ceteris paribus*, disbursement is better for shareholders.

3.7.4 Estimating benchmark cases for the model

Consider how premia affect shareholders' returns under the three cases. Since smaller, young firms are likely to have a higher ϕ, these firms should be more concerned about their excess cash. This model, by assuming that available cash flow, x, is proportional to firm's size, shows a breakeven point for all firms given an exogenously determined premium

Table 3.3 Model predictions when model variables are increased

Variables to be increased	Earnings retention	Earnings disbursement	Relative advantage from increase
q_0 – Investment quality	Increases	Increases	Earnings retention
q_1, q_2 – Investment Quality	Increases	Increases	Ambiguous (unless ϕ and P are known)
P – Probability of good investment	Increases	Increases	Most likely earnings retention
ϕ – External Finance Premium	Unaffected	Decreases	Earnings retention

(ϕ). Each case can be examined with a given ϕ in order to show a breakeven level of cash flow x. A breakeven level x would make earnings retention as attractive as earnings disbursement. After this breakeven level x is determined, further studies can determine the optimal policy.

In Figure 3.2, the model assumed that good investments, where q_1 and q_2 are both greater than unity, each occur with a probability of $P/2$ so the probability of a bad investment becomes $(1 - P)$. This assumption eliminates the certainty of project quality. Uncertainty modifies how the expected values of the two strategies compare – both P and f interact directly in the model.

Consider a large finite number of possible investments and the comparison becomes complex. For simplicity, assume there are only three possible investments as shown in Figure 3.2. By keeping probabilities endogenous to the model, the external finance premium can be related to the probability of good investment opportunities, P. Table 3.4 lists the various considerations in each case. To model specific instances of the three cases, assume that $\phi = 50,000$, but alternative ϕ values will be considered below.

Case 1, given an assumption that $\phi = 50,000$ and $q_0 = 0$, reveals that the breakeven point for the two strategies is $x = 100,000$. This can be found by substituting the given values into Case 1's second constraint (1B; see Appendix 1). However, with a premium of 50,000, constraint (1A) requires that $x(q_1 - 1) > \phi$. If $q_1 = 1.1$, the requirement suggests that $.1x > \phi$. This condition requires $0.1(100,000) > 50,000$; this constraint can never exist unless q_1 is greater than 1.5. Constraint (1A) now holds so that 100,000 can be the breakeven point. This exercise is limited by the interaction between the premium value and q_1. The two constraints will differ if these values vary. Case 1 shows that if these two constraints do indeed hold, then a strategy of full earnings retention has a higher expected return for shareholders. Firms have a higher expected value from retaining cash if $\phi \geq \dfrac{x(1 - q_0)}{2}$; therefore, as ϕ

Table 3.4   Summary of case studies: assumptions and modifications

Assumptions made in the three cases
Case 1 $\phi = 50,000$; $q_0 = 0$; $q_1 > 1.5$; breakeven level of x is 100,000 [Figure 3.4] Later modifications:$q_1 = 1.1$; breakeven level of x is 500,000 [Figure 3.5]
Case 2 $\phi = 50,000$; $q_0 = 0$; $q_1 = 1.1$; breakeven level of x is 55,555 [Figure 3.6] Later modifications: Varying levels of q_1; breakeven level is 200,000
Case 3 q_1 and $q_2 < 2$ and close to 1; $q_0 = 0$

increases and q_0 remains constant, the earnings retention strategy is better for an even larger investment x. A consequence of this finding is that firms with a higher ϕ should retain earnings up to the breakeven point to finance investment – this breakeven point increases concurrently with the external finance premium.

To show how investment opportunities influence the choice of strategy, reconsider constraint (1B) without assuming that $P = 2/3$. By simplifying the expression of the expected values, one finds that

$$P \geq \frac{x}{x+\phi} \quad \text{(see Appendix 2)} \tag{3.4}$$

if the earnings retention policy is dominant. By assuming the breakeven level of x equals 100,000, one can plot the relationship between P and ϕ. Below in Figure 3.4, the curve represents the breakeven relationship of P and ϕ. Given $x = 100,000$, any combination of P and ϕ lying above the curve will be an opportunity for the firm to gain by retaining all of its cash flow.[6] The downward slope of the curve fits the model intuitively, for as the premium of external finance increases, an earnings retention policy becomes more favourable and more valuable. Therefore, as ϕ increases, it takes a lower probability of good investment (P) to break even on the strategy.

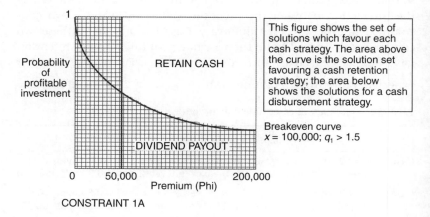

Figure 3.4 Relationship between P and the premium for Case 1

Given a breakeven x of 100,000 consider how the breakeven x will influence the relationship between ϕ and P. Figure 3.5 presents the breakeven curve relating P and ϕ, given $x = 500,000$. If $x = 500,000$ then $\phi = 50,000$ when $q_1 = 1.1$; thus, in this curve is the situation where both constraints are satisfied and $q_1 = 1.1$. One can see that the breakeven curve shifts nonlinearly upward with its vertical intercept fixed (compared with Figure 3.4 curve) as x increases. This is intuitive, for x represents the firm's cash flow at $t = 0$. When a firm's initial earnings increase, while ϕ remains constant, the possibility of misuse increases as Jensen predicts. Since the model includes the possibility of misinvesting (q_0), to break even with an earnings retention policy the probability of good investments, (P), must increase if ϕ remains constant and the total cash flow at $t = 0$ increases. Case 1 has revealed that for any firm's investment, there exists a wide range of possibilities in which it is better to retain and invest all of its cash. The assumption is that all earnings are retained or disbursed, but a more complex model could capture a firm's intermediate decisions at $t = 1$.

Since Case 1 was the most compelling situation against the earnings retention strategy, an examination of Case 2 should reveal more evidence that there exist conditions in which a firm should retain all of its earnings. Case 2's first constraint (2A), with $\phi = 50,000$, requires

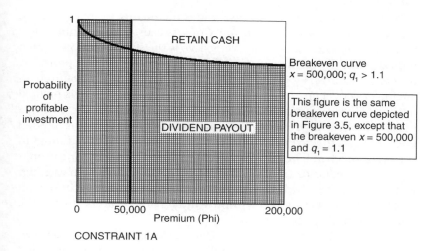

Figure 3.5 Modified breakeven curve

$x(q_1 - 1) < \phi$; therefore, again ϕ and x will interact to influence how constraining this assumption is. The second constraint (2B) states that $x(2 - q_1 - q_0) \leq \phi$. The assumption that f equals 50,000 makes inequalities $x(q_1 - 1) < 50{,}000$ and $x(2 - q_1 - q_0) \leq 50{,}000$ the requirements for an earnings retention strategy to be favoured. If q_1 is assumed to be 1.1, the first constraint is more easily met than in Case 1, for the inequality would hold for any investment x less than 500,000. However, the second constraint $x(2 - 1.1) \geq 50{,}000$ or $x(.9) \geq 50{,}000$ is absurd because it requires that $x > 55{,}555$. With $\phi = 50{,}000$, q_1 should be somewhere between 1.9 and 1.1 in order for both constraints to be satisfied and economically viable. With the assumption that $q_1 = 1.1$, the breakeven x becomes approximately 55,555 (see Appendix 2). As in Case 1, if the assumed ϕ is altered, there would be a correspondingly different breakeven x.

The second constraint is influenced by the probability of good investments and constraint 2B is met without substituting $P = 2/3$ (see Appendix 2 for details). The resulting expression describes the set of solutions in which the strategy for earnings retention is a superior policy:

$$P \geq \frac{2x}{\phi + q_1 x + x} \tag{3.5}$$

The set of solutions will depend upon the values of x and q_1. Figure 3.6 reveals the relationship between ϕ and P given varying levels of q_1. As the value of q_1 increases, the breakeven curve of the two strategies shifts downward.

This shift makes intuitive sense, for as the quality of investment q_1 increases there is a lower probability of loss caused by retaining cash. Since the area above the breakeven curve is the set of solutions which indicate earnings retention, as q_1 increases, it becomes more profitable to retain earnings. By increasing the initial cash flow x, a counterbalancing effect occurs, for as x increases the breakeven curve is pivoted upwards with its vertical intercept fixed. As in Case 1, an increase in x makes the cost of a misinvestment in q_0 (branch 3 of the model) greater. The expected value of earnings retention is reduced more in the event of a bad investment; therefore, the solution set for earnings retention is reduced. There is some range of values for which earnings retention provides the higher expected return. As in Case 1, this region of solutions for earnings retention will be reduced according to the limitations of the first constraint.[7]

Case 3 should be most likely to suggest earnings retention; however, its assumption in 3A is highly stylised. Constraint 3A requires that $x(q_2 - 1) < \phi$, and therefore, $x(q_1 - 1) < \phi$. Given differing levels of q_1 and

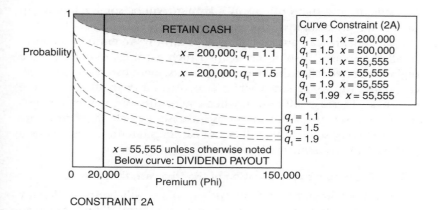

CONSTRAINT 2A

Figure 3.6: This figure shows various breakeven curves for $x = 55,555$ and $x = 200,000$, The different curves are found by varying the level of q_1 as shown in the figure. The shaded area above the $q_1 = 1.1$, $x = 200,000$ curve represents the set of solution for which an earning retention strategy is dominant. The area below the curve is the set of solutions for which an earnings disbursement strategy is dominant. Although these regions are only shown for one curve in this figure, the same type of solution set (above and below the breakeven curve) can be determined for each individual curve. As in Figures 3.4 and 3.5, constraint (A) will reduce the solution set must be to the right of the vertical constraint.

Figure 3.6 The relationship between P and premium for Case 2.

q_2, it is easy to see the difficulties presented by the constraint. If $q_2 = 2$, as in Figure 3.2, then the constraint requires that $x < \phi$. Since this requires the premium to be larger than the total investment itself, the underlying assumptions in this case reduce to absurdity.

However, a similar calculation can be attempted when q_1 and q_2 are both small enough to satisfy constraint 3A. The resulting constraint $\frac{q_0 + q_1 + q_2}{3} \geq 1$ (3B; see Appendix 1) shows that for Case 3 to hold, q_0 will also likely have to be greater than 0. If both constraints (3A and 3B) are met, earnings retention will always be superior to earnings disbursement. Since constraint 3B does not depend upon the breakeven value x or ϕ, one can recalculate the constraint to find how important P becomes. By including the probability P, the second constraint becomes: $P(q_2 + q_1 - 2q_0) \geq 2 - 2q_0$ (see Appendix 2). Case 3 depends upon the values of q_0, q_1, q_2. Assume that $q_0 = 0$, a proxy for the bad

investment, and that both q_1, $q_2 > 1$, there will be some relationship such that $P < 1$ will satisfy the constraint.

This model reveals an optimal level of earnings retention for a firm. In all three cases, a solution set for which earnings retention has a higher expected value than earnings disbursement can be determined. Generally, this set is larger when ϕ increases and smaller when the earnings x increase. Moreover, when the quality of the firm's investment increases, the set of solutions increases as well. Since firms are heterogeneous, some firms will favour earnings retention even when a positive NPV investment may not exist.

3.7.5   The model's incorporation of the free cash flow theory

Jensen's FCFT argues that firms with earnings will be institutionally biased to spend the retained earnings on poor projects. If firms retain all of their earnings and there are no investments they hold their cash. The model here suggests that all earnings are retained regardless of the available investments; therefore it is likely that firms which have some q_0 projects available will have excess cash. Jensen says that managers will purposely invest in the q_0 branch even if they know the true nature of the investment is equivalent to q_0's return or even less – the zero return in the third branch of the earnings retention strategy. The model here says that Jensen would be correct in this case since the earnings disbursement model would have a superior expected return. As seen in the various case relationships between f and P, as P declines the premium must increase in order to keep the earnings retention strategy dominant. For any firm whose premium is unlikely to change, the model predicts that if managers can foresee only q_0 projects, they should disburse earnings. It remains to explore situations in which the premium on external finance can upset the predictions of the FCFT. In these cases, it is likely that an optimal level of earnings retention exists.

3.7.6   The premium ϕ: costs of asymmetric information

The external finance premium rests upon asymmetric information in the capital market. Consequently, these asymmetric information effects can be considered in determining the external finance premium which a firm faces. By finding a feasible model for f, the difference between external finance and internal finance can be determined. As demonstrated in the model, there exist economic conditions and external finance premia, captured in P and f respectively, which favour firms which withhold all of their cash flow. Considering possible determinants of these premia suggests an optimal level of dividends for at least different types of firms.

The difference between internal finance and costs of external finance arise primarily due to three factors: firm's maturity, net worth (or collateral value), and amount of debt in its capital structure. Suppose that $\phi = f(w, m, d)$ where

- w = net worth
- m = maturity
- d = amount of debt in a firm's capital structure

As a firm's net worth increases, the asymmetric information premium decreases because it has a greater collateral level, thus $\dfrac{\partial \phi}{\partial w} < 0$. As a firm grows older and bigger, the amount of available information about a firm's management and its profitability also reduces the information costs. Small and young firms find it most difficult to obtain credit and are typically those rationed out of credit markets first, although partially because they have little collateral; therefore $\dfrac{\partial \phi}{\partial m} < 0$. Lastly, as a firm increases its debt burden, it also increases its bankruptcy costs. Intuitively, as firms with debt seek external finance for investment, new creditors require greater premium to compensate them for the possibility that a firm might collapse. The debt level is closely linked to net worth, since as debt increases, a firm uses up its collateral, or reduces its net worth to the new creditors; basically, the result that $\dfrac{\partial \phi}{\partial d} > 0$. An additional measure when modelling premia could differentiate between sources of external finance. For example, if the source of external finance is a bank, then the benefits of a banking relationship would effectively lower the premium over time.[8] For the present discussion, it is assumed that there are no such relationship effects due to the origin of the external funding. Since net worth, or collateral, influences the premium on external finance, strategies which increase a firm's net worth should lower the premium faced by the firm. Since the earnings are not distributed to the shareholders, it does not become an asset for the firm. If they were distributed as dividends, creditors would have no claim on these earnings. This implies that retained earnings is a good policy for a young firm. A paradox, according to the model, is that by retaining earnings and lowering the external finance premium, a firm increases the dominance of earnings disbursement. This apparent paradox can be reconciled within the context of a longer time scale. Earnings retention and collateral creation is more important for the younger, more immature firms. Earnings retention serves as a proxy for size and maturity. Perhaps the reduction of the finance premium is initially small, so that a firm continues to retain earnings. Once the firm exceeds a certain level of maturity and size, the size, maturity and net worth effects make retention no longer necessary to reduce the premium. It is at this point that a firm can switch primarily to earnings disbursement since the premium is now low.

In considering the premium of external finance, one can also find a reason for small firms to avoid misusing. If a small firm, which faces a premium for external finance, abuses its retained earnings, it reduces its access to external finance in future periods. Essentially, a bad investment of retained earnings by purposely choosing an investment with a q_0 return increases the premium that a firm will face. No sources would choose to provide external finance to this firm – i.e., f becomes prohibitively high. Such a firm will have to rely upon internal funds regardless of the state of the economy. Since the model predicted that earnings disbursement which requires external finance has higher returns when an economy is in recession, i.e., when (P) decreases, those firms which purposely make bad investments will suffer. A small firm with low return investment opportunities which decides to abuse retained earnings will suffer disproportionately in the long run. Small firms with good investments will use retained earnings productively. Large firms have the potential to abuse cash and still obtain external funds when needed because of net worth and size and maturity effects. This model incorporated both Jensen's predictions and asymmetric information as complementary ideas.

3.7.7   The case of recessions and booms

The model also allows an examination of the effects of economic conditions on a firm's financing strategy. By altering the probabilities corresponding to each investment, the effects of a recession may be captured. There are two general effects of a recession throughout the economy. The first is the balance sheet effect which causes both firms and banks to decline in net worth. The premium for external finance increases as firms' collateral is reduced and banks contract credit. Secondly, the recession should increase the uncertainty of investment project returns. In the model, it was assumed that each of the three investment qualities occurred randomly, but there will now be a bias towards bad investments so that the probability distribution of investments shifts towards the bad projects.

One effect of the recession is to make the bad projects more likely, i.e., the probability of a good investment (*P*) declines. According to the model, this means that firms should lean towards disbursing all of their cash and externally finance any good investments. This strategy maximises the shareholder's return during a recession. However, if there is a good investment opportunity, firms will face a much higher external finance premium. The reduction in collateral value increases the premium, but more importantly, during a recession, the probability of a firm defaulting on debt increases significantly. Regardless, the model suggests that during a recession firms should not retain cash to finance investment. There is only one type of firm which might consider retaining cash during a recession – small firms with highly rated investment opportunities.

Table 3.5 depicts the model's suggested strategies during stable conditions. Table 3.6 depicts a firm's cash strategy during recessionary conditions, and Table 3.7 depicts the same during a boom period.

In this framework, a low *q* firm is assumed to have poor investment opportunities, and a high *q* firm mostly good investments. Only small firms are the ones who should follow a cash retention strategy, and even then only given certain conditions and optimistic investment opportunities. A large firm with good investment opportunities will

Table 3.5   Firm strategies during stable conditions

	Small firm	Large firm
Low Q	Disburse cash	Disburse cash
High Q	Retain cash	Retain cash

Table 3.6   Firm strategies during recession

	Small firm	Large firm
Low Q	Disburse cash	Disburse cash
High Q	Retain cash	Disburse cash

Table 3.7   Firm strategies during boom

	Small firm	Large firm
Low Q	Ambiguous	Disburse cash
High Q	Retain cash	Retain cash

face a small external finance premium; therefore, even the slightest possibility of a q_o investment could make the earnings disbursement strategy dominant. This tradeoff remains an ambiguous prediction without further information on firm characteristics.

During a recession, only a small firm with a high probability of good investments might benefit from an earnings retention strategy. Although the recession decreases good investments (P) generally for firms throughout the economy, this effect only occurs if firms are uncertain about their investment qualities. For the small growing firm with good internal information about a project, the recession might increase the probability of investments with lower returns, but by definition a high q firm should have mostly $q > 1$ projects.

Table 3.7 shows the model's predictions in the event of an economic boom (P increases). Both types of high q firms, small and large, should retain earnings. Large firms are likely to be able to productively use their incoming cash flow through investment; therefore, although the boom market lowers borrowing costs, large, high q firms should never have to borrow unless they have more investments than their present cash flow can finance. By definition, high q firms will have profitable investment opportunities particularly in a boom. Small, low q firms could benefit from retention in a boom for they could build up slack for possible future investments even though good investment opportunities are presently unavailable. Although during a boom credit is more available, small low q firms still might have to pay a high external finance premium if other firms, i.e., small and large high q firms, borrow to finance investments which exceed their cash flow. Thus, it makes more sense to retain earnings as a source for future investment. With an increased P due to the boom, any small firm might profit from retention. Low q, large firms should still disburse cash since credit will always be easier for them to obtain regardless of the economic environment. Given such *ideal* behaviour in different conditions, it is possible to empirically examine the investment behaviour of firms and their strategies.

3.8   Empirical examination of earnings retention

3.8.1   Foundations for empirical investigations

Examining the use of retained earnings is empirically difficult especially since firms do not always publicly report their cash flow in excess of positive NPV projects; therefore, much empirical work seeks to examine firm investment as related to financial factors such as firms' net worth, their present cash flow, and dividend policies. Firms which follow an optimal retention policy, i.e., small, high q firms, find their investments are sensitive to cash flow. During a recession, they will require internal finance to invest; therefore, their investment's sensitivity to net worth should not be greatly affected. However, firms which should not retain earnings, i.e., low q firms, should have their investment become more sensitive to their net worth if external finance premia are increased during a recession. Another hypothesis is that firms which retain earnings should have investment be more sensitive to their cash flow. If they follow an optimal retention policy, these should be high q firms ($q > 1$) and cash flow will dictate their investment.

3.8.2 Examining actual firm investment behaviour

To test whether firms are actually following a strategy similar to that predicted in the model, the empirical work will examine data from firms in the non-financial sector listed on the Mumbai Stock Exchange. The data was primarily the result of firm balance sheets as well as directories of the Mumbai Stock Exchange during 1979–90. All firms which were missing data from 1979–90 were removed from the data set.[9] Since all Tobin's q values determined were less than unity and the market–book ratios were greater than unity, the data was separated according to relative investment quality.[10] Both Tobin's q and market–book ratio have been used as benchmarks for investment quality; this study will rely primarily the use of Tobin's q.

To separate the data, the relatively good investments were those which were greater than the mean in quality measures. Large firms were those which exceeded the mean value of gross assets. By employing this division, one could examine whether or not firms were indeed following cash strategies which the model suggests. According to the model, firms which are small and high q should rely primarily upon internal finance as a means of investment finance. All others with the possible exception of large, high q firms should release funds as dividends and seek external finance for investment funding.

From the non-financial sector, a representative sample of 317 firms has been used. The separation of the data reveals that 131 of 317 firms (42%) fit the category small, high q firms and that most of the firms in the sample are small (264 of 317; 84%). Table 3.8 shows the data classified by size and quality.

Table 3.8 Distribution of firms in non-financial sector

Frequency Overall percent Row percent Column percent	Small firms GA < Rs. 4,350,387	Large Firms GA > Rs. 4,350,387
Low Q	133 42% 82% 50%	29 9% 18% 56%
High Q	131 42% 84% 50%	24 8% 16% 44%

An examination of the dividend policies of the firms in the sample will show if they are indeed following strategies which the model suggests. For example, firms which are small, high q should not be issuing dividends whereas low q firms should be issuing dividends. Therefore, an examination of the dividend payouts to decipher whether or not firms are following optimal dividend strategies will prove quite beneficial for the present purposes.

From the common dividend policies of the firms, it does not appear as if firms are following the model's strategies. Table 3.9 reveals the distribution of firms having dividends. Dividing the data sample into relatively high q and low q firms, one finds that of the high q firms, 54% (84 of 155) issued dividends leaving 46% (71 of 155) which – as prescribed by our model – did not issue dividends. Of the relatively low q firms which should issue dividends, 40% (66 of 162) of the firms actually issue dividends. It appears as if, contrary to the model, firms are not acting optimally. The fact that a higher percentage of relatively low q firms do not issue dividends seems to support the FCFT – these firms are suffering from lower values due to a lack of dividends.

Table 3.9 Distribution of non-financial firms disbursing dividends

Firms giving (total) dividends	Small firms	Large firms
Low Q	60 (133)	6 (29)
High Q	66 (131)	18 (24)

From another perspective, by looking at the firm patterns of retained earnings in Table 3.10, a similar outcome emerges. All firms in the sample with lower quality investments retain some of their earnings, whereas of the good investment (high q) firms, 92% (145 of 157) retain earnings. The model predicts that all good investment firms should retain some cash for investment. A reason for this contradiction could be that firms do not choose either extreme policy, but instead opt for an intermediate cash strategy which mixes both a percentage of retention and disbursement – this allows dividends to appear in high q firms and retained earnings to appear in low q firms.

Table 3.10 Distribution of non-financial firms retaining earnings

Firms retaining (total) earnings	Small firms	Large firms
Low Q	133 (133)	29 (29)
High Q	121 (133)	24 (24)

To consider the influence of mixed strategies, it is instructive to examine both the dividend payments and the retained earnings after they have been normalised by firms' size (gross assets). If firms are acting optimally even though they play mixed strategies, the low q dividend firms should be paying higher dividends relative to the high q firms. Similarly, the low q firms which retain their earnings should be retaining less relative to the high q firms. Tables 3.11 and 3.12 list firms' relative dividends and retained earnings against the mean of these normalised variables. From the distribution of relative dividends, the model does not fare much better – a higher percentage of low q firms (55%) are below the mean of .2723 than high q firms (39%). Moreover, the mean of each low q cell is below the means of the other two cells. Since the model suggests that high q firms should be disbursing relatively less dividends than low q firms, the data does not substantiate the model. Moreover, the model implies that the small, high q firms are least likely to pay dividends if they follow an optimal cash strategy – the data shows their dividends are well over the mean.

A look at relative retained earnings, on the other hand, does provide evidence that firms might be optimising their cash holdings. From Table 3.12, one sees that several high q firms were below the mean of retained earnings while half of the small, high q firms were above the mean for retained earnings. Again, this does not indicate that theses firms are optimising as per the model, but in comparison with the low

Table 3.11   Distribution and means of non-financial firms' relative dividends

Firms below means (total) Mean of cell	Small firms	Large firms
Low Q	67 (133) .2295	22 (29) .2562
High Q	54 (133) .3021	6 (24) .3641
	Sample mean of relative dividends = .2723	

Table 3.12   Distribution and means of non-financial firms' relative retained earnings

Firms below means (total) Mean of cell	Small firms	Large firms
Low Q	60 (133) .6980	6 (29) .5636
High Q	67 (133) .7704	18 (24) .6194
	Sample mean of relative retained earnings = .7095	

q firms which ought to have followed a disbursement policy, the high q firms are relatively better. i.e., 53% high q firms are below mean of retained earnings vs. 55% of low q firms below mean for dividend payout. One can also note that the mean for the large, high q firms is below the mean for the entire sample. This is not odd, for large firms can always obtain external finance at a minimal cost. Since the mean retained earnings for small, high q firms is the only one above the sample mean, these firms are likely to rely heavily on retained earnings. A look at the distribution of normalised retained earnings suggests that firms might be retaining some optimal amount of cash even though they are nearly all paying dividends.

Although these findings appear to reveal non-optimal dividend policies, retained earnings may not actually be misused. Of the 317 firms, 221 did not undertake any significant investment in 1979 – the earnings were retained, yet these funds were not misinvested. Firms could be paying larger than optimal dividends because of the good underlying economic conditions in 1979 (GNP growth 6.3%). By also retaining some funds, external finance might have been cheap enough to provide marginally needed funds. The next step is to test for the effects of these very factors on investment.

Another possibility is that there is a relationship between dividend policy and firm profitability. Small, high q firms are releasing dividends and retaining earnings at the same time. These firms are likely to be more profitable than other firms in the sample because of their high q values. They do pay dividends, but, more important, they have a high level of retained earnings relative to the rest of the sample. The lack of dividend payments of the low q firms may simply be an artefact of their low q's – they are not very profitable so they have low earnings. They also retain less earnings on average, as the model predicts – they have no good investments. The odd dividend policies may not rule out the possibility that firms are acting optimally since the relative retained earnings coincide with the model's predictions.

3.8.3 Examination of past evidence from excess cash predictions

Given abnormally low q values during the 1980s, the relative q values can still be useful in examining the influences upon a firm's investment. To examine the influences on investment, it will be useful to look at an equation where investment is regressed on cash flow, gross assets (as proxy for size), common dividends, retained earnings, and q values. The results of the regression had both cash flow and retained earnings nearly significant at the 95% level. This finding suggests that the regression suffered from multicollinearity; therefore, the correlation between retained earnings and cash flow was computed. Intuitively, cash flow and retained earnings should be highly correlated. The Pearson correlation coefficient between the two variables was .84 as predicted; therefore, retained earnings were removed from the regression. The results of the new regression are presented in Table 3.13.

Table 3.13 Results of regression for investment with 1979 data

Variable	Coefficient	t-values
Intercept	0.005	0.404
Cash flow	0.052	1.105
Gross assets	0	–0.833
Common dividends	0.972	9.569
q values	–0.023	–1.277
	$R^2 = .989$	

This regression does not appear to be very good as only common dividends are significant at the 95% level even though the R^2 is .989. This R^2 is abnormally high – suggesting that perhaps multicollinearity is still present or that the regression is over-parameterised. The strongly significant positive effect of dividends upon firm investment contradicts the FCFT. According to Jensen, an increase in dividends should decrease investment. The positive relation between investment and common dividends could be explained by a signalling phenomenon – firms which expect future growth pay dividends. Perhaps the high q firms dominate the regression because of their profitability when compared to low q firms; thus, they might skew the regression. If this is true, when the sample is divided into low q and high q firms, it is expected that high q firms' dividends are positively related to investment and low q firms' dividends are negatively related to investment. Firms paying dividends are profitable and this profitability could be related to investment decisions and q values. Low q firms would not release dividends because of poor performance. Of the remaining results, the insignificance of cash flow is most surprising. Cash flow should be important to firm investment if there exists an external finance premium. The lack of such a premium could suggest perhaps that during this period there was significant credit available but very few investment opportunities where it might be used.

To investigate the model's assumptions which state that internal finance is cheaper than external finance, regressions similar to the above were performed on the same data set after dividing it into relatively good q firms and lower q firms. The results are presented in Tables 3.14 and 3.15.

Both regressions are not much better than the original – the high q firm regression had an abnormally high R^2 of 0.994 and the low q firm regression had an extremely poor R^2 of 0.087. In the high q firms, investment is positively but insignificantly related to cash flow and positively related to

Table 3.14   Results of regression for investment, 1979
  (high q firms)

Variable	Coefficient	t-values
Intercept	–0.0168	–2.954
Cash flow	0.033	0.436
Gross assets	0	1.115
Common dividends	0.964	6.653
	$R^2 = .994$	

Table 3.15 Results of regression for investment, 1979 (low q firms)

Variable	Coefficient	t-values
Intercept	0.005	1.674
Cash flow	–0.025	–0.777
Gross assets	0	0.931
Common dividends	–0.093	–0.681
	$R^2 = .087$	

common dividends. The positive coefficient for cash flow makes sense, for the cash flow of high q firms should strongly influence investment. It is rather surprising that cash flow is only significant at the 33% level. Gross assets do not appear significant probably due to the scaling of the variables. Gross assets should influence investment by affecting the external finance premium – as gross assets increase, the external finance premium should decline and more investment would be possible. Since the model predicts that high q firms should retain, they should avoid external finance as much as possible. This independence from external finance could be a reason for the insignificance of gross assets as well. The strong relationship between dividends and investments is probably an influence from the profitability of high q firms – these firms signal their optimistic futures by paying dividends.

The low q firm regression in Table 3.15 reveals that investment is negatively related to dividends and negatively related to cash flow. Since none of the variables are significant at the 95% level and the R^2 is only 0.087, this is a poor regression. These variables do not explain much of the variation in investment for these firms. However, it can still be instructive to examine the differences between the low q and high q regression. An interesting observation is the negative relationship between investment and dividends – albeit insignificant – in the low q regression. This finding suggests that either decreasing dividends increases investment – as Jensen predicts for low q firms – or that dividends are paid if there are no good investment opportunities. In either case, these findings contrast with the positive relationship between dividends and investment in the previous regression. Although gross assets should influence investment for low q firms since they rely upon external finance, the insignificance might be a simple lack of investment opportunities. Low q firms which choose not to invest will not need to seek external finance anyhow. Moreover, the lack of investment could also be the reason for the low R^2. The negative relationship between cash flow and investment reinforces this idea. These firms might be low q during the present period, and they might be building excess cash supplies for much later periods. i.e., financial slack. This negative relationship makes the positive relationship found in the high q regression more noteworthy. On the whole, both regressions seem to be influenced by firm profitability – high q firms being the more profitable and thus optimistic whereas low q firms being unprofitable.

3.8.4   Regression of investment after monetary contraction

It is useful to examine if the regressions changed after the downturn caused by a monetary contraction within the economy as India struggled to combat high inflation rates during 1980–2. The identical regressions were tested using 1982–3 data to examine whether there was a significant difference in the determinants of investment immediately following the recession. The results are presented in Tables 3.16 and 3.17.

After the recession, the high q firm regression still only has one significant variable at the 95% level, the dividends. This coefficient increased by approximately 0.01, a sign that dividends have become more important for these firms' investment. The recession has not altered the regression; rather, the cash flow and dividends become more significant in explaining the variation. Since these firms' dividends are correlated with investment, perhaps the unchanged regres-

Table 3.16   Results of regression for investment, 1982–3
(high q firms)

Variable	Parameter estimate	t-values
Intercept	–0.016	–1.239
Cash flow	0.033	0.528
Gross assets	0	–0.58
Common dividends	0.977	7.023
	$R^2 = .986$	

Table 3.17   Results of regression for investment, 1982–3
(low q firms)

Variable	Parameter estimate	t-values
Intercept	–0.004	2.325
Cash flow	–0.023	–1.372
Gross assets	0	1.784
Common dividends	–0.067	–0.889
	$R^2 = .178$	

sion is an indication that firms have managed their retained earnings in previous periods strategically. If they created a buffer of excess cash, as suggested for small firms, their investment could remain high and they could maintain dividend payments even in a recession. Releasing dividends would not affect investment if enough excess cash was accumulated. Looking at the data sample, it appears that firms do carry retained earnings over periods – cash flow in a previous period is carried over as retained earnings to the next. It appears that these firms actually retain earnings as a buffer; thus, these firms become less dependent upon the present period's cash flow for investment.

In Table 3.17, the low q regression, like the high q regression, does not change much after the 1980–2 economic downturn. Again, it appears as if the only effect was to increase the significance of the variables in the regression and to improve the R^2 to 0.178. The lack of change could be due to the same buffering strategy applied by high q firms, but this is unlikely if firms are acting optimally – this sample includes large, low q firms which do not need to buffer with excess cash. More likely, the low q firms still do not have many investment opportunities; therefore, they simply release dividends and invest less. The negative relationship between cash flow and investment, although insignificant, could be an indication that low q firms are forced to reconsider their survival. Although this view seems more viable in a recessionary environment, given the same negative relationship, this could indeed be a possibility. As cash flow declines, investment increases – firms retrench and re-invest in modern capital. This idea of a *cleansing effect* is possible because cash flow typically declines during a recession. Low q firms might be retrenching in an attempt to become high q firms. According to the regression, investment would be essentially increasing as the cash flow declined.

On the whole, the model cannot adequately capture the large but finite number of combinations between cash retention and cash disbursement policies, but it can help in examining the regression results. Although the monetary contraction of 1980–2 does not appear to alter significantly the determinants of firms' investment, the results of the regressions show how investment is influenced by financial characteristics.

3.8.5   Formula for retained earnings

Since the model described earlier is designed to show the potential of a dominant cash retention strategy, it only depicts the two extreme situations. Empirical work indicates that firms actually follow strategies which have policies that mix cash disbursement with cash retention. Although the data sample does have some odd or ambiguous results, it is assumed that throughout the period being examined, each firm is following its own optimal strategy. Based on this assumption, the same data sample is used to calculate the optimal cash formula for a firm. The key to this formula is the assumption that firms are behaving optimally. This assumption could be true as the regressions seem to indicate that the low q firms are not misinvesting (since their investment is negatively related to cash flow) but are retrenching. In the following exercise, retained earnings of the firm are first regressed on q values, gross assets, and the firm's growth rate. The q values serve to capture the relative quality of the investment, and the gross assets serve as a proxy for firm size. The results of this regression are presented in Table 3.18.

All the variables of the regression are significant; therefore, the optimal formula for retained earnings is as follows: $RE = -64.596 + 61.747q + 0.32GA + 48.948g$; where q is the q value, GA is the Gross Assets, and g is the growth rate of the firm. The R^2 of the regression is 0.9125, which suggests the regression can explain much of the variation.

Table 3.19 depicts two examples of how this formula can be used to determine how much cash a firm should retain. It is assumed that there are two firms: Firm A and Firm B. Firm A is a low q firm and Firm B is a high q firm. For Firm A, q = 0.8 and growth rate (g) = 0.02. For Firm B, $q = 1.2$ and (g) = 0.15. The formula predicts that generally high q, high-growth firms should retain more earnings than low q firms. This is true whether the firm is large or small – it is assumed that a large firm has Rs. 300 million and a small firm has Rs. 25 million in assets. The example shows the importance of retention for small firms. The normalised retained earnings suggest that large, high q firms retain more cash than large, low q firms, but not by a significantly greater amount. On the other hand, for the small, high q firm, the normalised RE far exceeds that of the small, low q firm. The negative RE of the small, low q firm can be rounded upwards to zero, but the robustness of this result remains.

Table 3.18   Results of regression for retained earnings

Variable	Parameter estimate	t-values
Intercept	−64.596	−6.314
Q values	61.747	4.785
Gross assets	0.32	71.919
Firm growth rate	48.948	2.336
	$R^2 = 0.912$	

Table 3.19 Formula predictions for small and large firms

Variable	Small firm		Large firm	
	Firm A	Firm B	Firm A	Firm B
Intercept	−64.596	−64.596	−64.596	−64.596
Q values	0.8	1.2	0.8	1.2
Gross assets	25	25	300	300
Firm growth rate	0.02	0.15	0.02	0.15
Predicted value (RE)	−6.219	24.843	81.781	0.376
Normalised RE*	−0.249	0.994	0.273	0.376

*Normalised RE is the retained earnings/gross assets. This is used so that one can compare how the strategy differs according to the size of the firm, i.e., a small, high *q* firm should retain considerably more relative to first a low *q* firm then a large, high *q* firm.

Since the period between the years being looked has undergone many changes in underlying economic conditions, the next exercise re-runs the regression of retained earnings while including an additional year variable (measured by the last two digits, i.e., 82 = 1982). The results of this regression suggest that the year is a significant factor in the retained earnings formula (Table 3.20).

The inclusion of the year variable increases the R^2 slightly to 0.9139. The year variable is significant at the 95% level, but the growth variable drops to 93%. This negative coefficient for the year variable might be an indication that firms require less retained earnings (investment) because of the recession in the latter years of the time period. During the later years, when underlying economic conditions worsened, the optimal strategy required lower earnings retention. The year variable functions as a proxy for deteriorating or fluctuating economic conditions. The regression could be re-run using a better proxy for the underlying environment.

Table 3.20 Results of regression for retained earnings including year variable

Variable	Parameter Estimate	t-values
Intercept	198.1211	2.139
Q values	56.1306	4.33
Gross assets	0.3212	72.171
Firm growth rate	39.0474	1.852
Year	−3.212	−2.853
	$R^2 = 0.914$	

Table 3.21   Results of regression for retained earnings including GNP growth
rate

Variable	Parameter estimate	t-values
Intercept	−59.907	−5.549
Q values	62.775	4.86
Gross assets	0.319	71.931
Firm growth rate	43.289	2.028
GNP Growth* (%)	−1.708	−1.218
	$R^2 = 0.913$	

* GNP growth rate is calculated as $(GNP_{t+1} - GNP_t)/GNP_t$. GNP figures are in constant dollars.

Table 3.21 contains the results of a regression in which the year variable is replaced with the GNP growth rate. The GNP growth rate should be a better indication of the economic conditions for a negative growth rate, such as the −1.7% in 1980 is unambiguously a recession year. All variables in the regression are significant at 95% with the exception of the GNP growth rate.

Both the coefficients of firm growth rate and the q value increase while the coefficient of gross assets declines slightly. By including the GNP growth rate, the formula for optimal retained earnings suggests that growth and high q firms should retain even more earnings. The GNP growth rate itself does not add much to the formula except in its effect of improving the significance of the other endogenous variables.

To further investigate this cash formula, it might be useful to re-examine a few cases looked at earlier. In Table 3.22, the exercise conducted in Table 3.19 is duplicated but now includes a year effect as captured by the GNP growth rate. The boom year of 1983 (GNP growth = 8.1%) and the recession year of 1980 (GNP growth = −1.7%) will be tested here.

Similar predictions as those in Table 3.19 can be noted after examining the years independently – high-growth, small firms should retain the greatest earnings. The formula suggests that firms should hold more earnings during a recession. The results that greater earnings should be held in a recession contradict the idea that more investment opportunities are available when the economy is in a boom unless firms have investments even during a recession. Perhaps in a recession the external premium is much higher so that retained earnings become more important. The inclusion of the GNP growth rate into the formula does not seem to alter the predictions.

Table 3.22 Formula predictions for small and large firms given the state of the economy

Variable	Recession (1980)				Boom (1983)			
	Small firm		Large firm		Small firm		Large firm	
	Firm A	Firm B	Firm A	Firm B	Firm A	Firm B	Firm A	Firm B
Intercept	−59.907	−59.907	−59.907	−59.907	−59.907	−59.907	−59.907	−59.907
Q values	0.8	1.2	0.8	1.2	0.8	1.2	0.8	1.2
Gross assets	25	25	300	300	25	25	300	300
Firm growth rate	0.02	0.15	0.02	0.15	0.02	0.15	0.02	0.15
GNP growth rate	−1.7	−1.7	−1.7	−1.7	8.1	8.1	8.1	8.1
Predicted (RE)	3.68	34.418	91.405	122.143	−8.601	22.137	79.124	109.862
Normalised RE*	0.147	1.377	0.305	0.407	−0.344	0.885	0.264	0.366

*Normalised RE is the retained earnings/gross assets. This is used so that one can compare how the strategy differs according to the size of the firm, i.e., a small, high q firm should retain considerably more relative to first a low q firm and then to a large, high q firm.

Overall, the regressions seem to indicate that q values, gross assets, and firm growth rate are all important in determining a firm's amount of optimal cash retention. Although this formula was derived from the assumption that firms mostly adhere to their optimal strategies, it predicts that even some low q firms will find it optimal to retain cash. Empirically, there do appear to be cases where cash should be retained even if it is excess cash. While the study examined various possibilities in an explicit two choice model, it is important to note that the data captures a characteristically more varied pattern of financial behaviour.

3.9   Conclusion

This chapter shows that in a dynamic situation, paying no dividends can be an optimal strategy for some firms. Jensen's FCFT is less useful with imperfect capital markets. Some firms which ought to disburse funds as dividends as per the FCFT can justify holding cash to add value based on the difference between the costs of internal and external finance. This finance premium varies according to individual firm characteristics and thus undermines the FCFT in certain instances.

This chapter shows how cash retention can be good given uncertainty and two choices: retaining cash or paying dividends. The expected values of the two alternatives depend on the external finance premium and the underlying economic conditions reflected in the probability of a good investment (P). The resulting breakeven curve between the two strategies suggests a set of solutions from paying all dividends to retaining all cash depending on ϕ, P, q_0, q_1, q_2. The model reveals that a high enough external finance premium justifies retaining excess cash.

The empirical analysis examined optimal mixed strategies. Since firms' total excess cash often exceed their excess cash in the current year, it implies a cash retention strategy. This finding suggests that firms are either ideally retaining excess cash as a buffer against negative economic conditions or that shareholders are risking managerial abuse as the FCFT predicts. It appears that by separating good and bad firms, there is a difference in treatment of retained cash and dividends. Investment in high q firms appears positively related to dividend payment and cash flow whereas the low q firms' investment is negatively related to dividend payment and cash flow. The difference in the determinants of investment suggests that firms should follow different finance strategies.

Calculating optimal retained earnings implies that firms are behaving close to the optimal during the time period examined. The results of regressions appear significant and suggest that high q firms and firms with high growth rates should retain more cash. The positive coefficient for retained earnings suggests that it might be optimal for some firms who do not presently retain cash to withhold future cash flow. Sometimes firms would have benefited from retaining excess cash from previous periods. The assumption that firms use their optimal cash strategies becomes central to these findings.

The critical determinant of optimal cash retention is the external finance premium. Low q firms have less reason to retain excess cash unless they expect to use it for investment soon; only small, low q firms which would face higher external finance premia should retain cash. If the primary determinant of the external finance premium is firm size, then large firms – even high q firms – would benefit less from retaining cash. Small, high q firms need to retain cash. Public information can make the high q firm appear to have very low-quality investments so that the capital market underestimates the firm's potential. These firms maximise their expected future value by relying on internal funds.

Firms find valid reasons to justify the retention of cash flow. Sometimes retained cash will be misused, but sometimes retention benefits the firms' shareholders. The explanation depends on firm characteristics. No firm which can obtain external finance at low cost can justify retaining excess cash as a buffer unless a large economic downturn is expected. Only firms which face stiff external finance premia can benefit from cash retention. Excess cash allocation must consider asymmetric information or remain incomplete. Excess cash is not always misinvested and this chapter developed a framework to examine possible abuses.

4
The Cost of Capital: Earnings Retention vs Leverage

4.1 Introduction

Firms have three main sources of finance: internal funds, bank loans, and finance raised in the capital market. In India, debt finance represents almost 40% of total finance raised by the largest 100 publicly traded Indian firms (Singh and Hamid, 1992).[1] The choice between debt and equity has always been critical for the overall value of the firm. However, financial economists have rarely hesitated to give advice on capital structure without knowing how firms actually choose their capital structures (Myers, 1984). This chapter addresses part of this problem by examining the determinants and effects of debt financing in Indian firms.

As in most developing country capital markets, India's debt market is complicated by institutional constraints and regulations with inefficient and distorted credit markets. Since 1951, the Reserve Bank of India (RBI) has required that for every rupee deposited in the banking system, 40% had to be held as reserves, and 24% as directed credit, leaving banks discretion over only 36% of all deposits. Government intervention in the form of directed credit and subsidised lending often favoured state-managed firms which crowded out the private sector's demand for credit. In this context, debt financing for firms in the private sector was one of the main concerns in the liberalisation programme undertaken by the Indian government. These reforms have attempted to influence domestic finance patterns by revitalising capital markets. Finance from state banks and development finance institutions emphasised project rather than corporate finance. Leverage ratios, financing requirements, and guidelines for lending were mostly based on project technology, capital intensity, and the perceived importance of the project within national priorities. However, since 1991, liberalisation has meant that the domestic market for corporate debt and equity has experienced substantial transformation. There has been a gradual shift from bank finance to capital markets while banks and development finance institutions are experiencing basic changes.

This chapter examines the recent history of capital markets in India and related financing decisions in Indian firms. How firms choose a given debt/equity mix and how they view the cost and risk of different sources of capital on firm performance are the basic issues addressed in this chapter. The chapter summarises recent literature on the cost of capital and capital structure, financing hierarchies, and leverage targeting models. It then outlines some general themes in an Indian context. In the following sections, two empirical models examine the determinants and profitability of leverage using Indian data. The first model concentrates on general determinants of leverage, and the second incorporates Jensen's FCFT to test the effects of leverage on firm performance. One of the aims of the empirical work is to test the FCFT's hypotheses regarding the significance and the type of relationship of leverage in Indian firms. It is hypothesised that due to agency costs and asymmetric information problems caused mainly by the different incentives of a state-managed banking system in India, the FCFT's predictions including the positive relationship between debt and firm performance need to be tested. The study concludes with policy suggestions for reducing inefficiencies. As foreign financial institutions enter the Indian capital market, they may exert competitive pressure on Indian firms. A crucial first step is the privatisation of state-owned banks already begun in 1991.

4.2 Background

4.2.1 Institutional characteristics of financial markets in India

After independence, the market for industrial securities in India was not well developed and commercial banks were the only important financial intermediaries in industrial financing. At the time, commercial banks provided only short-term finance for working capital. In 1958, commercial banks began to undertake some-term lending activities, and provided medium-term finance which was re-financed by a special institution set up for the purpose.[2] Therefore, industry was largely dependent on internal sources for finance as well as on government-controlled finance.

For long and medium-term finance for industry, government-sponsored special development finance institutions (DFIs), i.e., development banks, were established in the post-independence period.[3] Policy-makers thought that due to imperfections in the capital markets, new firms, relatively smaller firms, and certain sectors of industry did not have easy and adequate access to term finance and therefore needed special attention. Capital shortage was said to justify such institutions to fill the gap. In India, there was the additional objective that both the amount and the allocation of investment be in accordance with plan priorities. Gupta distinguishes the characteristics of these institutions (Gupta, 1969):

1. They were restricted to providing finance for new investments in fixed assets.
2. Although they were expected to work on commercial lines they were also expected to pay 'due regard to the public interest' and work in accordance with the official plans.
3. They were not expected to compete with the traditional providers of finance and their role was that of 'gap fillers'.

These DFI's were also expected to meet the equity capital and foreign currency resource requirements of industry and they grew rapidly during the 1980s. All the finance provided by them goes to industry. Disbursal of credit by the DFIs grew almost 20% per annum during the 1980s whereas overall bank credit to industry grew at an average annual rate of 17% during the same period. In spite of their 'priority sector' commitments involving non-industrial activities, approximately 50% of the commercial banks' finance also goes to industry. However, even today commercial banks largely fulfil only the traditional function of providing short-term finance for working capital requirements.[4]

The financial system has enjoyed an almost total lack of competition. Long-term lending has very few participants. In addition, since they are all government owned, the term lending institutions have generally acted as a consortium and have the characteristics of a lending cartel. If a loan is refused by the consortium, there is no alternative. Further, there is virtually no competition between the term lending institutions, which concentrate on medium and long-term finance, and the commercial banks with their emphasis on working capital. With the nationalisation of the 14 large commercial banks in 1969 about 85% of the assets of the banking system were under public control.[5] Long-term lending by these nationalised commercial banks had been restricted to smaller enterprises and their share in consortium lending had been restricted to 25%.

Given political objectives of maintaining low interest rates and directing credit towards certain preferred sectors, there was until recently a complex system of administered interest rates.[6] In commercial banks both deposit and lending rates were regulated. Credit provided at lower rates to the priority sectors is cross-subsidised by the rest. The administered interest rate structure was characterised by an inverted yield pattern with Long-term interest rates being lower than minimum short-term lending rates of the commercial banks. The Narasimhan Committee noted in 1991: 'The inverted yield pattern is largely a consequence of inflation and the desire of the Government to shield Long-term investments from the penalty of high interest rates caused by inflation' (Narasimhan Committee, 1991). Although the reasoning contained in the first part of this statement is not compelling when applied to a relatively long period, the statement itself is indicative of the way in which the problem of the yield curve was being viewed. DFIs provided credit at relatively stable lending rates during the 1980s. The prime lending rate of the major DFIs during the 1980s was 14% whereas the regular short-term lending rates of commercial banks were in the range of 16–19.5%. Inflation rates based on the Wholesale Price Index ranged from 4.5% to about 8% during this period.

Nonetheless, although the GDP deflator was somewhat higher between 6.5–9.3%, at least real interest rates on non-concessional loans remained positive. The fiscal system has also encouraged debt finance over equity; therefore, Indian firms have been highly leveraged and dependent on the DFI's for capital. Figure 4.1 indicates that the overall industry average debt/equity ratio over this period has been 80.1% for all listed firms.

Before gradual deregulation of the financial sector, both the mobilisation and allocation of savings were heavily regulated. For example, the opening, expansion, and closure and location of bank branches were tightly controlled. In addition, interest rates on loans and deposits and the direction of credit were also regulated with wide interest rate differentials across sectors and loan sizes. Firms' access to capital markets was also strictly regulated. Regulations notwithstanding, the last four decades witnessed a considerable widening and deepening of the Indian financial system as shown by the improvements in the financial ratios (see Table 4.1).

However, most financial institutions are still government owned and guided by so-called 'public interest considerations' which are likely to

86

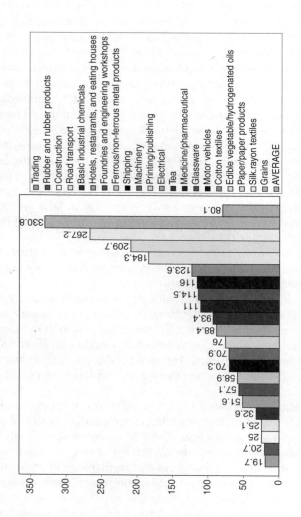

Source: Based on data from Reserve Bank of India

Figure 4.1   Industry average debt/equity ratio

Table 4.1 Financial development ratios

Ratio	1951–1956	1966–1969	1980–1981	1989–1990
Finance ratio	4.9	13.8	32.7	43.9
Financial interrelation ratio	0.63	0.93	1.93	2.5
Intermediation ratio	0.27	0.33	0.41	0.45

Note: Finance ratio = total financial claims/national income; Financial interrelation ratio = increase in stock of financial claims/net capital formation; Intermediation ratio = claims issued by financial institutions/issues of non-financial sectors.
Source: adapted from Rangarajan and Jadhav (1992).

entrench poor incentives and a misallocation of resources. These institutions are not under pressure to foreclose a mortgage when a borrower defaults. Thus loans are rescheduled more often than if the financing institution were guided purely by commercial motives. For this reason, liquidation of insolvent firms which often continue to enjoy government-sponsored losses continues to be rare in India, as described in the following chapter.

4.2.2 Capital structure: theory

The value of a firm is the discounted stream of expected cash flow generated by its assets financed by investors with various types of claims on the firm's cash flow. Debt holders have a first and relatively safe claim on the stream of cash flow through contractual guarantees of a fixed schedule of payments. Equity holders have a claim on the residual stream of cash flow and accept more risk. The mix of debt and equity funds defines a firm's capital structure. Firms combine debt and equity, subject to certain constraints, to maximise their market value.

Theories of capital structure are well documented in the literature. Modigliani and Miller's seminal paper on corporate financial structure embodies the original value-invariance proposition. It states that the weighted average cost of capital remains constant as leverage changes. So why do firms focus on their financial structure? Miller says: 'perhaps we should have put more emphasis on the other, upbeat side of the *nothing matters* coin: showing what *doesn't* matter can also show by implication what *does*' (Miller, 1988). Modigliani and Miller's hypothesis was founded upon a number of restrictive assumptions ignoring transaction costs, taxes or inflation, the quality of borrowing and lending rates, and independence of financing and investment decisions. The consequences of relaxing one or more of these assumptions, especially if firms alter their discounted cash flow (i.e., value) by varying leverage, is now well covered in the literature.

Literature following Modigliani and Miller implies an internal solution to the problem of optimising leverage (Modigliani and Miller, 1958). The internal solution, i.e., target leverage ratio, is the mix of debt and equity which maximises the value of the firm. Firms equilibrate the costs of debt, relative to equity, to determine optimal leverage. The alternative view is distinguished by the implication that internal funds are always cheaper than funds raised on external equity markets. Therefore, leverage is determined by the demand for funds in excess of the limited internal resources. These *fund cost hierarchy* models focus mostly upon a single determinant of costs of alternative funds.

4.3   Financing hierarchies

Some evidence of corporate financial structure suggests that internally generated cash flow is the cheapest form of finance. Debt is more expensive, and external equity is the most expensive. To minimise total cost, managers use the cheapest source first. However, given that internal funds are limited, firms often resort to credit and equity markets and pay premia for these external sources. Fund cost hierarchies are consistent with a variety of exceptions in the Modigliani–Miller framework with asymmetric information issues most commonly discussed. However, transaction costs, liquidity constraints, and ownership dilution can all lead to a preference for internal funds.

In their most basic form, asymmetric information theories say that managers have more information about the firm than investors. Investors assume this and infer that managers are more likely to raise equity when a firm's share prices are overvalued so investors price equity issues at a discount. This discounting of share issues can force firms to forgo good projects with positive net present values. The costs of external equity can be avoided, however, if firms use retained earnings. The problem can also be partly overcome in firms with a reputation for accurate reporting. Asymmetric information can also generate a premium on debt funds through the same mechanism. Again, the premium can force firms with exhausted internal funds to forgo projects with positive net present values. However, premium on debt will be less than that on equity mainly because debt is less prone to sharp fluctuations at valuation. As a result, firms may tend to use internal funds first, then debt, and lastly externally raised equity (Myers and Majluf, 1984; Harris and Raviv, 1991).

Market imperfections also explain variations in the different costs of finance. First, costs and delays involved in raising funds on equity markets, e.g., broker charges, underwriting fees, issue of prospectuses, may lead to a preference for internal cash and debt over external equity. The Modigliani–Miller value invariance proposition assumes that capital markets are frictionless (there are no transaction costs and transactions occur instantaneously). But, as Allen notes, 'many firms stated that equity issues were costly and time consuming...debt funding had the advantage of being quick to obtain' (Allen, 1991). Firms may prefer internal funds and debt because transaction costs are lower, especially for smaller firms, and firms can respond quickly to investment opportunities. Furthermore, the 1993 Indian Industry Commission's *Availability of Capital* report says implausibly that the larger the equity issue, the cheaper are the unit fees associated with issuance thus imposing higher costs on smaller firms. Debt means slower access and higher transaction costs than internal funds which can be used almost immediately. Second, some firms may prefer to maintain informational asymmetries since using internal funds does not subject the firm to external scrutiny. Similarly, with debt finance, information is provided for the banks, but there is no required disclosure of information to capital market competitors, or to shareholders. The advantage of confidentiality and the costs of releasing information may generate a financing hierarchy, as discussed in the earlier chapter. Third, new equity issues may dilute the claims of existing shareholders. Pinegar and Wilbricht list the dilution of shareholder funds as an important consideration in the capital structure decisions of US managers (Pinegar and Wilbricht, 1989).

A finance hierarchy implies that the mix of debt and equity reflects firms' cumulative requirements for external finance, and this, in turn, reflects the relationship between surplus cash flow and projected investment. Which factors are primarily responsible for the observed preferences for internal funds over debt is debatable. However, it is likely that each factor has some influence and the empirical support for financial hierarchies is strong. Fund cost hierarchies imply a negative relationship between net cash flow and leverage, since as cash flow increases, firms are able to rely more on internal funds. Also, if firms operate under a fund cost hierarchy, those with rapid growth expectations should assume larger debt burdens after exhausting internal funds. In the US, more than half of the firms surveyed preferred internal funds and the rest a mix of internal funds and debt (Allen, 1991). Where new finance was required, debt was preferred to equity. This was confirmed by Pinegar and Wilbricht who also found that 84% of US firms ranked debt as their first choice of external finance (Pinegar and Wilbricht, 1989).

However, an important caveat for fund cost hierarchy models is that there are significant costs associated with extreme reliance upon a single fund source. For example, a strong preference for internal finance, resulting in very low levels of debt, may expose a firms to takeovers financed by the firm's own debt capacity. Nevertheless, the cost structures underlying the fund cost hierarchy may affect firms' preferred fund sources over moderate ranges.

4.4   Target leverage models

Modigliani and Miller and others consider the effects of introducing taxation into the original framework. Other studies consider costs associated with bankruptcy, financial distress, transaction and agency costs in the models of financial structure. All of these costs are influenced by leverage.

Taxation means that net cash flows are divided between debt holders, equity holders, and the government. By incorporating a tax on profits, Modigliani and Miller show that profit and tax deductibility of interest payments make it optimal for firms to rely entirely upon debt (Modigliani and Miller, 1963). Miller shows the gain from leverage when different tax rates are applied to corporate profit, personal earnings from stocks, and personal interest earnings (Miller, 1977). The incentive to finance completely through debt disappears under a variety of tax regimes. Moreover, the gains from leverage are zero if full dividends are paid and the marginal income tax rate for the investor is equal to the corporate tax rate. DeAngelo and Masulis emphasise that the tax induced gains from leverage are reduced if a firm's expected income stream against which interest expenses can be deducted is less than the firm's total interest costs (DeAngelo and Masulis, 1980). They note that deductions from taxable income, other than interest payments, reduce the expected gains from leverage. These non-interest tax deductions are generally known as *non-debt tax shields* and include accelerated depreciation allowances and investment tax credits, both of which can finance investment regardless of the choice of financing. Despite these offsetting factors, the tax system is an important influence on capital structure choice. Two implications of the influence of taxation on capital structure choices are: (a) optimal leverage may increase as corporate tax rates rise; (b) optimal leverage may increase with the amount of income against which firms expect to be able to offset interest expenses.

In the Modigliani–Miller model there are no bankruptcy costs.[7] In the event that a firm is unable to meet contractual obligations, the firm is transferred without cost to its bondholders. In reality, bankruptcy imposes both direct and indirect costs on the firm. Direct costs include legal expenses, trustee fees, and other payments which are due to parties other than bondholders or shareholders. Indirect costs include disruption of operations, loss of suppliers and market share and the imposition of financial constraints by creditors. These indirect costs of bankruptcy and the financial distress costs which may occur even if the firm does not enter bankruptcy can be very significant. The following chapter discusses these costs and their implications for capital structure choices.

Castanias, and Bradley, Jarell and Kim find a negative relationship between leverage and business risk but Long and Malitz found it positive (Castanias, 1983; Bradley, Jarell and Kim, 1985). Titman and Wessels concluded there was no significant relationship (Titman and Wessels, 1988). Optimal leverage ratios may be positively related to firm size and reflect economies of scale. Bankruptcy costs include a fixed payment and these costs constitute a larger fraction of the value of a firm as firm size decreases (Ang, Chua and McConnell, 1982). Large firms may also have lower risk through diversification, more stable cash flows and established operating and credit histories. These factors provide large firms with better access to alternative sources of finance, especially during times of financial distress. This may reduce the present value of expected bankruptcy costs for large firms, thus encouraging them to take on relatively higher debt levels. Lastly, leverage may be positively related to the value of a firm's collateral assets or liquidation values. Higher liquidation values reduce the expected losses accruing to debt holders in the event of financial distress, thus making debt less expensive (Chaplinsky and Niehaus, 1990).

4.5   Agency costs of leverage

Agency costs of debt for firm owners arise from potential conflicts between debt and equity holders and between managers and equity holders. The choice of capital structure can in some cases reduce the costs arising from these conflicts. Jensen and Meckling (1976) highlight the agency costs associated with equity holders' limited liability and debt holders' fixed maximum returns. In the event that an investment is successful, equity holders capture more of the profit. If the investment is unsuccessful, however, debt holders share the burden with equity holders. As discussed in the previous chapter, this asymmetry of expected returns may provide incentives for managers acting for equity holders to pursue more risky investments with expected negative net present values. Alternatively, agency costs may arise between managers and equity holders if projects are financed using debt. Managers stand to lose their jobs, their reputation, and their firm specific capital in the event of financial failure, and because they cannot diversify this risk, managers may choose not to engage in projects with positive net present values if they must use debt finance (Lowe and Rohling, 1993). This type of agency cost can be reduced by the use of equity fund sources.

Jensen (1987) proposes a *control hypothesis* which focuses upon an agency cost which can be reduced by high debt levels. He says that if a firm has large excess cash flow then managers may spend funds on projects with negative net present values to increase firm size or market share. Jensen suggests that managers have an incentive to waste funds in this way because management remuneration is positively correlated with firm size. High debt may diminish this incentive because the interest burden reduces excess cash flow. Jensen postulates that this incentive towards debt eventually offsets the other agency costs associated with high debt levels to determine the firm's optimal leverage.

While the agency cost literature boasts several theoretical models, tested hypotheses are scarce. One testable hypothesis is that a negative relationship exists between leverage and firms' growth opportunities (*q* values). This negative relationship arises in two ways. Titman and Wessels note that since growth opportunities are not considered collateral (they are very difficult to monitor and value), creditors demand a relatively high return when providing finance for these opportunities (Titman and Wessels, 1988). Thus, firms with growth opportunities are expected to look to equity rather than debt as a source of finance. Similarly, firms in growing industries may have greater flexibility in their choice of investments, allowing equity holders greater freedom to expropriate wealth from bondholders. Either way the costs of debt in rapidly growing firms may lead to a preference for equity.

Therefore, agency cost theories imply that leverage is chosen in a rather complex fashion to reduce the power of equity holders to act against the welfare of bondholders and to reduce managers' capacity to act against equity holders' interests. Titman and Wessels find that leverage is inversely related to firms' growth opportunities while Kester does not find a significant relationship (Titman and Wessels, 1988; Kester, 1986). The results in Malitz are inconclusive (Malitz, 1985). The hypothesis that leverage is positively related with default probability and with excess cash flow is rejected by Castanias and Chaplinsky, and Niehaus respectively (Castanias and Chaplinsky, 1990; Niehaus, 1983).

4.6 Research methodology

To understand the effects and determinants of leverage, two empirical models will be tested. The first concentrates on the more general determinants of leverage for all types of firms. The second splits the sample into two, i.e., firms with high and low growth opportunities, and uses a profitability model with leverage and equity as the key explanatory variables. Furthermore, these firms will be further split into sub-groups based on their cash retention behaviour based on Jensen's FCFT. Jensen recommends debt as a disciplinary and market value enhancing device for all firms, but especially low q, low dividend firms which retain a substantial portion of earnings. Similarly, the FCFT also suggests that high q firms with greater investment opportunities should increase leverage but at a relatively lower rate than their low q counterparts. In either case, however, as the FCFT hypothesises, leverage ought to increase both the market value and performance of firms of all types as it signals lower agency costs and lower information asymmetries.

The previous sections revealed some general principles which have empirical support and are tested here. Within moderate ranges, firms should exhibit a preference for internal funds over external securities.[8] Again, within moderate ranges, when external funds are required, firms should prefer debt to equity. The preference for internal funds should be evident in a negative relationship between firms' cash flow and their reliance on debt. The various costs associated with external finance may be lower for those firms with less informational asymmetry between the various stakeholders (debt holders, equity holders, managers, creditors, customers, and employees). They may also be smaller for larger firms. If firms require external funds, then their leverage is determined by the tradeoff between the relative costs of debt and equity, as mentioned before. That is:

(a) Leverage would be negatively related to firms' inherent riskiness through the effect of risk on the expected costs of bankruptcy and financial distress. This implies that leverage may be positively related to collateral and negatively related to cash flow volatility.

(b) Leverage would be set by firms to minimise their effective tax rates. This link ought to vary between firms but it will not be clearly observable. Also, the tax advantages of debt should decline if interest payments cannot be fully deducted from earnings.

(c) The relationship between growth and leverage depends upon the relative importance of the fund cost hierarchy or the target leverage approach.

Beyond firm-specific factors, more general institutional and macroeconomic factors might affect leverage. General macroeconomic factors such as real asset prices, consumer price inflation, and the differential between the real cost of debt and the real cost of equity may affect capital structure decisions by altering the availability and the relative costs and benefits of alternative funds and by changing the demand for funds. Institutional factors such as the degree of regulation may also affect firms' capital structure choices.

4.6.1   Data

Data here comes from the Mumbai Stock Exchange Directory supplemented with Reserve Bank of India (RBI) bulletins. The measure of financial leverage used in this study is used by the RBI and the Stock Exchange Directory in surveys of listed firms, namely the debt equity ratio. Debt comprises of (a) all borrowing from government and semi-government financial institutions other than banks and other institutional agencies; (b) borrowing from banks against own debentures and other mortgages; (c) other borrowing against own debentures, other mortgages, deferred payment liabilities and public and other deposits. Equity comprises paid up capital including ordinary, preference, deferred shares, etc., forfeited shares, and all reserves. This measure of the debt equity ratio is based on book values and is subject to the limitations of book values.

4.6.2   Statistical model

Based on the former review, a number of factors may influence financial structure. Some of these vary exclusively between firms while others vary exclusively over time and others vary across both firms and time. In the first empirical model, the following linear relationship is assumed between leverage and its determinants:

$$\frac{D_{it}}{A_{it}} = \alpha + \beta' X_{it} + \rho' Z_t + \pi' W_i + u_{it} \tag{4.1}$$

$\dfrac{D_{it}}{A_{it}}$ = leverage is firm debt, D_{it} is expressed as a percentage of total assets, A_{it}. Both debt and total assets are measured at book value.

X_{it} = vector of determinants that vary across both firms and time.

Z_t = vector of determinants that vary only with time.
W_i = vector of determinants that vary only across firms.
α, β, ρ, π = vectors of coefficients that are assumed in the standard model to be constant over time and across firms.
u_{it} = residual comprised of a firm specific component, μ_i, a time specific component, λ_t, and a component that varies over both firms and time, v_{it}. i.e., $u_{it} = \mu_i + \lambda_t + v_{it}$

X_{it} includes the following variables that vary both between firms and over time:

Cash flow – earnings before interest, tax, and depreciation have been deducted and expressed as a percentage of total assets*
Growth – the percentage rate of growth in real total assets*
Size – natural log of total assets*
Real tangible assets – measured as a percentage of total assets*
Potential debt tax shield – income against which interest expenses can be deducted and expressed as a percentage of total assets*

* all real values adjusted for inflation

At this stage, it is hypothesised that in firms with a fund cost hierarchy, cash flow is negatively related with the dependent variable, D/A. As cash flow increases, more internal funds become available and firms reduce their reliance on more expensive debt. Similarly, firms with a fund cost hierarchy are likely to have a positive relationship between leverage and their rate of growth. Higher growth rates mean a greater demand for funds, which forces firms to use external fund sources including debt. An increase in real tangible assets, by increasing the quality of collateral, is expected to lead to higher leverage. The coefficient of firm size is expected to have a positive sign because of the increased access to credit markets which is available for large firms. The potential income against which firms can deduct their interest expenses is predicted to have a positive sign, since the benefit from debt is reduced if interest cannot be deducted in the current period.

The complexity of the potential debt tax shield variable (referred to as E_{it} henceforth) requires further explanation. DeAngelo and Masulis (1980) and Titman and Wessels (1988) consider the relationship between non-interest tax deductions and the leverage of firms. *Non-debt tax shields* are non-interest tax deductions as discussed earlier, e.g., accelerated depreciation allowances, investment tax credits. They hypothesise that as these 'non-debt tax shields', S_{it}, increase, firms have less incentive to incur debt to reduce tax. It is also recognised that firms focus on the amount of income that can be shielded from tax using interest payments, E_{it}. To determine this amount, the non-debt tax shields, S_{it}, need to be calculated.

If the amount of tax paid by firm i in period t, T_{it}, is greater than zero, then S_{it}, can be obtained by calculating from the expression for the tax payable[9]:

$$T_{it} = \begin{cases} \tau_c(Y_{it} - I_{it} - S_{it}) & if \quad Y_{it} - I_{it} - S_{it} > 0 \\ 0 & if \quad Y_{it} - I_{it} - S_{it} \le 0 \end{cases} \qquad (4.2)$$

Therefore, if a firm pays tax, the non-debt tax shields can be expressed as:

$$S_{it} = (Y_{it} - I_{it}) - \frac{T_{it}}{\tau_c} \qquad (4.3)$$

Y_{it} = gross earnings I_{it} = interest payments τ_C = corporate rate of tax

However when firms pay no tax, i.e., tax exhausted, the extent to which non-debt tax shields plus interest payments exceed gross earnings is not observed; thus, non-debt tax shields are not observed. However, since the earnings against which interest payments can be offset, E_{it}, are equal to gross earning less non-debt tax shields, the following expression arises for E_{it}.

$$E_{it} = \begin{cases} (Y_{it} - S_{it}) = I_{it} + \dfrac{T_{it}}{\tau_c} & if \quad T_{it} > 0 \\ 0 & if \quad T_{it} = 0 \end{cases} \qquad (4.4)$$

E_{it}, the measure of the potential debt tax shield, is unobserved when a firm is paying no taxes, since the relative proportions of income shielded by interest payments and by non-debt tax shields cannot be determined. To allow for this, tax exhaustion is included as a dummy variable which is set at one when no tax is paid by a firm.[10]

Z_t includes the following variables which vary only over time: real asset prices; consumer price inflation; fund cost differential – the difference between the real cost of debt and the real cost of equity where both costs are measured as aggregates for the Indian economy.[11] For variables under vector Z_t, it is expected that increases in real asset prices will generate upward pressure on firms' demands for funds and thus raise leverage. Consumer price inflation is predicted to have a positive relationship with debt if higher inflation transfers wealth to debtors through tax deductibility of nominal interest payments. A negative relationship is expected between the fund cost differential variable. As the relative costs of debt rises, profit maximising firms would restructure their finance to reduce their leverage.

Lastly, the importance of the tax burden cannot be understated. Tax burden depends on the tax status of shareholders, the non-debt tax shields associated with investment projects, earnings retention ratios, rate of inflation, and the tax system (Ross, 1991). Since information is not readily available on investment projects or the tax status of shareholders, effective tax rates are not observed here.

W_i includes the following variables which vary only across firms: industry dummy variables; listing category dummy variable. Many factors that influence individual firm's capital structure are common within organisational structures and industrial groupings. Also, many characteristics of firms may be similar within industry groupings but whose effects are not captured elsewhere. For example, industry classifications are strongly correlated with cash flow volatility. Also, firms in the same industry which face common product and factor markets are likely to have similar capital requirements. For these reasons, the industry classifications are included in the specification. Moreover, previous studies support the importance of including industry groupings for capital structure decisions (Bradley, Jarell and Kim, 1985).

4.6.3 Estimation

Where there are no firm or time specific effects, $\mu_i = \lambda_t = 0$, OLS is appropriate. However, it is hypothesised that both unobservable firm-specific and unobservable time-specific factors will relate to leverage. Managers of one firm may be consistently more risk averse than others so the firm they manage may have consistently low gearing ($\mu_i < 0$). Similarly, changes in tax regulations may make debt relatively more expensive in some years than in others. As a result, desired leverage would be lower in some periods and firms ($\mu_i, \lambda_t < 0$). In estimating the equation, unobservable effects need to be accommodated. The unobservable effects can be included in the error term. The variance covariance matrix of the resulting errors must be transformed to obtain consistent estimates of the standard errors. In this case, the 'random effects' estimator is appropriate (Hsiao, 1989).[12]

4.7 Results

The results of the leverage equation are listed in Table 4.2. Estimates are presented for a simple regression as well as those which include both firm and time fixed effects. The results mostly support the hypotheses and suggest that firm, institutional, and macroeconomic factors combine to affect capital market structure decisions.

The estimated coefficient on cash flow is negative and significant. The fixed effects model has a coefficient of –0.18. This is consistent with other studies, including Chaplinsky and Niehaus (1990), Titman and Wessels (1988), Kester (1986), and Allen (1991). It is also consistent with the predictions of the financing hierarchy models described earlier. The importance of cash flow and the availability of retained earnings in determining leverage reflect the agency costs of using external finance. Other factors are also responsible, in part, for the preference for internal finance. These include the need for financial flexibility and for reducing the flow of information to outsiders. Also, firms prefer internal finance because it reduces monitoring by the market and it prevents the dilution of existing shareholder claims. A reliance on internal funds also reflects

Table 4.2   Results of leverage model

Variables	Ordinary least squares	Fixed effects (firms and time)
Constant	5.44*	3.25
	(5.71)	(3.32)
Cash flow	–0.36*	–0.18*
	(0.14)	(0.09)
Firm growth	0.06*	0.03*
	(0.01)	(0.01)
Real tangible assets	0.23*	0.11*
	(0.03)	(0.03)
Firm size	2.88*	5.46*
	(0.44)	(0.89)
Potential debt tax shield	0.36	0.15
	(0.15)	(0.11)
Tax exhaustion	5.06*	4.71*
	(2.41)	(1.64)
Real asset prices	5.41	
	(2.08)	
Fund cost differential	0.2	
	(0.12)	
F-value	3.54	
R^2	0.63	

* Significant at 5% level.
Values in parentheses are standard errors.

the inability of some firms to access external capital markets. All of these factors potentially explain the negative coefficient on the cash flow variable in the leverage equation.

The coefficient of firm growth variable is also significant and positive. The fixed effects model has a value of 0.03. The positive relationship between leverage and firm growth is consistent with the view that rapid growth exhausts firms' internal fund reserves. This may result in increased dependence on debt, the next least expensive source of finance. In this light, the positive coefficient of firm growth is consistent with a conventional fund source hierarchy. Alternatively, assuming that past growth is a proxy for future growth, the positive coefficient of firm growth suggests creditors anticipate higher future cash flow. However, this view is contrary to the agency cost literature which says that rapidly growing firms are not able to use their growth potential as collateral for borrowing. Agency cost theories also suggest that firms in growing industries have greater flexibility in their choice of investments and, thus, shareholders gain at the expense of bondholders. Therefore, this increases agency costs of debt and creates a negative relationship between leverage and growth. Consequently, the evidence presented here conflicts with this aspect of the agency cost view of financial structure.

The coefficients of the real assets variable and firm size variable are both positive and significant. This supports the view that there are agency costs and financial distress costs associated with the use of external funds and that these costs may be moderated by size and collateral. Large firms often have more diversified and longer credit histories. Likewise, firms with quality collateral can obtain debt at lower premia because they are more secure for creditors. The ratio of real tangible assets to total assets is significant in an economic sense. The coefficient of firm size is more difficult to interpret. As the natural log of real assets, percentage change comparisons cannot easily be made. Instead, as real assets increase, so does leverage but at a diminishing rate. The leverage of a firm worth Rs. 100 million is expected to be 3.8 percentage points higher than the leverage of a firm worth Rs. 50 million. In comparison, the leverage of a firm with 250 million rupees is expected to be only 1.2 percentage points higher than a firm worth 200 million rupees, as indicated in Figure 4.2.

The coefficient of the potential tax shield variable is insignificant, suggesting no detectable role for the tax system in corporate leverage. But the tax exhaustion dummy variable is significant and positive; perhaps distortions caused by the tax system are more important to firms that are tax exhausted.

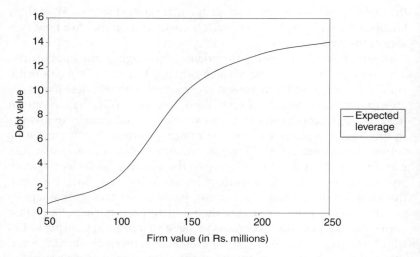

Figure 4.2   Expected leverage for different firm values

The results suggest a relatively insignificant role for macroeconomic variables. The insignificance of the consumer price inflation variable suggests that general goods price inflation has played a minor role in increasing leverage. This may be because creditors are able to compensate themselves for the wealth transfer to debt holders created by inflation through increases in nominal interest rates. The fact that the aggregate fund cost differential fails to add explanatory power to this model may reflect the difficulty in measuring the relative costs of debt and equity rather than the insignificance of relative funding costs. With appropriate data, further tests might actually examine these same macroeconomic factors before and after financial deregulation when some firms were able to take advantage of liberalised credit markets and expand their lines of credit.

As a first step towards examining the model's specification, White tests for heteroscedasticity were conducted. In both the fixed firm and time effects specifications, these tests reject the null hypothesis of homoscedasticity at the 5% level. Tests of the null hypothesis for the presence of first or second order autocorrelation were conducted on the residuals from the fixed effects model. In each case, residuals were regressed on the independent variables from the original model and the first and second lags of the residuals. The joint significance of the lagged residuals using the Wald test rejected the null hypothesis of no autocorrelation at the 5%level. These results support the view that an autoregressive process is present in the error structure. These might be the result of adjustment costs for which firms may alter their financial structure slowly over time as opportunities for new investments arise and as excess cash flow becomes available to retire undesired debt.

4.7.1   Discussion

For a better understanding of the effects of the variables on leverage consider Figure 4.3. Figure 4.3 indicates the levels of change in the variables required for the set changes in leverage. Chart 1 indicates for set changes in leverage percentage points: i.e., –10, –5, –3, 0, 2, 4, 10, the level of change required in some of the independent variables, e.g., the chart suggests that for a 10 percentage point decline in leverage for a firm, a decline of almost 300 percentage points in a firm's growth or a decline of 100 percentage points in a firm's real tangible assets is required, other factors being held constant.

The magnitude of the coefficient on the firm growth variable indicates that a 33 percentage point increase in growth is required to induce a 1 percentage point rise in leverage. Therefore, differences in the predicted leverage of firms with growth rates within the usual 5 to 10% band tend not to be driven by firms' growth rates. Also, the coefficient of the real

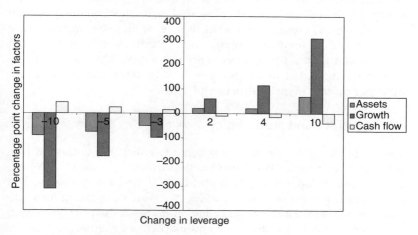

Figure 4.3   Factors affecting leverage

tangible assets relative to total assets suggests that an increase of 10 percentage points is required to increase leverage by 1 percentage point. Given that real tangible assets vary between 0 and 100% of firms' assets, such 'quality collateral' is capable of explaining up to 10 percentage points of the variation in leverage predicted by the model.

The results suggest that a number of firm-related and some macro-economic factors influence the leverage of Indian firms. The dominant factor driving variation in leverage across firms is firm size. The results suggest that larger firms have considerable advantages over smaller in credit markets. Cash flows, real tangible assets, and growth in the real size of firms also play important roles in explaining the variation in leverage across firms. The results also showed the insignificance of consumer price inflation in the model's specification. This suggests that the importance of tax deductibility of interest charges has been exaggerated. Instead, the insignificance of inflation is consistent with creditors simultaneously adjusting nominal rates of interest on a more than equal basis with changes in inflation.

More data on leverage of firms before and after the deregulation of credit markets in India might have helped to explain better the movements in leverage over time. It would be expected that prior to deregulation, increases in asset prices had less influence on leverage because firms were credit constrained. Following deregulation, higher asset prices would stimulate firms to increase their leverage and the size of their balance sheets. Rates of return from assets would be increasing and firms would increase their asset accumulation using credit. These newly acquired assets could then be used as 'quality collateral' against further credit. Therefore, since market prices would be rising and these values would be used to evaluate credit worthiness, so higher asset prices would spark a rising dependence upon debt. Although deregulation is not included in this model, it must have had a significant influence on the financial structure of firms.

4.8   Leverage and profitability

The second empirical model considers the effect of leverage on firm performance in India. The sample is split in two, i.e., firms with high and low growth opportunities. A profitability model uses leverage and equity as the key explanatory variables. Firms are further split into subgroups based on their retention behaviour to test Jensen's FCFT. Jensen recommends debt as a discipline and market value enhancing device for all firms, but especially low q, low dividend firms who retain a substantial portion of their earnings. Similarly, the FCFT also suggests that high q firms with greater investment opportunities should increase leverage but at a slower rate than their low q counterparts. In either case, the FCFT hypothesises that leverage increases both the market value and performance of firms of all types as it signals lower agency costs and lower information asymmetries.

4.8.1 Theory

Several theories relate the level of debt to firms' performance. Most have been discussed above. Ross argued that a firm with better growth opportunities, can issue more debt than one with lower growth opportunities since the issue of debt by the latter will result in higher probability of bankruptcy due to the higher debt servicing costs (Ross, 1977). The level of debt is believed to signal the growth opportunities of a firm to outsiders or others who do not enjoy the benefits of insider information available to managers exclusively. Similarly, when managers are also shareholders of their firms, higher debt promotes investment and inhibits managerial consumption (Jensen and Meckling, 1976). Equity dilutes profits to shareholders by requiring all profits to be divided evenly amongst all shareholders including managers. This dilution of profits leads to the classic agency problems discussed in the previous chapter. However, fixed debt service payments provide less incentive for managers to shirk their responsibilities when all profits beyond a certain fixed level are shared by fewer shareholders. Grossman and Hart combine the former explanations and assume managerial discretional behaviour (Grossman and Hart, 1986). Debt serves as a signal as well as a check on managerial discretion. Not only is the market able to make inferences about a firm's growth opportunities and the quality of its investment prospects, but the market perceives that management will pursue profits rather than discretionary behaviour. Therefore, debt compels managers to align their interests with those of shareholders, reducing the principal agent problem. Each of the former explanations shows why higher levels of debt will be associated with higher performance levels.

4.9   Research methodology and data

4.9.1   Data

The data here is from the Mumbai Stock Exchange Directory. The firm data are cross-sectional, collected from each firm for one of the years between 1987 and 1994 depending on the availability of all key variables thus avoiding any missing value problems. Some firm balance sheets were updated using additional data from the Reserve Bank of India. The sample contained 237 firms at the start, but further classification reduced the number used in the model whose main goal is to examine performance effects on high and low growth firms with similar levels of debt. So the sample was limited to firms with similar levels of debt in their financial structure.[13] The average level of debt for this sample was 35–40%. Of the 237 firms, only 92 fell into this category.

There needs to be some way to distinguish investment quality. Both Tobin's q and market–book ratio have been used; this study relies primarily on Tobin's q. Relatively good investments were those with a greater than mean quality measure. Employing this division shows if firms followed predictable cash strategies.

According to Jensen's FCFT, debt is a disciplinary and market value enhancing device for it signals that managerial interests are aligned with those of shareholders. This holds especially for low q, low dividend firms who retain a substantial portion of their earnings. Firms classified as high debt were those with greater than average debt. Similarly, firms classified as excess cash firms were those with greater than average retained earnings in their financial structure. Similarly, the FCFT also suggests that high q firms with greater investment opportunities should increase leverage but at a relatively lower rate than their low q counterparts. Therefore, in order to test the sample as per the FCFT, high q and low q firms were further classified into those high q firms which retained greater than average earnings and those high q firms who had greater than average levels of debt in their financial structure; similar divisions were made for low q firms.

Tables 4.3 and 4.4 show the distribution of the 92 firms used in the data set as classified by their q ratios as well as cash holdings. In this sample, 36 out of 92 were high q and 56 were low q firms. Out of the 36 high q firms, 17 were classified as holding excess debt and 11 retained an excessive level of earnings. For the low q firms, 35 held excessive debt and 16 held more than the average level of retained earnings. In total, for both low and high q firms, 29% of the firms retained excessive earnings whereas 56% retained excess debt.[14]

Table 4.3 Distribution of high q/low q firms

Type of firm	Number	Percent
High q	36	39
Low q	56	61

Table 4.4 Distribution of high q/low q firms with excess retained earnings and debt holdings (in percent)

Type of Firm	High q	Low q
Excess retained earnings	31%	29%
(no. of firms)	11	16
Excess debt	47%	63%
(no. of firms)	17	35

4.9.2 Statistical model

To assess the impact of leverage on firm performance, debt/equity will be used as the primary independent variable in a model where the dependent variable will be profitability. Profitability is measured as the ratio of profit to sales based on analyses done by Cowling and Waterson (1976). The model to be estimated includes the following independent variables: debt/equity ratio, liquidity, sales growth, overhead expenditures, and size. The principal independent variable is the debt/equity ratio; however, in explanations of economic performance, a number of other factors may have an influence. These factors may be firm related, industry related, or related to aspects of the institutional environment. If the impact of other factors are not controlled, the relationship between profitability and leverage may be spurious.

Debt/equity, the primary independent variable, should in theory have a positive influence on firm profitability due to its ability to monitor managers along with the other reasons discussed above. However, in India, term lending institutions are government owned and the loans made to commercial firms effectively come out of public funds. Therefore, just as state-owned enterprises have been known to compare unfavourably with private sector firms in performance, within private sector firms a greater level of debt might tend to reduce incentives, allowing managers to enjoy less accountability with respect to a large amount of capital invested in their firms. Therefore, the relationship between profitability and the debt/equity ratio should be negative.

The size of a firm affects performance in many ways. Key features of a large firm are its diverse capabilities, the abilities to exploit economies of scale and scope and the formalisation of procedures. These characteristics can make the operations more effective and allow larger firms to perform better relative to smaller firms (Penrose, 1959). Alternative views suggest that size is correlated with market power and any associated inefficiencies leading to relatively inferior performance (Leibenstein, 1976). Overhead expenditures include the ratio of advertising, marketing, and distribution expenditures to total operational expenditures. These ratios control at once for firm-related and industry-related factors. Some firms may spend heavily on advertising, distribution, and marketing activities to increase market share and profit. Therefore, these variables capture firm-level idiosyncrasies as well as industry-level settings which require all firms within a certain industry to spend more on the aforementioned activities.

Liquidity is another variable which reflects industry-level and business-cycle effects. Liquidity is the ratio of cash to total current liabilities. Cash requirements may be affected by industry practices but also by overall economic conditions. Liquidity also helps capture firm-specific attributes, so that the ability to manage working capital while maintaining a certain level of cash balances relative to current liabilities reflects superior skills. Jensen's FCFT supports this view and says that shareholder value will reflect the benefits of these superior skills. Sales growth is the rate of change in sales between the observation year, and the preceding year and also captures business-cycle effects and general market volatility. In markets where sales growth is high, there are possibilities for firms to make larger profits; however, such growth may attract new entrants and reduce profits for all players in the market. In fact, since reforms in India, there has been an increasing presence of smaller new entrants into industries with high sales growth.

4.10 Results

As discussed earlier, separate regressions are carried out for each of the cases under examination. Table 4.5 shows the results of the regression model where the sample was divided into high q and low q firms. For both types of firms, the relationship between the debt/equity ratio and firm performance is negative and significant; furthermore, the coefficient for the debt/equity variable for low q firms is more significant and lower.

As hypothesised, this finds a negative relationship between debt and performance for Indian firms, unlike their Western counterparts. It also substantiates part of the FCFT's hypothesis that debt is relatively more significant for the performance of low q firms than for high q firms; however, equally important is that the FCFT's predictions fail to capture the negative relationship. Again, as mentioned before, this may be the result of the misaligned incentives in India's banking system and is discussed in detail below.

Table 4.5   Regressions of high q and low q firms

	High q	Low q
Debt/equity	−0.923	−1.63
	*(1.83)***	*(2.03)***
Size	1.03	0.936
	(0.27)	*(0.62)*
Overhead expenditures	−0.438	−0.829
	(0.42)	*(0.93)*
Sales growth	−0.07	−0.26
	*(1.72)***	*(0.92)*
Liquidity	−0.893	−0.673
	(0.32)	*(0.29)*
F-value	4.35	3.42
R^2	0.705	0.626

[*]   Significant at the .10 level.
[**]   Significant at the .05 level.
[***]   Significant at the .01 level.

The coefficient for size is positive for both high and low q firms. As the results indicate, large firms in India have not only been able to escape the discipline of market valuation, but many of them were able to generate greater than average profits. Until serious reforms began in India, there were no reasons for these large firms to minimise costs or strive for efficiency as a result of state intervention in the market through licensing and other direct controls removing any threats of competition. Bhagwati (1993) has remarked on such inefficiencies.[15] Overhead expenditures have a negative relationship with firm profitability as expected. The coefficient of sales growth is negative but significant at the 0.05 level for high q firms, suggesting that perhaps firms in high growth industries attract increased competition by new entrants because of their high levels of sales thus reducing their profits. Liquidity has a negative but insignificant relationship with both high and low q firms, suggesting that further subdivision within each category of firm types might be useful. The explanatory power of these regression models is 0.705 for the high q firms and 0.626 for the low q firms.

In the next sample low q firms were separated from the entire sample and tested separately. Table 4.6 indicates how they were further sub-divided into firms which retained more than the average levels of debt and earnings for all low q firms. These low q firms, the

FCFT suggests, should increase debt in order to signal managers' effort to maximise shareholder value; therefore, it is particularly interesting to examine the results of these sub-divided firms in the context of the Indian banking system.

Table 4.6   Regressions of low q firms with excess debt and excess retained earnings

	Excess debt	Excess retained earnings
Debt/equity	−4.29	−3.68
	$(3.89)^{***}$	$(3.52)^{***}$
Size	0.893	0.629
	(0.73)	(0.92)
Overhead expenditures	−0.923	−0.631
	$(0.98)^{*}$	$(1.83)^{**}$
Sales growth	−0.163	−0.221
	(0.38)	(0.19)
Liquidity	−0.681	0.706
	(0.42)	$(2.93)^{***}$
F-value	5.36	2.67
R^2	0.398	0.693

[*]   Significant at the .10 level.
[**]   Significant at the .05 level.
[***]   Significant at the .01 level.

In contrast to the FCFT, debt/equity ratios for low q firms of both types have negative and significant relationships with firm performance. Further, the negative effects of the debt/equity ratio are more significant on firms with excess debt in their financial structure, as indicated by a lower and more significant coefficient. For low q firms, the significance of debt levels on firm performance is apparent, but the nature of the relationship is negative rather than positive as is predicted by the FCFT. Table 4.6 also indicates the negative and significant relationship between overhead expenditures and firm performance. The relationship is more significant for low q firms with excess retained earnings supporting their excessive retention policies. Either as firms they need to spend heavily to increase their market share or as part of a certain industry they have greater overhead costs. The coefficient for liquidity is positive for low q firms with excess retained earnings, suggesting another reason for the high level of retained earnings. As greater liquidity for these firms leads to better performance, it is apparent that the FCFT's predictions do not hold true, since the FCFT suggests that low q firms of all types should not retain cash under any conditions. Thus, the FCFT has been correct in predicting the significance but not the direction of relationship between liquidity and firm performance.

Table 4.7 shows the results of the regressions after the high q firms were separated and sub-divided into their different groups. The relationship between the debt/equity ratios remains negative for both types of high q firms, reaffirming the previous negative relationships between debt and firm performance. Sales growth has a greater and more significant coefficient than for low q firms, suggesting that the effect of new entrants on the performance of high q firms is less predatory than for low q firms. For high q firms with excess retained earnings, liquidity has a positive and significant relationship with firm performance. Furthermore, it is more significant and greater than the coefficient for its low q counterpart, suggesting that since these firms might have greater and more positive investment opportunities, the excess retained earnings might help to finance them.

Table 4.7 Regressions of high q firms with excess debt and excess retained earnings

	Excess debt	Excess retained earnings
Debt/equity	−2.42	−2.09
	(0.72)	(1.38)*
Size	0.273	0.418
	(0.52)	(0.12)
Overhead expenditures	−0.381	−0.263
	(0.49)	(0.13)
Sales growth	−0.121	−0.132
	(3.46)***	(3.87)***
Liquidity	−0.282	1.69
	(0.91)	(3.13)***
F-value	7.32	3.82
R^2	0.842	0.473

* Significant at the .10 level.
** Significant at the .05 level.
*** Significant at the .01 level.

4.10.1   Evaluation

Contrary to the FCFT which emphasises the positive influence of debt for all firms and the possible value of liquidity for high q rather than low q firms, the evidence from India is different. Not only are there negative effects of debt on firm performance, but levels of liquidity and other factors depend more on a firm's financial structure than on its growth opportunities. Liquidity has played a more significant role in affecting performance for Indian firms with excess retained earnings than for firms with excess debt. The positive coefficients for liquidity for firms with excess retained earnings and the negative coefficients for liquidity for firms with excess debt suggest that firms with excess debt suffer from lower performance when they simultaneously maintain high liquidity levels. These difference marks a critical departure from the fundamental predictions of the FCFT for determining firm value. Under the FCFT, firms with higher debt have greater value whereas the results from India indicate the opposite. Similarly, under the FCFT, firms with high levels of retained earnings maintaining additional liquidity would most certainly be downgraded in value by the market, whereas results here have suggested otherwise. The FCFT gives opposite results to this study in India specifically in its predictions for the nature of the relationship between debt and firm performance, perhaps because of the crucial peculiarities underlying India's financial lending institutions.

4.11   Policy implications

The financial sector in India is dominated by state-managed institutions. Unlike more developed capital markets in the West where financial institutions themselves are subject to capital market discipline and control, Indian financial institutions do not face such constraints. Since Indian banks and financial enterprises are not subject to the discipline of their owner-principals, which is the government, firms which borrow from these financial institutions do not feel the need to change their own incentive structures by the bonding behaviour which Grossman and Hart have documented in developed markets (Grossman and Hart, 1986). The banks and financial institutions which are owed debt by firms are not likely to be called upon to suffer from bad debt because the government has deep pockets. The encouragement of industrial development has been a major policy goal of the Indian government. Therefore, banks and financial institutions have reduced incentives for monitoring their debtor firms. From the debtor firms' point of view, the knowledge that debt holders' presence is essentially non-existent encourages managers towards discretionary behaviour with negative consequences on firm performance.

Under normal circumstances, this situation should not exist since banks and financial institutions' ownership is normally vested in one government department which retains all shares on behalf of the government. Thus, ownership is not diffused but vested in one owner which can exercise the appropriate control. From the debtor firms' perspective, this fact ought to encourage bonding because their debt suppliers are likely to face strong monitoring and performance pressures themselves. However, this is not the case in India since there is some fuzziness as to the identity of the exact owners. The government department owning shares in financial institutions is itself an agency for citizens who are therefore the legal owners of the financial institutions. As a collection of many principals, citizens of a state face severe agency problems. As citizens, they neither have the proper incentives due to 'free riding' problems, nor are they able to control the managers of the state-owned financial institutions. Consequently, financial enterprises become proprietary organisations owned for all intended purposes by civil servants and politicians who seek their own rents (Bardhan, 1984). Meanwhile, managers in these institutions know that they are free of both market discipline or sanctions from the ultimate principals, the citizens of the state. For debtor firms' managers, debt is felt to be owed to the public at large who can effectively do nothing. Therefore, the greater the level of debt in firms' financial structures, the greater is the lack of effort on the part of the Indian managers, leading to a significant negative impact on firm performance.

There is one critical implication for India's reform process. India is liberalising many of its closed markets within the financial sector and privatising commercial and industrial Indian state-owned financial enterprises albeit at a very slow rate. Although a number of foreign and domestic financial institutions have entered the capital market, they have entered as portfolio investors in equity and only recently were allowed to become debt suppliers. If the norms of corporate governance as seen in developed capital markets are to be applied in India, banks and financial institutions need to be privatised. Perhaps then the presence and size of debt in the financial structure of firms might have a disciplinary impact on firm managers. Besides the agency problem, the evidence suggests that the capabilities of Indian banks and financial institutions do not meet the minimum standards, since a high debt/equity ratio is associated with low performance. By no means are these problems unique to India, as apparent from the experiences of other countries. Banking systems only work if they are allowed to suffer the costs of their bad decisions, i.e., bankruptcy.

The decision process of Indian banks and financial institutions needs to be re-examined given the many loans approved for inherently unprofitable projects. In many cases, political consideration determined loan approvals and banks were merely a channel for government largesse to specific parties. As agencies of the government, many of these banks had to continue funding these unprofitable projects or face the negative consequences of calling in the low-performing loans. Furthermore, a more active role should be sought for bank managers appointed to the boards of highly leveraged firms. As representatives of the financial institutions, they should have appropriate corporate governance structures including incentive schemes and appraisal skills which encourage them to question loans and projects. Lastly, there may be a great deal of variation in the quality of capabilities which the financial institutions and banks possess. Some may be highly capable whereas others might suffer from low performance levels. The large number of these banks and financial institutions in India warrants more detailed empirical research which would identify the relationship between the explicit sources of debt capital and the profitability of firms. On a larger scale, more attention needs to be focused on the regulatory structures under which these banks operate to promote greater financial accountability, transparency, and discipline.

4.12   Conclusion

This chapter considered the debt/equity mix and how different sources of capital affect firm performance in India. The first model looked at the more general determinants of leverage, and the following model incorporated Jensen's FCFT to test the effects of leverage on firm performance. The results of the first model suggest that the dominant factor in determining leverage between firms is firm size. The results indicate that larger firms have considerable advantages over smaller firms in credit markets. Macroeconomic factors, cash flows, real tangible assets, and growth in the real size of firms also play important roles in explaining the variation in leverage across firms. Further, although deregulation was not included in this model due to data limitations, it would have had a significant influence on the financial structure of firms. The second model examines the FCFT's hypotheses regarding the significance and the type of relationship for leverage in Indian firms. Contrary to the FCFT, results indicate that not only are there negative effects of debt on firm performance, but also that chosen levels of liquidity and other factors depend more on a firm's financial structure than on its growth opportunities. Liquidity has played a more significant role in affecting performance in firms with excess retained earnings than in firms with excess debt. These differences mark a critical departure from the fundamental predictions of the FCFT, specifically the positive influence of debt on firm value. These results imply that the FCFT's predictions are inapplicable in weak capital markets such as India's, and that the underlying assumptions need to reassessed given the misaligned incentive structure of India's state-managed banking system.

5
Earnings Retention as a Specification Mechanism in Predicting Corporate Bankruptcy

5.1 Introduction

Chapter 4 estimated a model for finance strategy based on firm quality using Indian data. Chapter 5 extends this analysis by assessing the influence of a firm's capital structure on the probability of bankruptcy. The aim is to find if retained earnings are more significant relative to bankruptcy in firms with fewer investment opportunities (i.e., low q vs. high q firms). Bankruptcy theory provides a framework combining corporate financial structure, relationship between debt and equity, the composition and ownership of corporate debt, and the structure of share ownership. Leverage becomes an important consideration as it can shift the balance of bargaining power during bankruptcy. This exacerbates asymmetric information between debtors, creditors, and equity holders encouraging low-quality firms to continue overinvesting.

This chapter contains seven sections. Sections 5.1 and 5.2 cover the legal and economic framework within which unhealthy firms can seek assistance from the Indian government. This includes a theoretical discussion of the reasons for information asymmetries in India. The following sections are empirical and test the validity of the hypotheses on Indian corporate data. The chapter defines corporate bankruptcy and the role of the state in liquidation and debt renegotiation. It specifically covers Indian bankruptcy restructuring procedures under the Sick Industrial Companies (Special Provisions) Act of 1985 (SICA) and its regulating body, the Board for Industrial and Financial Reconstruction (BIFR). It then considers the theoretical arguments to examine the interaction between a firm's financial structure and its position when caught in bankruptcy proceedings. Much of this theory is applied to Indian bankruptcy procedures including an empirical look at leveraging practices of formerly bankrupt firms. Corporate data is used to closely examine the violations and weaknesses in India's financial sector practices especially as they apply to the treatment of bankrupt firms. A logistic model is developed for bankruptcy prediction using firm quality as well as earnings retention to improve forecasting. The final sections assess the 1992 reforms in bankruptcy proceedings and offer some policy recommendations.

5.2 Bankruptcy management in India: SICA and BIFR

The Sick Industrial Companies (Special Provisions) Act of 1985 (SICA) establishes the legal framework for reorganising a sick firm. According to definition, a 'sick' firm must (a) be registered for at least seven years, (b) have suffered cash losses for two consecutive years including the current year, (c) have cumulative losses destroying its net worth. An amendment to this legislation in December 1993 stated that (a) firms need to be registered only for five years, and (b) cash losses involved no time constraint. The main objective of the SICA was the *timely detection of sick and potentially sick firms*. However, even with the 1993 amendment, late detection continued to inhibit efficient rescue policies. It is difficult to plan a viable rehabilitation scheme before firm losses have wiped out their equity and reserves.

The Board for Industrial and Financial Reconstruction (BIFR) is the main legal body appointed by SICA for restructuring sick firms. The BIFR has often been quite slow in responding and arbitrating cases. If SICA does not register a firm as unhealthy due to rigid rules, the firm must petition the BIFR. The BIFR received 1,673 petitions from firms since it was established in 1992. Of these, only 1,221 were registered so that their cases would be heard by the Board. Representatives of the company, trade/labour unions, financial institutions and banks, and state governments plead their case in a prima facie enquiry. Between 1987 and 1992, almost 27% of these firms were classified as sick and 'non-maintainable'.[1]

After the firm has been labelled 'sick', the BIFR considers the following two options:

(a) Rehabilitation in which the firm itself convinces the BIFR that a recovery scheme will be viable within ten years. If ratified, under Section 17(2) of SICA, the BIFR sanctions the firm's plans for recovery. Two notable features of such schemes include the limited participation of the BIFR in the recovery/restructuring plans and that they do not necessarily provide any funds or subsidies. In most cases, the firms have already entered refinancing arrangements with banks and financial institutions.

(b) Rehabilitation when the firm is unable to support itself, but the BIFR decides it is in the 'public interest' to keep the firm afloat. Under Section 17(3) of SICA, the BIFR appoints a bank or financial institution to examine a possible recovery of the firm.[2] This bank re-examines the BIFR's decision regarding the viability of the firm and reports. If the report agrees with the BIFR to rehabilitate the firm then under Section 18(4) the process continues. However, in some cases, the bank decides that liquidation is the best solution.

Liquidation occurs when the BIFR decides after petitions of outside parties that the firm ought to face bankruptcy. Table 5.1 shows a distribution of the petitioned cases before the BIFR between 1987 and 1992.

As evident in Table 5.1, the problem with the BIFR's process is the time it takes for decisions. Of the 1,014 petitioned cases before the Board, nearly 44% faced an uncertain future.[3] Such delays are costly for all parties concerned. Unhealthy firms deal with the BIFR more than with the SICA. Unfortunately, the SICA was often too late to identify sick firms. Officials claimed that the SICA suffered from identification problems as well as discouraging the BIFR from stepping in. By the time the SICA had identified a problem, a firm had lost almost 10 to 20 times its net worth so it was often too late for a fair chance of recovery. As a result, SICA concentrated on the most sick firms doomed to liquidation; however, only 242 of 1,014 cases between 1987 and 1992 were liquidated, suggesting that too many 'sick' firms were being supported.[4]

Table 5.1 Distribution of petitioned cases before the BIFR, 1987–92

Registered		Not disposed or pending (in percent)					
Year	Number	1987	1988	1989	1990	1991	1992
1987	266	98	84	59	46	22	15
1988	215		96	76	43	23	18
1989	166			96	74	41	33
1990	127				94	76	64
1991	137					99	93
1992	103						100
Total	1014						44

Source: Government of India, BIFR (1992).

5.3   Firm and capital structure management

5.3.1   Alignment of managerial incentives

The extent to which shareholders were able to monitor managers of public firms in India can be compared with a more developed market like the US. Effective monitoring is more difficult with differing share ownership and firm structure in both countries. The spread of equity ownership means higher monitoring costs for public shareholders (Ananth, Gangopadhyay and Goswami, 1992a, 1992b; Ananth, Chaudhuri, Gangopadhyay and Goswami, 1994).

In the US. until the 1930s, leading investment banks and financial institutions owned most of the equity and were also major creditors in the same firms. This gave rise to serious conflict of interest, i.e., very little discrimination between lenders and borrowers. It allowed financial institutions – as dominant equity holders – to monitor US firms quite closely. However, in the 1930s and the 1940s, the introduction of the Securities and Exchange Commission Act (1930), the Glass Steagall Act (1933), the Investment Company Act (1938), and the Chandler Act (1939) restricted banks' and financial institutions' shares of corporate equity. So, public shares of large to medium size US firms had a large number of small shareholders with neither individual influence nor resources for mechanisms to monitor management. Jensen concludes that this change of ownership from shareholders to managers dramatically reduced firm value:

> The result of these regulations has been to leave managers increasingly unmonitored. In the U.S. at present, when institutional holders of over 40 percent of corporate equity in small lots become dissatisfied with management, they have few options other than to sell their shares. Moreover, managers' complaints about the churning of financial institutions' portfolios ring hollow: one can guess they much prefer the churning system to one in which those institutions actually have direct power to correct a management problem. Few CEOs look kindly on the prospect of having institutions with substantial stock ownership sitting on their corporate board. That would bring about monitoring of managerial activities by people who more closely bear the wealth consequences of managerial mistakes and who are not beholden to the CEO for their jobs. As financial institution monitors left the scene in the post 1940 period, managers commonly came to believe that companies belonged to them. (Jensen, 1987)

He shows how companies which generated large excess cash flow acquired diverse activities often not remotely related to the core area and expertise which managers claimed to possess (Jensen, 1986, 1987). Jensen proves the value-destroying activities of managers by pointing out that during the takeover period in the 1980s, bids averaged almost 50% more than the prices quoted on US stock exchanges, indicating that managers diluted firm activities and reduced share prices.

A similar situation has occurred in India for different reasons. Since colonial days, management agencies performed several functions, from the initial share offering to its ultimate management and control. Furthermore, management were careful both to underprice shares to attract investors and to sell these shares in small lots so that no one shareholder could exercise control. Thus, agencies garnered maximum control with minimal ownership exacerbating asymmetric information. This system continued after independence and eventually spread to many industries. Government attempts to solve this problem only worsened the situation. By addressing the most transparent problem, i.e., that managers became wealthier relative to shareholders, they failed to solve the underlying problem of asymmetric information. So the Indian government passed laws prohibiting management from owning more than 40% of corporate equity. As in the 1930s in corporate US, managers in India continued to exercise the same control but at lower costs to themselves. Needless to say, as described by Jensen, activities by management were not the only factor which reduced the value.

Corporate bankruptcies were rare in some industries, e.g., textiles, because successive governments disallowed sick firms from one of the following options: (a) takeover–merger–reorganisation or (b) liquidation–exit–migration. Instead of reducing the social and economic costs of sick firms through rapid reorganisation or immediate liquidation, the Indian government would continue to subsidise these large-scale operations with credits. So these sick firms were protected legally by government regulations which had little regard for performance and by government funds with little consideration for returns. Consequently, in some ways, corporate bankruptcy was government sponsored in India. The system has, for almost forty years, protected unhealthy firms and their management from bankruptcy through financial subsidies and regulations. An examination of the intertwined relationship between India's *development finance* and management monitoring schemes illustrates these problems.

In 1969, India passed a *Development Finance Act* which nationalised banks and focused on term lending and full working capital exposure.

This Act meant that monitoring, discipline, and the quality of loans was of secondary concern. Most public financial institutions bought large equity positions into many private firms to protect their loans. The result was that financial institutions owned from 40 to 45% of corporate equity by the late 1980s and concurrently supplied a large portion of their long-term debt. Concentration of ownership in firms should have allowed for greater control over management; unfortunately, this was not the case. Public financial institutions were often the largest shareholders and creditors at the same time, but the focus of government policy was wrongly focused on credit quantity rather than quality. The Indian government admitted as much in 1993:

> There was excessive focus on quantitative indicators; growth of total lending, sectoral deployment of credit and the outreach of banks were main indicators of dynamism and strength in banking. There was inadequate concern with issues of credit quality and the capacity of borrowers to service loans. In such a climate, poor lending decisions were taken.[5]

To illustrate this misguided focus, consider interest payments in the profit and loss accounts of financial institutions. Until 1992, banks recorded interest payments even when they were not made, concealing any poorly performing accounts; moreover, writing off loans was a rare occurrence on balance sheets. Consequently, most, if not all, of these banks seemed solid. In this environment, effective monitoring of management became an option rather than a necessity, since the ultimate creditors, the banks, were not considered a threat. In fact, most banks cared less about weeding out inefficient management and were more concerned with increasing their overall exposure to adhere to government policy. As a result, inefficient and overvalued firms increased because of the inefficient behaviour of these managers. Banks – with critical support from the government – were more interested in increasing the quantity rather than the quality of their loan portfolios. Now even the government admits that

> The bank managements became more susceptible to outside pressures to make loans. Influential borrowers brought external pressure to bear on banks to tolerate defaults, and these were tolerated because prudential norms were lax.[6]

By the late 1980s, investment banks and financial institutions held almost 70% of India's corporate equity. Managers rarely feared takeovers by more efficient operators as the Indian courts – with the support of the government – almost always ruled in favour of the *preferential rights* of the existing management, ensuring the continuation of incapable and faulty management.

These factors did not help shareholders monitor management. Consequently, in these years, there was a massive increase in the number of over-leveraged and under-performing firms which fostered inefficiency with the full support of government policies. Management continued to exercise greater control with minimal ownership, ignoring discipline whether from the market, i.e., takeovers, or from their creditors, i.e., the banks.

5.4   Bankruptcy effects of corporate leveraging in Indian firms

Most sick firms within India are excessively leveraged by almost any debt measurement ratio. The ideal measure of leveraging should compare the value of debt to the market value of the firm, i.e., the debt-to-value ratio. However, imperfections in the Indian capital market do not allow the use of share prices as proxies for value. Accurate estimation of debt value requires more information than is readily available. This debt–equity ratio can have two definitions:

(a) deferred or long-term liabilities divided by net worth (i.e., value of equity and preference shares plus free reserves) if reserves are greater than or equal to zero; or deferred or long-term liabilities less reserves divided by net worth less reserves, if reserves are less than zero.
(b) deferred or long-term liabilities plus the excess of current liabilities over current assets divided by net worth, if reserves are greater than or equal to zero; or deferred or long-term liabilities plus the excess of current liabilities over current assets less reserves divided by net worth less reserves, if reserves are less than zero.

The first definition is a more narrow definition of corporate debt and includes only two classes of claimants: banks and term-lending financial institutions. The latter is a more broad definition which accounts for irregularities in working capital and non-payment to suppliers. Firms within the textile and engineering sectors indicate that for both debt measures, there are certain common features. The post-1980s period saw a vast difference in leveraging habits between those firms which were healthy and those close to bankruptcy. After 1980, the former group had significantly lower debt ratios than their bankrupt counterparts. Figures 5.1 to 5.4, based on data from Ananth, Gangopadhyay, and Goswami (1992a), indicate this pattern, for engineering and textile firms.

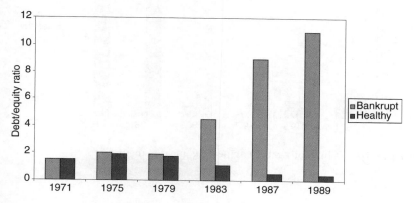

Figure 5.1   Debt/equity ratio, textiles: measurement A

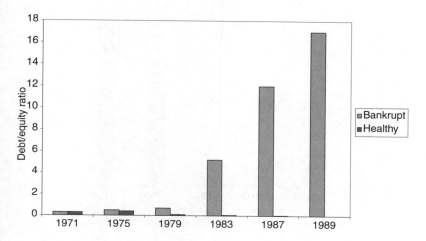

Figure 5.2   Debt/equity ratio: textiles, measurement B

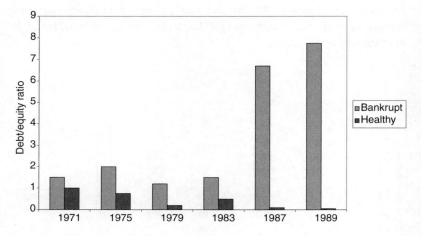

Figure 5.3   Debt/equity ratio: engineering, measurement A

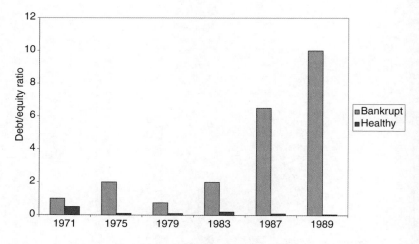

Figure 5.4   Debt/equity ratio engineering, measurement B

Source for Figures 5.1 to 5.4: Ananth, Gangopadhyay andGoswami (1992a).

Furthermore, in each of the above cases, another interesting trend can be picked out. Since the comparison within each industrial sector is between healthy and firms close to bankruptcy, there is an obvious relationship between the interest costs per unit sold and the level of leveraging. A simple regression similar to those conducted by Ananth, Gangopadhyay and Goswami in each of the two industrial sectors between the levels of debt and the interest cost per unit shows that leveraging more seriously affects the unit interest cost for firms closer to bankruptcy than their healthier counterparts.

Among the two industrial sectors, the effect of greater leveraging is more onerous to the engineering firms, as indicated by a higher debt–equity coefficient and significance, i.e., 0.6422 > 0.1732 (Tables 5.2 and 5.3). This might be the result of the need for greater cash outlays on the part of these types of firms which are involved to a greater extent in research activities. Consequently, they not only have to pay the regular interest payments but are required to fund unforeseen projects and produce the appropriate investment outlays.

Table 5.2   Interest cost per unit sales, engineering firms, 1970–89

Dependent variable	Bankrupt firms	Healthy firms
Debt–equity ratio	0.6422*	−0.0478
	(0.132)	(0.089)
Intercept	−4.153	−2.958*
	(0.0023)	(0.153)
R^2	0.91	0.93

*Significant at the .05 level.

Table 5.3   Interest cost per unit sales, textile firms, 1970–89

Dependent variable	Bankrupt firms	Healthy firms
Debt–equity ratio	0.1732*	−0.0026
	(0.253)	(0.003)
Intercept	−2.452	−1.752*
	(.0142)	(0.326)
R^2	0.92	0.89

* Significant at the .05 level.

5.5   Corporate bankruptcy procedures in India

5.5.1   The treatment of bankruptcy by India's financial sector

For a long period, India's corporate restructuring schemes often encouraged increases in the leverage ratios of ultimately bankrupt companies; moreover, these plans often went ahead without any opposition from the provider of loans. An examination of the overall goals and aims of financial sector practices might help to answer these questions. Specifically, this section will address the following concerns: the motives of financial institutions behind their decisions to extend loans to already bankrupt firms; whether the BIFR restructuring plans helped to improve the financial structure of these firms in terms of economic incentives and principles; the treatment by the BIFR of firms with low vs. high leverage ratios.

The presence of nationalised banks and other similar development financial institutions has no doubt played a great role in the lending practices of Indian banks. However, it would be rash to blame nationalisation for all of India's corporate lending and restructuring problems. The crux of the issue lies in the economic costs of mistakes made by these public sector banks. Of course, private banks have also made comparable errors as apparent in the US savings and loan crisis or the Mexican debt crisis, but the difference lies in the consequences of these decisions. Public sector banks represent the ultimate problems in the ownership and control debate, for it is assumed that government subsidies will cover any wealth effects of wrong decisions. On a more practical note, experience in India and other countries has proven that it is in these banks' interests to continue to renegotiate with those firms with whom they have larger exposures. These highly leveraged firms are more important to banks than firms with smaller debt burdens, and consequently, banks have very little bargaining power with them. It might be worthwhile modelling this outcome using a game theoretical approach (Table 5.4).

Table 5.4   Bargaining power: bank returns for leveraged firms[7]

Bank returns		
Firm type	*Liquidate*	*Renegotiate*
Low leverage ratio	$1 - X/L$, X/L	$1 - RX/L$, RX/L
High leverage ratio	$1 - X/H$, X/H	$1 - RX/H$, RX/H

X = Liquidation value
L = Debt of low leverage firm
H = Debt of high leverage firm
Rx = Post renegotiation liquidation value

In this one-stage model, it is assumed that both firms are valued equally; moreover, the liquidation value of each firm is also the same. However, in considering the bargaining power of banks, it would seem that the firm with the higher leverage ratio has greater probability of re-negotiation than the lower leveraged firm. That is, from the bank's perspective, the higher leveraged firm will always have a lower return, i.e., $x/L > x/H$. In specific terms, since the marginal difference between $RX/H - X/H$ is significantly greater than the difference between $RX/L - X/L$, the final pay-off for the same renegotiation effort is greater with the higher leveraged firm . The post-renegotiation value of the higher leveraged firm will have greater marginal increases in returns for the bank than from the lower leveraged counterpart. Consequently, there will always be greater incentive for banks to renegotiate with higher leveraged firms in hopes of increasing their returns. As evident in Table 5.4, the bank would choose renegotiation with the higher leveraged firm and liquidation with the lower leveraged firm. It is in the banks' interests for these more indebted and unhealthy firms to restructure themselves in hopes of recovering at least some of the outstanding loan value. Therefore, banks are willing to give these higher leveraged firms greater leeway as they also have considerable incentives to preserve the value of the firm.

5.5.2   Bargaining power between banks and firms

The loss of bargaining power for banks when dealing with the higher leveraged firms often leads to what Jensen labelled as an overinvestment problem. Highly leveraged firms found themselves not only taking on greater debt, but applying this available credit to projects deemed risky at best which ultimately proved to be value reducing rather than value enhancing. This overinvestment problem had two main causes, as seen in evidence of the reports describing rehabilitation schemes sanctioned under section 18(4) of the SICA: managers of these highly leveraged firms pressured banks to re-finance them; the largest creditors often designed the restructuring plan leading to a moral hazard problem. Creditors often gave their consent to such risky projects for reasons suggested earlier, whereas managers of these firms continue to (in Jensen terms) 'abuse' the excess funds. Banks and financial institutions were forced not only to try and rehabilitate and preserve whatever value the firm already had, but also to extend further credit in hopes that the eventual turnaround would cover their rescheduled claims. The experience of many textile mills which had been initially rehabilitated and then ultimately failed typifies this over-investment problem.

Furthermore, when rehabilitation schemes were designed, they were often based on unrealistic expectations which assumed recovery. The textile mills provide a good example of how overinvestment by these firms continued unabated by banks as a result of false expectations. Rehabilitation schemes for the textile mills were based on the assumption of a defined number of working days per year. The Indian Cotton Mills Federation sets the maximum number of working days per year in textile mills between 325 and 330. In many cases, banks planned for 340 working days, almost 15 days more than the industry average.[8] Extreme cases of 350 working days were also noted in some reports. Similarly, in forecasting sales projections, firms which had been unhealthy for almost 10 years, were forecasted to flourish with 380% rise in sales revenue in the next five years, so that after losing Rs. 32 million per annum it was expected to increase its profits to Rs. 134 million within three years of restructuring. Although this is an extreme case, on average, formerly unhealthy firms were projected to increase their sales by almost 50% within two or three years of restructuring. As expected, most of the rehabilitation schemes were extremely sensitive to these optimistic sales projections. Small falls of even 5% and 10% in actual sales figures and costs would mean that those projects with once positive NPV created further losses.

The lack of adequate allowances for loan assets and rules against writing down debts magnified the moral hazard problem. Not only were the designers of the rehabilitation schemes the largest creditors, but they were also forced to provide for past dues. Consequently, these banks often rigged the post-restructuring cash flows high enough to not arouse any suspicion from the BIFR. Sales forecast was set at $1.33[D + L(1+r)]$. *(D = past debt, L = new loans, r = rate of interest.)* This way the extra 33% could be used to pay the service coverage of the new debt. Such creativity meant that banks seemed to have covered their exposure, the firms could claim that they had every intention of paying their past debts, and the BIFR served its public interests by rehabilitating yet another sick firm. Unfortunately, reality seemed to show otherwise when most firms under these types of plans eventually faced bankruptcy.

5.5.3   The public interest: subsidies, sacrifices, and accounting practices

Since most commercial banks and financial institutions were encouraged to preserve the meagre value of over-leveraged bankrupt firms, the objective of suppliers was to maximise deposits, working capital and cash-credit loans, and project financing. Most lending often occurred with inadequate project appraisal and those projects which fit in with government objectives rather than profit motives were often undertaken. The monitoring of debtors was deemed unnecessary as there seemed to be a constant supply of subsidised budgetary support for the banking system. In addition to Reserve Bank of India (RBI) regulations disallowing the write-off of bad loans, the accounting system booked interest in the profit and loss account regardless of actual receipt. The accounting system itself was regulated through a highly complicated and often inexplicable method of classification called the Health Code System.

Needless to say, in such conditions, bad debts continued to rise. As an approximate measure, in 1993 the total non-performing advances of public sector banks for limits above Rs. 25,000 was Rs. 370 billion or 21% of the domestic plus foreign loan portfolio. In more profitable banks, the share of non-performing assets was between 8% and 10% of total assets while it was from 35% and 40% in their weaker counterparts.[9] Furthermore, many of the reported profits were non-existent. In the 1991–92 financial year, the 28 public sector banks reported operating profits of Rs. 55.4 billion. Upon further inspection and after these supposed profits had been examined, the figure dropped by almost 86% to Rs. 8 billion. In the following year only 15 of the 28 banks could declare net profits, and even these profits were insufficient to cover the losses of the 13 which had suffered greatly.

To understand the aforementioned often perverse accounting and lending practices, it might be useful to reconsider the conditions in which most of these corporate lenders operated. Success was measured in terms of maximising the number of loans, and the declaration of bad loans as a non-performing asset implied a reduction in the size of the bank's loan portfolio. Therefore, bankers were often eager to loosen credit policies and advance more funds to firms in difficulty. Consequently, leverage ratios grew even higher and so did the risks of the ultimate defaults. In fact, there were strong managerial incentives within banks and financial institutions which supported higher leverage ratios for firms regardless of their recovery potential. It was agreed to a large extent by the lack of any market discipline that the losses of these firms had to be covered by greater funds. This provides yet another reason for the increasing leverage ratios as described in the earlier section throughout the 1970s and 1980s.

During this period, large interest rate subsidies were justified by the government and the RBI as sacrifices to be made for the good of rehabilitating and restructuring bankrupt firms. The discounted interest rates and concessions available to these unhealthy enterprises even encouraged firms to finance risky investments. Such allowances by the government in the interest of the public fell under section 18(4) of the SICA. Specifically, a review of the document reveals the following allowances:

State governments
(a) Exemption or deferment of sales tax, purchase tax and electricity tax for two to five years or when net worth turned positive. The deferment was either free, or at simple interest of 12%, with a moratorium of one to two years after sanctioning. Sales tax on loans could carry subsidised interest rates.
(b) Deferment of duty and water charges.
(c) Deferment of energy dues, including turnover tax or sales on electricity.
(d) Waiver of compound interest and penal charges levied on state dues.
(e) Deferment of recovery of past state excise dues.
(f) Deferment of interest payment, or funding of interest on outstanding term loan dues of state financial corporations at subsidised rates.
(g) State governments not only should provide guarantees for fresh loans but also waive bank guarantee requirements for arrears.
(h) Protection from revenue recovery action.
(i) Price preference, quota reservations, and assistance in the supply of controlled raw materials.
(j) Equity contribution, even where the firm was not taken over by the state government.

Central government
(a) Exemption or deferment from central excise duty for two to five years.
(b) Income tax relief for a specified period.
(c) Deferment of provident fund payments, and waiver of penalties on non-payment of provident fund and employees state insurance dues.
(d) Preferential supply of canalised items.

Banks and financial institutions
(a) Interest on term loans reduced.
(b) All penalties, compound interest, and damages for non-repayment waived.

(c) Unrealised interest capitalised at subsidised rates of 10%, 6%, or even 0% per year in exceptional cases. The normal repayment of funded interest was three to five years, extendable to six or seven years.

(d) The irregular component of a firm's cash credit (other than unadjusted interest) converted into a working capital term loan. On this subsidised interest was charged.

(e) The defaults on payment to workers and towards other statutory dues and overdue trade creditors were shared between the participating banks and financial institutions on a 50/50 basis. Anticipated cash losses during the rehabilitation periods were borne by the banks, who also provided the marginal money for working capital.

(f) Although additional assistance for working capital was on commercial rates, these were reduced if state governments offered concessions.

(g) Cost of rationalising labour was met by banks on a 50/50 basis.

These allowances coupled with unrealistic assumptions regarding future sales hid the dubious results of improper financial structures and interest rate subsidies. Controversial methods were often used in calculating projected profits. As the RBI, BIFR, and other financial institutions required that the debt coverage service ratio be 1.33 times past dues, calculations would be reversed guaranteeing that projected sales and profit targets would be met. Most firms had well-defined debt components (past debt, interest on past debt, new term loans, and interest on these loans), and since these could not be written down, numerators which were 1.33 times the denominators were created using revenue and cost figures to match the numerators.[10] Therefore, instead of using realistic production and sales projections and then calculating the appropriate outcomes, the procedure had been reversed.[11]

5.5.4 Violations of the 'absolute priority rule'

In an Ananth, Chaudhuri, Gangopadhyay (1994) study, the authors examine whether 'sacrifices' in the interest of the public often implied the sanctioning of financially unviable projects. They also examined whether subsidies forced public financial institutions to bear losses while equity holders, firms and their managers earned positive returns on the same investments; clearly, this would be in violation of the absolute priority rule (APR) which was intended to restrict the type of assistance offered by the government. The Chaudhuri *et al.* study illustrates how the APR continued to be abused so that secured creditors experienced major losses while others simultaneously benefited from the same restructuring and refinancing schemes.

They consider projected profit and loss account sheets which contain the projected net earnings of a firm. Specifically these include (a) sales net of indirect taxes plus other income, (b) variable costs such as raw materials , consumables, fuel, electricity, interest on working capital, and variable costs in production, (c) fixed costs, and (d) corporate income tax. In the end the net earnings are: $Y_t = (a) - [(b) - (c) - (d)]$ where Y is the NPV of the Y_t stream discounted at the market rate. In discussing the preservation of failing firms, past debt (V_d) and new investment (I) are often the restructured variables. I is mainly funded either by equity contributions (P) from new investors or new term loans (N) from financial institutions. The rates of return are respectively r_p and r_n for the former variables and the authors assume that there is neither a risk premium nor agency costs for the issue of equity.

Using the following equation to examine the conditions which define 'rehabilitation' and 'public interest' under section 18(4) of the SICA:

$$V_n(1 + r_n) + P(1 + r_p) < Y < V_n(1 + r_n) + P(1 + r_p) + V_d \qquad (5.1)$$

The left-hand side of the inequality defines the condition under which the proposed earnings are greater than the equity and interest costs for the firm, whereas the right-hand side of the inequality includes a past debt (V_d) variable. If the inclusion of this variable reduces projected earnings so that the firm's costs exceeds its profits and it decides not to invest, the 'public interest' funds subsidise the difference or write-off the past debt.

The problem occurs when firms are endowed with subsidies. In other words:

$$Y = V_n(1 + r_n) + P(1 + r_p) + wV_d \qquad (5.2)$$
$$\text{where } 0 \leq w \leq 1$$

if w^* is considered the exact w which satisfies the above equation, when the subsidy provided is (w) and $w > w^*$, the BIFR is writing-off too much debt and thus servicing the equity of negative net worth firms. The evidence proves that this occurred in several cases. In a sample of 21 firms, the BIFR wrote-off too much debt for 17 firms. On average, these excess subsidies were almost 26% greater than the appropriate amount. Again, the evidence shows that the BIFR and its APR allowances were abused repeatedly.

To decipher to what extent the BIFR was subsidising firms with negative net worth, consider the relationship between firms rescued under section 18(4). Table 5.5 presents a list of firms under rehabilitation schemes and their various rates.

Even if the BIFR had customised and adjusted normal accounting procedures, the data shows that there were serious violations of the APR in favour of equity holders in 10 out of the 23 cases. In Figure 5.5, there is evidence of perfect correlation between excess write-offs and high returns on equity so that all firms with high returns on equity were those with large debt write-offs.

Table 5.5   Rates of return for firms under Section 18(4)*

Firm	Return on equity (in %)	Rate of interest on new loans (V_n) (in %)	Excess write-off (in %)	APR violation
1	115	–8	31	Yes
2	52	2	–3	No
3	–34	8	8	No
4	90	–7	24	Yes
5	10	–5	60	Yes
6	208	2	62	Yes
7	20	–2	84	Yes
8	508	NA	55	Yes
9	50	NA	–13	No
10	26	3	–12	No
11	63	NA	16	No
12	104	9	33	Yes
13	–13	NA	16	No
14	325	–4	42	Yes
15	34	–27	55	Yes
16	43	NA	13	No
17	31	NA	12	No
18	–19	NA	27	No
19	48	–1	–95	No
20	–29	NA	16	No
21	49	9	19	Yes
22	44	NA	NA	No
23	73	NA	NA	No

* NA – Not applicable. Either firm did not take fresh loans or the projects only involved rescheduling without loan
(Anant, Chaudhuri, Gangopadhay and Goswami, 1994).

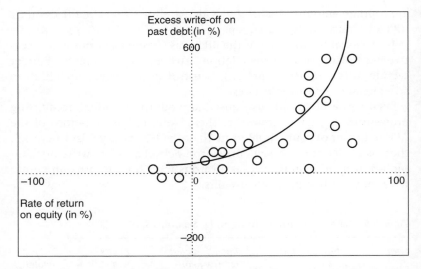

Figure 5.5   Comparison of excess write-off on debt and projected rates of return on equity

Thirteen of 23 firms had new loans (V_n's) and in none was the projected rate of return higher than the assumed opportunity cost of 9%; in fact in 4 of the firms the new loans were targeted to earn negative rates of return.

There have been many reasons for the aforementioned lack of discipline in both BIFR and its affiliated entities as well as in firms and managers who earned profits from the very institutions from whom they had sought restructuring assistance. The BIFR tried to solve this asymmetric information problem by encouraging a greater equity stake by firm owners during restructuring plans; however, 'sacrifices' and excessive subsidies in the so-called 'public interest' contradicted whatever discipline they may have intended. As a result, the system sent incorrect signals to the market and coupled with poor monitoring mechanisms it allowed certain equity holders to reap unwarranted benefits.

5.6   Earnings retention in logistic bankruptcy models: a test of the free cash flow theory

5.6.1   Introduction

Not all firms fail in a sudden manner. Many causes explain ultimate failure: namely, faulty management, lack of knowledge of the market, and illiquidity. Unfortunately, such information is not readily available to shareholders and creditors. In most cases, the probability of bankruptcy is implied in the firm's financial statements and may be revealed through financial ratio analysis before it actually occurs. Furthermore, assessing the quality of investment opportunities for individual firms in the recent past and then using this crucial difference as a classification technique helps to predict bankruptcy more efficiently; it allows better comparisons with similar firms. Industry relative ratios measuring the position of a firm within the industry also helps to understand financial indicators (Platt and Platt, 1990). Izan (1984) working on Australian firms found in comparing the characteristics of firms within an industry rather than a more general group of firms from all industries produced better results.

5.6.2 Purpose

The object of this section is twofold: to develop a better model for predicting corporate bankruptcies; to test Jensen's Free Cash Flow Theory's (FCFT) validity. This model adds a screening device by incorporating the FCFT to further categorise and compare similar firms within a single industry. The FCFT can divide firms based on their investment opportunities. The model serves its second purpose by testing the FCFT to confirm or deny whether retained earnings are indeed more significant in the context of bankruptcy to firms with a smaller set of productive investment opportunities.

The model for forecasting bankruptcy in this section builds on the former work done in statistical and accounting methods in an Indian context. A closer examination of the FCFT in context of the relevant statistical modelling follows. The methodology and the actual model will be tested and compared with previous results. The last sections discuss this particular model as a predictor of corporate failure in India.

5.6.3 Background

5.6.3.1 Review of the free cash flow theory

When firms raise equity in the market, the object is greater future cash flow for shareholders. When this cash flow is not paid out as dividends, it is said to be retained by firm managers for further investment. In a world without asymmetric information, shareholders would trust managers. With asymmetric information the abuse of earnings by firm managers is possible. So dividend policy plays a crucial role as a signal which might alleviate some asymmetric information costs.

The interpretation or even misinterpretation of this signal – good, bad, no effect – in India is addressed below.

Jensen's FCFT is an extension into principal–agent costs since managers' incentives are not always aligned with the interests of the shareholders. In Jensen's view, increased leverage or increased dividends can assure manager efficiency and lower the cost of asymmetric information between managers and shareholders; therefore, excess cash flow, the after tax cash flow in excess of the amount needed to fund positive NPV projects, should be disbursed as dividends in order to maximise the firm's value. This is difficult to refute given perfect capital markets because only positive NPV projects have any chance of increasing firm value. Other possible excess cash policies, such as excess cash flow for acquisitions or non-value enhancing investments, can only maintain or decrease a firm's value. It is the uncertainty inherent in project evaluation which makes excess cash flow retention advantageous to a firm.

The FCFT suggests an increase in dividends or debt for growth firms which have excess cash flow. Although these 'Genetech' fast-growing firms would have many positive NPV projects to absorb cash flow, it is possible that a firm could have excess cash flow. Considering future time periods, research could reveal the possible extra requirements of new positive NPV projects on cash flow. To finance all projects, the firm might have to reduce its dividend or forgo other good investments. Evidence generally shows that a fall in dividends reduces firm value in share price (Pettit, 1972). Capital markets are not perfect according to theories of asymmetric information. These asymmetries predict that credit rationing could occur in the capital market where firms are heterogeneous. Asymmetries allow an excess cash retention policy to become a superior strategy. Incidentally, Tobin's q ratio will be used to distinguish between firms with a greater and poorer set of investment opportunities.[12]

The FCFT explores firm characteristics which affect the choice of best policy for shareholders and examines the conditions under which earnings re-investment might seem preferable. The objective of the FCFT is to balance both the benefits and costs of investing earnings. As examined in Chapter 3, the optimal strategy should vary according to the individual firm's cost of borrowing which depends on asymmetric information and private information held by the firm.

5.6.3.2   Previous studies on bankruptcy models

Beaver's *Financial Ratios as Predictors of Failure* examined the predictive power of thirty different financial ratios to predict failure five years in advance (Beaver, 1966). Unfortunately, Beaver used failure synonymously with bankruptcy. In legal terms, bankruptcy is the final legal event which may have been postponed for years, whereas accounting failure may have occurred several years prior to this official legal condition. Predicting bankruptcy too late leaves little chance and time to take evasive action.

This important technical difference between bankruptcy and failure is important in India where failing firms were often taken over by governments avoiding bankruptcy proceedings. So, what exactly defines a failing company in India? At a political and executive level in India, corporate failure is recognised as a problem only when an enterprise is on the brink of closure, creating a serious employment problem. The government cares if a firm closes, regardless of its financial performance, and creates temporary unemployment. Lending institutions seem more concerned with a failing firm when they consider default of loan repayment. This plays an increasing role in India where bankruptcy laws cannot be enforced as in the UK or US. Shareholders are probably more sensitive to a firm's performance, perhaps more so than lending institutions. Bankruptcy is signalled to them when no dividends are disbursed and the prospect of dividend payments seems bleak. Shareholders are vigilant of such signalling given the background of dividend payments in Indian firms where it varies more than in the UK or US. Each of these views must be taken into account in developing a prediction model for bankruptcy in India.

Altman tried to improve Beaver's work by combining several financial ratios into a single index (Altman, 1968). He developed the Z score based on multiple discriminant analysis (or MDA). The problem with the application of MDA was in its strict applicability to judging the financial strength of a firm. MDA has been used for classification when dependent variables are qualitative. However, the score variables should ideally yield continuous degrees of risk of bankruptcy, and Z scores as bi-variate statistics were unable to do so. Altman's later model used a cut-off point for the Z score; moreover, he treated private and publicly traded firms independently.[13] The Z score was developed so as to minimise the overlap between potentially bankrupt and potentially non-bankrupt groups. Altman's approach was both novel and highly reliable but only for one year prior to bankruptcy. The error in classification was about 28% for two years before bankruptcy and this error subsequently increased for more years before bankruptcy. Applying Altman's model in India means data would be required at least one year prior to bankruptcy for all firms. Unfortunately, most published financial statements of firms in India are not available for six months after the end of the accounting year. This delay would further obfuscate Altman's one-year prior performance record, as the data would simply be unavailable. But, again, this is not as much a problem with Altman's model as with the availability of data on time.

Wilcox developed the *Gambler's Ruin* approach (Wilcox, 1976). The model assumed that at any moment a firm's financial state is defined by its adjusted cash position or net liquidation value. Wilcox rather arbitrarily defines the liquidation values for the different assets of a firm (Table 5.6).

Table 5.6 Liquidation values of assets (based on Wilcox)

Asset	Liquidation value (%)
Cash equivalents	100
Other current assets	70
Long-term assets	50
Debt	100

In this model, the firm is the gambler and a firm's probability of winning a bet is r and the probability of a firm losing a bet is l; S is the size of the bet. The interval to bankruptcy is based on the inflows and outflows of liquid resources. However, this model is disappointing, especially because it assumes that periodic cash flows are independent of each other. Wilcox replaced the functional form of this model in later years with one with better forecasting abilities.[14]

5.6.4   Research methodology and data

5.6.4.1   Financial ratio selection

When a financial ratio is highly sensitive to changes in a firm's behaviour and is able to correctly measure a firm's ability to handle unexpected conditions, it is considered to be an efficient indicator of financial performance. Profitability ratios are sensitive to bankruptcy risk, while the sustainability level of a firm is usually measured by its balance sheet ratios. The more sensitive a measure is to bankruptcy risk, the more quickly can it reflect changes in a firm's health, and therefore the more effective it will be as an early warning device. Ratio selection is a difficult task due to the information overlaps in the different ratios. A study by Caruthers, Pinches and Mingo (1973) used factor analysis to categorise the financial ratios into seven sets: return on investment, capital turnover, financial leverage, short-term liquidity, cash position, inventory turnover, and receivable turnover. Table 5.7 shows the ratios

Table 5.7   Industry-relative ratios tested for analysis

Receivables turnover	Capital turnover
Receivables/Inventory	Cash flow/Sales
Receivables/Sales	Net income/Sales
(receivables+inventory)/Total assets	Current assets/Total assets
	Sales/Total assets
Short-term liquidity	
Current assets/Current liabilities	*Financial leverage*
Net fixed assets/Total assets	Total debt/Total assets
	Total debt/Net worth
Cash position	Current liabilities/Total debt
Cash/Current liabilities	Common equity/Net worth
Cash/Total assets	
	Inventory turnover
Return on capital	Sales/Working capital
Cash flow/Total assets	Current assets/Sales
Net income/Total assets	
Net income/Net worth	*Other*
EBIT/Total assets	Retained earnings/Total assets

which fall under each category. Again, since this model aims to stabilise the data and specify its categories for classification to a greater degree, it uses the Platt and Platt method of specification to convert all ratios to industry-relative ratios.[15]

To avoid potential multicollinearity only one ratio from each category was to be included in the final model. In the end, various combinations of ratios across all categories were tested on the Indian data set and the final selection was based on the statistical significance of the estimated parameters. Furthermore, it was predicted that the probability of bankruptcy would be positively related to financial leverage and negatively related to return on capital, inventory turnover, cash position, receivables turnover, short-term liquidity, and sales growth. These results concurred with previous tests. Also, it was expected, as suggested by the FCFT, that Retained Earnings/Total Assets (RE/TA) ought to be more positively and more significantly related to the probability of bankruptcy for Tobin's low q firms than their Tobin's high q counterparts.

5.6.4.2   Statistical model

In this study, the logit regression technique will be used to analyse the choice probabilities. Lo (1986) has already indicated the advantages in applying this type of model to multiple discriminant analysis. The logit model has the form:

$$P_i = \cfrac{1}{\left(1 + \cfrac{1}{e^{(B_0 + B_1 x_{i1} + B_2 x_{i2} + \ldots\ldots\ldots B_n x_{in})}}\right)}$$

P_i = probability of failure of the ith firm
X_{ij} = jth industry – relative ratio of the ith firm

$$\text{Odds ratio} = \frac{P_i}{1 - P_i} = e^{(B_0 + B_1 + x_{i1})} = e^{B_0}(e^{B_1})^{x_{i1}}$$

(5.3)

The logit model is a non-linear model. Estimation of b can be carried out by the method of non-linear maximum likelihood methods. This model will be used because it possesses a number of advantages over the linear regression model. First, it is well known that the linear regression model, if applied to a dichotomous dependent variable, will suffer from heteroscedasticity whereas the logit model will not. Second, extrapolation of the linear function would yield probabilities outside the (0,1) range. However, the logistic curve is bounded by the values 0 and 1. Third, the logit model is consistent with random utility maximisation as shown by McFadden (1973). On both statistical and theoretical grounds, the logit model is preferred here. Another feature of the logit model is the *odds ratio*, which is a ratio of the probability of the event occurring, i.e., bankruptcy, to the probability that it will not occur. This exponential relationship provides an interpretation for β: the odds increase multiplicatively by e^{β} for every single unit increase in x. Therefore to summarise, the coefficients give the change in the log of the odds ratio of bankruptcy per unit increase in the respective ratios. Taking the antilog of this coefficient provides the%age change in the odds per unit increase. However, to calculate the probability of bankruptcy itself per unit change in a ratio, the following equation is used:[16]

$$\frac{\partial P_i}{\partial x_i} = B_i P_i (1 - P_i)$$

(5.4)

Greater use of the odds ratio will be made later as it will help to show the marginal increases in the probability of bankruptcy as the different ratios increase and decrease.

5.6.4.3 Data

The firms included in this sample were limited to the textile industry in India.[17] Again, it is important for comparative purposes to remain within one industry so as to not overestimate or underestimate the magnitude of certain ratios, since each industry has its unique characteristics.[18] All bankruptcies were recorded for the period between 1964 and 1973. The failed firms were matched with successful firms with similar asset size and within the same period. In a sample of 93 firms almost 40% had failed. As mentioned earlier, the Platt and Platt industrial relative ratios were used to try and achieve as much stability as possible in all of the variables. As a general rule for the following analysis, there needs to be some system which can distinguish between investment quality. Both Tobin's q and market–book ratio have been used to reflect investment quality; this study will rely primarily on Tobin's q. Relatively good investments were defined as those with a greater than mean quality measure. Large firms were defined as those which exceeded the mean value of gross assets. Employing this division shows whether or not firms were indeed following predictable cash strategies. According to the model, small firms with high q should rely primarily upon internal finance for financing their investments. All others with the possible exception of large, high q firms should release funds as dividends and seek external finance for investment funding. The hypothesis for the present model implies that Retained Earnings/Total Assets (RE/TA) has greater significance for low q firms which are closer to failure. In this sample, 46 firms were classified as low q and 47 were high q firms (Table 5.8). Out of the 46 low q firms, 31 firms were classified as small, and from the 47 high q firms, 29 were large firms.

Table 5.8   Distribution of textile firms

Type	Small firms	Large firms	Total
Low Q	31	15	46
High Q	18	29	47
Total	49	44	

5.6.5   Results

The final model included five variables, one from each of the above categories (Return On Capital: EBIT(earnings before interest, taxes)/total assets; Leverage: total debt/total assets; Cash Position: cash/total assets; Capital Turnover: current assets/total assets; Other: retained earnings/total assets). The coefficients and t-statistics are shown in Table 5.9 for the entire sample. The following tables, Table 5.10 and Table 5.11, show the results of the same data after it had been further specified and separated based on their Tobin's q ratio into high and low growth firms.

Failed companies were assigned a 1, whereas survivors were assigned a 0. Therefore, a negative coefficient suggested that an increase in a ratio would reduce the probability of bankruptcy, whereas a positive coefficient suggested that there was a direct relationship between the probability of bankruptcy and an increase in the ratio.

Table 5.9 shows results of the entire sample before separation into low q and high q categories. The probability of bankruptcy increased for a firm if it had lower cash flow/sales and lower cash flow/total assets, whereas it increased if it had a higher total debt/total assets ratio. The coefficient for RE/TA has a positive sign, which indicates, as predicted by the FCFT, that the probability of bankruptcy increases as this ratio increases. The%age change in odds suggests that for a unit increase in the RE/TA the log of the odds ratio of bankruptcy increases by about 7.3%. The signs of the coefficients for the entire sample are as predicted. The coefficient of total debt/total assets is large and quite significant. But as mentioned earlier, failing firms are expected to have greater financial leverage than their healthy counterparts, since these high fixed loan service payments are usually a precursor to eventual bankruptcy. Of course, this is well known and has been demonstrated in many empirical and theoretical surveys; moreover, most optimal capital structure literature mentions the increase in risk for firms as they increase their debt burden. The forecasting accuracy for this model using the entire sample was 84%.

Table 5.9   Results for entire sample

Variable	Estimated β	t-statistic*	Exp(β)	% Odds change
EBIT/ Total assets	−.1031	.2406	.9020	−9.8
Total debt/Total assets	3.3921	2.2934*	29.6659	2866.59
Cash/ Total assets	−.8295	3.4273*	.4363	−56.37
Current assets/ Total assets	−.0443	2.133*	.95666	−4.334
Retained earnings/ Total assets	.0708	.7111*	1.07336	7.336

* Significant at .01 level of significance.

Classification results
(*percentage correctly classified*)
Bankruptcies: 75
Survivors: 92
Overall: 84

In the next model, the high *q* firms were separated from the entire sample and then tested separately. As listed in Table 5.10, the accuracy of the model improves slightly (88%) but not enough to confirm the higher quality of this method of sample specification.

Table 5.10   Results for high *q* firms

Variable	Estimated ß	t-statistic*	Exp(ß)	% Odds change
EBIT/Total assets	−3.4153	1.1434*	.04305	−95.69
Total debt/ Total assets	3.3427	.0026	28.2956	2729
Cash/Total assets	−4.8798	1.3085*	.0076	−99.24
Current assets/ Total assets	−.1787	.1406	.83635	−16.36
Retained earnings/ Total assets	−.0297	.1251	.9707	−2.92

* Significant at .01 level of significance.

Classification results
(*percentage correctly classified*)
Bankruptcies: 90
Survivors: 85
Overall: 88

Short-term liquidity, i.e., Cash/Total Assets, and the ROC, i.e., EBIT/Total Assets, have significant coefficients. As far as the short-term liquidity ratio, according to the FCFT, given imperfect capital markets and asymmetric information problems, high *q* firms should remain more liquid than their low *q* counterparts, for high *q* firms have a more value-enhancing set of investment opportunities. In fact, it may even be advantageous for them to retain some of their earnings to increase their liquidity, as they might be faced with unforeseen investment opportunities for which they must have cash readily available. An example might illustrate this need for earnings retention. Perhaps a quick-growing firm researching frontier technology is close to a breakthrough but cannot reveal its investment information without losing its competitive advantage. Assume also that its past cash flow had exceeded its investments in prior years (before the new technology was considered). An imperfect capital market could evaluate this firm as having no positive NPV projects without any further information. If a similar firm in the industry obtained funds but invested them in a positive NPV project which ultimately had a lower NPV than the original firm, capital markets have been inefficient. In this case, if the first firm had retained its earnings in liquid assets, it would have had more internal finance to invest in the secretive research. But if it had released its earnings as dividends, it would fall short of investment funds. Given imperfect capital markets, earnings retention can serve as a buffer of liquidity for investment funding when capital markets do not or cannot accurately evaluate projects with the publicly available information.

The following model used the low *q* firms from the sample. As listed in Table 5.11, the coefficients on all of the ratios are statistically significant. It is interesting to note that in comparison to the former models (Table 5.9, Table 5.10), leverage plays a much greater role in determining the probability of bankruptcy when low *q* firms are concerned. Furthermore, the RE/TA coefficient is significant. The positive sign indicates that as the ratio increases, the probability of bankruptcy increases. Furthermore, the %age change in odds shows that for every unit increase in RE/TA there is almost a 273% rate in the log of the odds ratio favouring bankruptcy. Clearly, this is a much greater increase than the previous model where a unit increase in RE/TA yielded 7.33% and –2.92% in Table 5.9 and Table 5.10 respectively. Again, this is just as the early hypothesis had predicted: retained earnings play a much more important role in determining the probability of a low *q* firm's bankruptcy. The remaining coefficients have negative signs as expected, so that any increases in their values imply a lower probability of bankruptcy. Clearly, the accuracy of this model improved so that the specification techniques being used seem to be successful (89%).

Table 5.11   Results for low *q* firms

Variable	Estimated β	t-statistic*	Exp(β)	% Odds change
EBIT/ Total assets	–.8549	2.3510*	.4253	–57.47
Total debt/ Total assets	4.23	3.693*	68.717	6771
Cash/ Total assets	–.9946	1.2824*	.3699	–63.01
Current assets/ Total assets	–.0521	1.6335*	.9492	–5.07
Retained earnings/ Total assets	1.319	2.248*	3.7396	273

* Significant at .01 level of significance.

Classification results
(percentage correctly classified)
Bankruptcies: 87
Survivors: 91
Overall: 89

In following the overall strategy employed in this study, the final model attempts to gain greater accuracy through further specification. It now not only separates the firms by their q values but also by their sizes. The type of firms (small, low q) with the greatest vulnerability to bankruptcy are described in Table 5.12. As noted, leverage (TD/TA) and retained earnings (RE/TA) have the numerically highest positive coefficient in comparison to the other models. In this case, the%age change in odds is greatest and indicates that for every unit increase (in RE/TA) for these types of firms, there is a 335% increase in the log of the odds ratio favouring bankruptcy, by far the most severe. Again, this is as hypothesised earlier. Not only are these low q firms, but they are small on average so that they cannot rely on other resources to bail them out during bankruptcy. This type of *bail out* is quite common in the Indian corporate arena where some large firms are usually part of a bigger conglomerate and thus can rely on other divisions to help them in their times of sickness. The level of accuracy is also the greatest for this final model, so that this model seems to be the most useful for forecasting purposes (93%).

5.6.5.1 Evaluation

In light of the earlier discussions on previous bankruptcy models, it might be useful to compare the final model developed in this analysis with the other benchmark models. Specifically, the same data sample

Table 5.12 Results for small low q firms

Variable	Estimated β	t-statistic*	Exp(β)	% Odds change
EBIT/Total assets	−.0535	.0104	.9479	−5.21
Total debt/ Total assets	12.362	1.7772*	233374	23374725
Cash/Total assets	−1.0860	1.4189*	.3376	−66.24
Current assets/ Total assets	−.0649	1.5281*	.93716	−6.28
Retained earnings/ Total assets	1.4706	2.2314*	4.35184	335

* Significant at .01 level of significance.

Classification results
(percentage correctly classified)
Bankruptcies: 90
Survivors: 95
Overall: 93

will be tested for several different failure models including the one developed in this section. As all of the data is from the textile industry, industry-relative ratios will be used in all cases. The results are presented in Table 5.13.

Table 5.13   Classification accuracy one year prior to bankruptcy

Model	Statistical method	Percent correctly classified		
		Bankruptcies	*Survivors*	*Overall*
Altman (1968)	MDA	92%	73%	82.5%
Altman (1983)				
Public:	MDA	90%	87%	88.5%
Private:		91%	85%	88%
Betts and Belhoul (1987)	MDA	80%	83%	81.5%
Platt and Platt (1990)	Logit	87%	93%	90%
Pantalone and Platt (1987)	Logit	89%	93%	91%
Zmijewski (1984)	WESML probit			
	Even weight	57%	93%	75%
	20:1 weight	42%	89%	65.5%
Wilcox (1976)	MDA	72%	82%	77%
Dhumale (1997) (a)*	Logit	89%	88%	88.5%
Dhumale (1997) (b)*	Logit	90%	95%	92.5%

*   (a) Includes Q classification
    (b) Includes size and Q classification

Table 5.13 shows the classification results of the different models. The model under examination in this section seems to perform quite well. Specifically, the final model which uses both size and q values in its testing methodology carries a 92.5% overall accuracy rate. Other models also performed well including the Platt and Platt and Pantalone and Platt specifications.

As a final analysis, it is worth considering the plots of low q and high q firms vis-à-vis the logit function (Figure 5.6). The RE/TA will be used as the horizontal axis and the other variables will be set at their mean values.

The first observation is that the low q logit function rises much faster than the high q function in the domain beyond 0. Furthermore, the low q firm function reaches the 0.5 probability level – the last assumed feasible point at which bankruptcy is avoidable – when RE/TA is less than zero (–0.031), whereas with high q firms the function approaches the 0.5 level at a positive RE/TA level (0.0006). This implies and confirms that for low q firms to avoid the onslaught of bankruptcy i.e., the 0.5 probability level, they must retain no earnings and even

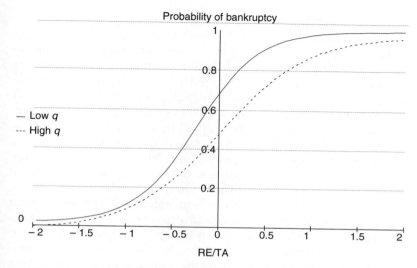

Figure 5.6 Plot of estimated probabilities as functions of RE/TA by using low *q* and high *q* firms

disburse any unearned income. Of course, the latter condition is not feasible, but it re-emphasises the importance of non-retention policies for low *q* firms. For high *q* firms, the curve shows that at the 0.5 probability level a firm can retain a minimum RE/TA ratio (.0001) and not enter the bankruptcy level (0.5). Similarly, at the RE/TA = 0 level a low *q* firm has a .72 probability of bankruptcy while the high *q* firm has a .48 probability. Clearly, the findings from these functions confirm the hypothesis that low *q* firms can enter bankruptcy levels at much lower levels of RE/TA than their high *q* counterparts. The increase in the slopes of both functions after they pass the critical level of 0.5 is also noteworthy. The slope of the low *q* firms approaches $P = 1$ asymptotically at a much faster rate than the slope of the high *q* function. Again, this suggests that if low *q* firms retain earnings and continue to do so increasingly after they pass the 0.5 level, they will face bankruptcy much sooner than their high *q* counterparts. As mentioned earlier, these functions further demonstrate the validity of the hypothesis regarding the importance of the RE/TA ratio to low *q* firms.

5.6.5.2   Discussion

The results have demonstrated that the FCFT does indeed hold true especially in its treatment of low q firms close to bankruptcy. The model demonstrates that for those firms with fewer positive NPV investment opportunities, it is more important to retain less earnings lest they risk bankruptcy at a much faster rate than high q firms. Similarly, in dealing with high q firms, the model showed that a certain level of retained earnings might be useful in liquid form, especially given asymmetric information and imperfect capital market conditions. As mentioned earlier, these conditions especially hold true within markets where all firms do not receive similar advantages, whether in the forms of creditor leniency or temporary help from another division within its conglomerate.

Furthermore, this study also demonstrated that the use of such methods of specification is associated with increasingly accurate forecasting, so that the last model which had specified firms by both their size and growth opportunities seemed to be most accurate. To confirm that the aforementioned increases in accuracy were not simply a natural consequence of sample truncation, the data was divided and tested based on other attributes and it did not yield any useful results. Clearly, there is some order to the prescribed specification methods and this study has tried to demonstrate it. The model is a direct consequence of work done previously on improving forecasting techniques, and although there is still much room for improvement, the growth potential of firms should certainly be considered in future work.

5.7   Policy implications of reforms in Indian bankruptcy proceedings

There have been many financial sector reforms specifically aimed at India's banking sector since 1992. These revisions have tried to define higher banking standards in India including the treatment and procedures for firms facing bankruptcy. The following list tries to point out specific attempts to improve various aspects of the aforementioned financial sector problems:

(a) Sharp reduction in the number of centrally administered interest rates. In 1989, there were more than 50 lending categories with administratively determined interest rates depending upon size of loan, location of the firm, usage, and type of borrower. These were brought down to two base rates in 1994 when a new policy provided for substantial deregulation of interest rates.

(b) Banks are no longer allowed to book interest income on non-per-forming assets (NPAs).

(c) Asset classification and provisioning requirements have changed in line with Bank for International Settlements (BIS) criteria. A sub-standard loan asset is now defined as an NPA for no more than two years. Such assets must be written down by 10%. Doubtful assets are those which are NPAs for more than two years. The entire unse-cured portion of such loans has to be written off. Moreover, the secured portion has to be written down by 20% in the first year, 30% in the second, and 50% in the third. For loss assets (a pure bad debt), the entire value has to be written off.

(d) The provisioning schedule has also been tightly defined. All loss assets had to be provisioned for by 31 March 1993. Moreover, 30% of the substandard and doubtful assets had to be written down according to (c) above by that cut-off date, with the remaining 70% provisioned for by 31 March 1994.

(e) Capital adequacy. The value of loan portfolios of banks initially had to consist of at least 4% risk-free loans which increased to 6% and tapered off at 8% by 1996.

(f) New private sector banks may be established to foster a competi-tive environment. There are still too few to create strong competi-tive pressures, but the number of highly efficient entrants is rising.

(g) Legislative changes were made in the Banking Companies (Acquisition and Transfer of Undertakings) Acts of 1970 and 1980 and the State Bank of India Act to facilitate public sale of bank equity. This enabled the State Bank of India (the largest nation-alised bank) to raise Rs. 22 billion through a public equity issue and another Rs. 10 billion through bonds.

(h) To supervise the banks and financial institutions, the RBI has recently set up a Board for Financial Supervision. This Board became operational in 1994 and has to ensure that banks comply with the new guidelines for credit management, asset classification, income recognition, capital adequacy, provisioning and treasury operations.

The changes listed above will indeed significantly improve present con-ditions, but unless there are fundamental alterations in the behaviour and workings of both banks and sick firms, these reforms will not live up to their fullest potential. That is, if these changes are not coupled with solid institutional reforms, there could be unexpected outcomes in the short run. For example, merely insisting on more transparent accounting procedures, stricter provisioning for non-performing assets, and higher capital adequacy ratios as well as high liquidity ratios and priority sector lending at subsidised rates drained almost 55% of banks' deposits. Although the objective of this particular reform was to encourage more profitable loan portfolios, banks reacted by shifting a larger part of the remaining 45% of their deposits into 12.5% treasury bills. Due to the 6% capital adequacy ratio and higher NPA provisioning, *t*-bills were the ideal short-term solution for banks to adhere to the new guidelines.

Unfortunately, these *t*-bills only marginally reduced portfolio risk, but added greatly to India's sovereign debt. Clearly, without the greater stringency for provisions as well as the continuation of subsidies, these funds could have been more efficiently allocated by the banks themselves. In this case, the low cost of *t*-bills attracts the banks to risk-free sovereign debt whose returns are comparatively less than average at best. As a result, banks and financial institutions find that they must charge higher rates to firms just to cover their basic costs. In the end, the more reputable firms will opt to leave these banks and find other sources of finance. Given the gradual deregulation of corporate debt instruments, these firms would rather invest in these new debt issues. The signalling and self-selection mechanism will eventually separate these more profitable firms and the banks will be left with their less prosperous counterparts. As stated earlier, the ultimate objective of this particular reform was to improve loan portfolios of banks so that the healthy firms remain and bad ones are removed. However, in the end, it seems that banks would be left with *t*-bills comprising a large part of their portfolio and unhealthy firms who were not able to enter the secondary debt market. Therefore, such consequences need to be considered prior to establishing conflicting reforms into law.

Other 1992 financial sector reforms discuss the corporate restructuring process. As discussed previously, pre-1992 conditions essentially allowed and often encouraged ultimately bankrupt firms to survive through subsidies and concessions, as banks were more interested in maximising loans regardless of quality.[19] In many cases, these sick firms should have been allowed to face bankruptcy, thus creating less of a burden to their banks who ultimately were subsidised through BIFR/SICA. Unfortunately, the focus of the reforms has been unduly placed on maximising cash turnover and recovery, so that in post-1992, banks have greater incentive to take bankruptcy action against otherwise sound firms who might really be facing difficult times. In this situation, banks have greater incentive to close firms at their first sign of default regardless of quality. Such mistakes are comparably inefficient and are not necessarily an improvement from the pre-1992 era.

At a more logistical level, the banking procedures in India are outdated and inefficient. Ordinary business which these days is conducted by computers is often carried out arduously by hand. Moreover, the ritual of filing numerous forms on a daily basis further impedes any potential progress. Unfortunately, changes in these procedures will occur slowly at best, for they involve difficult decisions for two very politically powerful groups: namely, the trade unions representing the bank officers and workers. These groups not only resist any efficiency-based changes for fear of losing their jobs, i.e., computerisation, performance-based pay, elimination of non-profitable branches, but they are often ready to strike for the slightest reason. Given these conditions, real improvements can be made only when attitudes change and disciplinary measures are respected. That is, if the government is willing to subsidise unhealthy firms under severe circumstances, banks must try and select only those with the greatest potential for recovery rather than include more merely to increase their loan portfolio. This implies that regulations have to be aware of such circumstances, and the government and the banks have to strike an equitable contract where the government does not face a moral hazard problem and banks have an incentive only to be far more selective amongst sick firms.

5.8 Conclusion

This chapter tried to decipher the role of a firm's capital structure during and before possible bankruptcy. In doing so, it first looked at a firm's financial structure as a possible predictor of bankruptcy, and it then examined how a firm's treatment differed after bankruptcy, based on its leveraging ratios, equity ownership, etc. The chapter began by considering the definition of corporate bankruptcy and then explaining the role of the state in liquidation and debt renegotiation. It then described Indian bankruptcy restructuring procedures under the SICA Act of 1985 and its legal body, the BIFR. An analysis of these legal and administrative procedures revealed that India's definition of corporate sickness is too narrow and consequently any assistance entitled to these sick firms often arrives too late. Further complications are added by delays caused by inefficient bankruptcy reorganisation procedures which only hinder and lessen the likelihood of a possible recovery.

The following section examined the theoretical factors involved in the interaction between the capital structure of a firm and possible restructuring schemes. It provided proof of how bargaining power can shift away from banks to firms as the leveraging ratio increases leading to a possible overinvestment problem. In the latter part of this section, empirical evidence using corporate data is tested against the aforementioned theory. It considers the effects of subsidies, sacrifices, and irregular accounting practices within the Indian context. A detailed description of several violations under the auspices of restructuring and refinancing in the public interest is presented. In the fifth section a logistic model for better bankruptcy prediction was developed using earnings retention as a specification mechanism. It used results from the previous chapter, specifically the potential quality of investments for firms to further classify firms before any such analysis. This specific model is tested against previous work using the same Indian data set, and its classification techniques do improve prediction rates to a certain degree. The chapter concludes by first mentioning the various reforms which have occurred since 1992. It then specifically addresses certain policy changes which might fit within a market-driven framework and better align the incentives of both sick firms and their potential rescuers.

The post-1992 reforms have resulted in improving certain procedures and practices in bankruptcy proceedings. Government regulations have granted greater rights to creditors which can be enforced through constitutional legislation. The government has recently decided to establish debt-recovery tribunals for banks to try and recover their debts. The government has endowed these banks with greater power on both the economic and legal fronts. The aforementioned commissions address the legal issues, whereas new rules allow banks to convert written-down debt into equity and then sell such equity in secondary debt markets thus potentially creating a market for takeovers. The government's allowance of private market participation implies that it must believe that no regulation is able to effectively discipline firms as well as the pressures in a market for corporate control. However, it is important in the initial stages of financial sector reform for the Indian government to strike a balance between a freely functioning market for corporate control and the concentration of industry. To further explore these and other issues, the following chapter examines some of the effects of a market for corporate control in India from the perspectives of firms and the shareholders involved.

6

Factors Affecting the Market for Corporate Control: The Role of Excess Cash, Diversification, and Predation during Mergers and Acquisitions

6.1 Introduction

A a microeconomic level, the information value of a firm's financial structure is relevant for its behaviour in takeovers and acquisitions; however, this information can be misused at great cost to the market. Consequently, takeovers and mergers could exact negative externalities on the market through short-termism, greater concentration of industry, and agency costs. This chapter examines the signalling effects of earnings retention and diversification on returns during acquisitive activities and considers the benefits and disadvantages of a more active market for corporate control within India at a macroeconomic level.

One of the risks in developing an active market for corporate control lies in its tendency to increase the concentration of industry in a market already dominated by large conglomerates. If a market for corporate control becomes prevalent in India, not only could the survival of small and medium-sized firms be threatened, but any successfully emerging small firms would surrender to such predators even before they had a chance to operate in the market. Due to the inexperience of the Indian government with laws concerning such activity, it is possible in India with a minimum 10% stake in a company to acquire controlling interests in a firm by making an open offer of a further 20% of the equity of the target firm. In fact, recent legislation, December 1996, reduced this level from higher levels to 20% to solve the problems of fund flow and thus facilitate the takeover process. The aims of the Bhagwati Committee who suggested these recommendations were to ensure that the provisions did not prevent all takeover activity. However, they hoped to provide enough protection to minority shareholders so that this group of atomistic investors would not implicitly bear the greater costs in any takeover arrangements. A more detailed review and suggestions for improvement for these laws will follow in due course. However, recent takeovers in India, albeit small compared with those in the US and the UK, indicate the disparate treatment of small firms under present rules. The recently publicised takeovers of Damania Airways by Skyline NEPC and Cox and Kings Travel provide two valid cases where the shareholders of the smaller takeover targets have been put at risk. In the former case, shareholders who were fortunate enough to be included in the 20% buy-out are still awaiting payments, while Cox and Kings struggle to survive with the threat of being taken over by one of many groups of investors with significant positions in Cox and Kings Travel's equity. That such takeovers promote efficiency is debatable but often at a significant cost to firms and their shareholders.

The chapter surveys the merger and takeover experience in India – especially economic and legal peculiarities – before encouraging an active market for corporate control. The following sections consider empirical evidence from takeover activity and model returns to shareholders using data from the Indian market. Specifically, it examines signalling effects of earnings retention and diversification on bidder and target returns during acquisitive activity within a FCFT framework. The next part of the chapter addresses the signalling effects of the financial structure for smaller firms which often deal with the consequences prior to being taken over, acquired, or even driven out of the market . In many cases, it is believed that these smaller target firms reveal their true financial information for efficient market valuation which bidders unfortunately use against them. The informational value of a small firm's financial structure becomes crucial when bidder firms plan to take over or drive out smaller rivals. Using the long-purse theory of predation, attempts are made to mitigate some of these predatory forces by modelling an observable contract between small firms and banks which might remove some of the financial constraints used by predatory bidders against them during takeovers. Banks would serve as mediators in these contracts who it is believed are able to handle asymmetric information problems and agency costs more efficiently than stock markets alone. The analysis in this chapter attempts to reconcile the advantages and disadvantages of further promoting India's market for corporate control. It considers the benefits of the Japanese and German examples of greater reliance on banks against the Anglo-Saxon efficiency arguments underlying markets for corporate control. The chapter concludes with possible suggestions to improve the current status of takeover regulations with greater roles for banks rather than stock markets alone so that indeed India's market for corporate control might promote corporate efficiency rather than impair it.

6.2 Takeover policy in India

Takeovers are common in an economy like India whose financial and corporate sector is maturing and integrating with the world economy. During 1988–92, there were almost 121 successful takeovers and mergers with 37 unsuccessful takeover bids. Some of the successful cases included the takeovers of Ashok Leyland and Ennore Foundries by the Hindujas, and the Goenka's takeover of Ceat Tyres, Herdilia Chemicals and Polychem, and the unsuccessful 1988 attempt by Swaraj Paul and Sethia groups to take over DCM and Escorts. One of the reasons for the increase in the activity in the market for corporate control was the introduction of the MRTP (Monopolies and Restrictive Trade Practices Act) Amendment Act. This act abolished the rule which required prior government approval of all takeovers. Indeed, since 1969 the MRTP Act restricted takeover activities through its various rules and regulations. For almost twenty years, these rules along with Reserve Bank regulations disallowed banks from financing takeovers. They limited the participation of banks by placing a ceiling on the amount which could be loaned as well as requiring collateral shares upfront. Often, these shares were held by government financial institutions who always ensured that share ownership was never contested. As a final barrier, ultimate control often rested in the hands of the Boards of Directors of firms who refused to surrender their shares under any circumstance. Proponents of takeovers suggest that the development of a market for corporate control provides the financial community within and outside India with major opportunities for growth. The reasons for the recent increase in the number of Indian takeovers are not unlike those in more developed markets, including synergy, greater market share, agency dilution, and efficiency.

Before liberalisation, the MRTP Act, FERA, and other licensing regulations restricted business expansion to their core areas of expertise, and thus forced firm management to grow through unrelated diversification schemes.[1] Post-liberalisation marked the end of the licence *raj* and other restrictive policies, meaning a sudden increase in the number of new firms going public. Luckily, most of these nascent firms were funded through the large inflow of post-liberalisation portfolio flows into India's capital markets (*Economic Times*, 1992). Unfortunately, most investors were caught in the market euphoria paying little attention to efficiency and productivity. These problems were further exacerbated when further financial deregulation opened Indian equity and debt holdings to Euro markets in 1991. Again, the unrestrained growth led to careless decisions fostering low productivity, inefficient capacity use, and diversified asset portfolios. As growth rates slowed due to higher corporate taxes, many firms listed on the stock markets fell to three-year lows in the mid-1990s. Banks and financial institutions (FIs) became less generous, so firms experienced poor performance and low share prices. Consequently, firms realised that they must think of economies of scale, specialisation, and scope. Firms and their promoters have begun to consolidate and to specialise while shedding their diversified interests. As a result, there are several domestic players in the market seeking to consolidate by acquiring firms in their core areas and shedding their non-core activities. Furthermore, foreign firms with similar incentives create even more competition in the market for corporate control.

Another reason for the recent takeovers in India is the perceived need for size and synergy. Banks and FIs are encouraging dominant players in industries to take over weaker counterparts and increase their focus. Large conglomerates are gradually selling off smaller ventures and using the proceeds to increase market share in their core areas. The takeover of Hindustan Gases by Praxair, and Lakme by Hindustan Lever, are typical examples of deals where bidders have realised that taking over smaller entities is more profitable than setting up new operations. Unlike before, management cannot now block these takeovers, due to the abolition of Section 22A of the Securities Contract Act. Previously, FIs shared a cosy relationship with the old management, paying little attention to performance. However, in recent years, FIs like the ICICI (Industrial Credit and Investment Corporation of India), UTI (Unit Trust of India), and the IDB (Industrial Development Bank) find themselves listed and concerned with the value of their own shares. Historically, most of these FIs have been at the heart of India's financial system and they regard the FIs support of a market for corporate control as inconceivable. These opponents of takeover promotion cannot believe that FIs would ever surrender their shares and ultimately their controlling interests to a hostile bidder. Unfortunately, recent evidence has proven otherwise. The takeover bids for the Indal Steel Corp. by Sterlite Corp. and for Raasi

Cements by India Cements are only two cases where the FIs – major shareholders in both target firms – seem to be ranking their own interests above that of their clients. The same FIs who coddled promoters in the 1980s and early 1990s are not only demanding greater performance but are also threatening to sell underperforming firms through outright solicitation. The chapter now turns to empirical evidence from the Indian takeover market and examines returns to shareholders of bidder and target firms using amongst other things their rates of earnings retention as measures of quality.

6.3   The signalling effects of earnings retention and diversification on bidder and target returns during acquisition activity

6.3.1   Introduction

Several studies examine the relationship of bidder and target firm returns to Tobin's q in successful tender offers.[2] In these analyses, Tobin's q represents the value of investment opportunities under current management and is a measure of both investment and managerial quality. These studies suggest that bidder gains are greatest in takeovers of poorly managed targets by well-managed bidders. Lang, Stultz and Walkling (1989) analyse the possibility of a relationship between tender offers and Tobin's q ratios of targets and bidders. They find that bidders with high q ratios have significant positive abnormal returns, whereas bidders with low q ratios show negative abnormal returns. The highest returns for both bidders and targets occur when a high q bidder takes over a low q target. Again, if q values are used as a measure of managerial quality, these studies suggest that firms with greater performance make better bidders, and firms with lower performance ratings are more valuable as targets. Some studies of takeovers examine the impact of agency costs of excessive retained earnings during the announcement of a tender offer. These analyses indicate that the expected negative reactions for bidder and target returns are more likely and significant when shareholders expect amongst other factors increased agency costs. These costs can be minimised through reputation building by bidder management so as to reduce asymmetric information costs. In Jensen's terms, managers build a favourable reputation in spite of their abuse or rather the lack of excessive retained earnings. Nachman and John investigated this problem of reducing agency costs and showed how underinvestment can be offset by reputation building (Nachman and John, 1985).

6.3.2   Purpose

This study extends these above analyses by combining firm quality and managerial reputation building to examine the effects of the combined variables in tender offers. The study attempts to test Jensen's FCFT as it applies to takeovers. First, it questions whether the quality of firms – bidder and target – involved in a takeover transaction is reflected in the level of returns for shareholders. A further screening device which classifies these high and low quality firms into high free cash flow/high retained earnings or low free cash flow/low retained earnings categories is used to examine how bidders and targets can be further specified. Second, the study will consider how acquisitive activity, i.e., into a related or unrelated area of business, affects returns to shareholders in both target and bidder firms. To achieve the former purpose, abnormal returns in a series of firms receiving tender offers during the takeover process are examined. In cross-sectional regressions, the differences in q values can explain some of the abnormal returns, but the relationship is more significant when firms are classified as high retained earnings/high free cash and low retained earnings/low free cash types. In several cases, the abnormal returns of both targets and bidders under this classification system are larger and more significant. Second, it is hypothesised that managers build reputations by pursuing only tenders related to their core area of business. Consequently, abnormal returns should be lower for those firms which are undertaking diversification programmes.

This study is one of the first to examine recent takeovers in India. During recent years, mergers and takeovers have become the preferred choice for growth and consolidation in India. The recently introduced reformed takeover code will encourage such activity in the market for corporate control. This study will help shareholders, firms, and financial institutions to assess at least one aspect of takeovers and its efficiency. The model uses data from takeovers and mergers in India during the years 1988–92.

The first part of this study develops a hypothesis for bidder and target returns based on the FCFT. This section reviews the FCFT and examines previous empirical literature on abnormal returns in takeovers, and surveys the merger and takeover experience in India – especially its economic and legal aspects – before encouraging a more active market for corporate control. In the succeeding sections, the measurement of abnormal returns, firm quality, and acquisitive activity will be examined. The last sections discuss the results and implications of takeovers and mergers for both bidders and targets.

6.3.3   Background

6.3.3.1   Takeovers within the free cash flow theory

The FCFT assumes agency conflicts exist between shareholders and managers. Free cash flow is the excess cash flow over and above the necessary amount required to fund NPV projects. The FCFT implies that managers can acquire assets for their own interests even if it means investing in negative NPV projects. That is, without an incentive structure to constrain their behaviour, managers will take actions that maximise their own utility. Jensen argues that cash disbursements, i.e., dividends, limit the funds available to managers and thus reduce agency costs. Moreover, in an efficient capital market, the value of a firm is discounted by the amount of these funds or 'free/excess' cash available to managers (Jensen, 1986).

Managers have incentives to reduce the uncertainty implicit in their terms of employment, i.e., employment risk. They attempt to reduce this risk by increasing and diversifying the firm's real asset portfolio, which might involve the purchase of real assets unrelated to a firm's primary line of business and lead to non-Pareto optimal performance for the conglomerate firm as a whole.[3] Jensen notes that takeovers are often undertaken based on expansionary arguments with little regard for efficiency. Jensen even states that the FCFT 'implies that managers of firms with unused borrowing power and large excess cash flow are more likely to undertake low-benefit or value-destroying mergers'. For managers, such diversification measures reduce employment risk by increasing the asset portfolio along with the security of their positions and provide them higher compensation. Most executive pay and promotion schemes are positively related to firm size. Therefore, if shareholder and manager interests diverge as the FCFT predicts, it is important to constrain the behaviour of these agents through bonding, monitoring, proper organisational forms, i.e., limited partnerships, and appropriate incentive structures.

The capital market and the market for corporate control become the most effective constraints on managerial abuses. Excessive retained earnings committed to debt service payments or dividend payouts increase firm value. This is especially important for firms with poor and limited set of investment opportunities since the market cannot monitor these firms as well as their higher-growth counterparts. The latter are actively involved in investment activity which is continuously appraised by the market.

Mitchell, McCormick and Maloney (1993) found that bidder returns were positively related to leverage and insider holdings. Applying these findings in an agency theoretical framework, these results indicate that debt is used as a monitoring device and that managerial shareholdings improve incentives. Managers can also show their commitment to shareholders' interests by investing in reputation building. A manager builds a good track record by expanding only into related lines of business. Such expansion signals to shareholders that managers have acquired assets that fit integrally into both the firm's and their areas of pre-existing expertise. This reputation building inclines against diversification which ultimately implies to shareholders that managers are not wasting their firm's excess cash. (Morck, Shleifer and Vishny, 1990) find that bidder returns are lower than average in diversification bids when the target is performing well or when the bidder is performing poorly.

6.3.3.2   *Determinants of successful takeovers*

Having considered the use of excess cash or retained earnings to finance unproductive takeovers, it is natural to consider high free cash flow/high retained earnings firms as takeover targets. Financial economists tend to view takeover possibilities as a constraint on managerial decisions – inefficient firms will be taken over and run more efficiently. In this case, if firms are investing retained earnings poorly, they become good targets for acquisition. By acquiring a firm with significant excess cash or retained earnings, the bidder can use the newly obtained retained earnings to finance the leverage required to facilitate the buyout; moreover, by increasing leverage, the value of the firm should increase due to the debt benefits proposed by the FCFT (Browne and Rosengren, 1987, 9). Leveraged buyouts serve as effective control devices in capital markets which cannot effectively govern firms with excess cash or retained earnings. Typically, the bidding firm's management acquires a larger stake of equity after the merger, thereby further reducing agency costs. A merger creates value reflected as an increase in stock price, as retained earnings or excess cash from the acquired firm can now fund better available investment opportunities in the bidding firm. This extension of the FCFT, however, creates a paradox: managers enjoy utility in retaining earnings, yet in doing so they attract predatory acquiring firms. If managers value job security, they will maximise firm value rather than risk being acquired (Frydl, 1987, 145). But high free cash flow firms tend to be mature firms; therefore, it may be difficult to obtain sufficient funds to finance a hostile takeover. Managers of these firms will still retain earnings if the probability of being acquired is low. Therefore, investors are rightly suspicious of managers who use their retained earnings and raise additional equity to fund such diversified acquisition activity. Consequently, as shown by Mikkelson and Parch (1985), Pettway and Radcliffe (1985), Asquith and Mullins (1986), and Masulis and Korwar (1986), the average abnormal returns for such bidders in the two-day announcement period is negative and statistically significant. On the other hand, when managers acquire or merge with firms in related lines of business, investors have greater confidence in their managers, and such confidence ought to be reflected in the share price. Shareholders learn more about managerial behaviour by observing their past actions. If managers want to prove to shareholders that they do not want more excess cash or retained earnings, they establish a track record of investing only in related lines of business.

Myers and Majluf (1984) define *financial slack* as the sum of cash, marketable securities, and risk-free debt.[4] In this instance, they contradict Jensen and argue that restricting dividends is a good means of accumulating financial slack. Slack does not merely increase managerial discretion; it also allows managers to avoid the lemons premium which would occur if a firm had to seek external finance, either equity or debt. Although retained earnings and excess cash are a good source of financial slack, it must be used properly. Again, the FCFT can be reconciled with Myers and Majluf's findings. Implicitly, it is the larger mature firms which will misuse excessive retained earnings. Large firms, which Jensen's theory targets, should face a more symmetrical capital market anyhow, if the sudden need for external finance were to arise. These firms will essentially have more financial slack since capital market asymmetries affect them to a lesser degree. The smaller, dynamic firms have more growth options, and the build-up of financial slack as a buffer against possible credit shortages , or against the need to issue equity at a price below the fair market value, is a tenable financial strategy. Private information, as in technologically advanced industries, also warrants the build-up of slack due to asymmetric information. Financial slack allows firms to maximise the value of the manager's inside information, an important part of its human capital, without facing the cost of educating possible investors (Myers and Majluf, 1984, 196).

6.3.4   Research methodology and data

The firms included in this sample were all involved in takeovers in India between 1988 and 1992. Of the 158 successful and unsuccessful takeover attempts, the final sample included 83. Many firms were excluded from testing since they failed to meet the minimum data requirements (notice of public announcement, balance sheet information, daily stock return data).[5] Balance sheet information is required to calculate Tobin's q and the announcement date and daily stock returns are required to estimate the market model and to compute the abnormal returns. As a general rule in the following analysis, there needs to be some way to distinguish investment quality. Both Tobin's q and market–book ratio have been used to reflect investment quality; this study relies primarily on Tobin's q. Relatively good investments are defined as those with a greater than mean quality measure. Employing this division shows whether or not firms were indeed following predictable cash strategies. According to the present hypothesis, firms with high q should rely more on internal finance for financing their investments. All others should release funds as dividends and seek external finance for investment funding.

Tables 6.1 and 6.2 show the distribution of the 83 target and bidder firms used in the data set as classified by their q ratios as well as their excess cash holdings. In this sample 39 were target firms and 44 were bidders. Out of the 16 low q target firms, 9 firms were classified as high liquidity (HL) and 7 as low liquidity (LL).[6] Out of the 28 low q bidder firms, 12 were HL and 16 were LL, and for their high q bidder counterparts 9 HL and 7 LL.

In classifying these firms within the FCFT framework, firms were grouped according to high or low levels of liquidity relative to their growth prospects. Firms with high liquidity/low growth prospects, i.e., HL and Low Q, were considered to have potential high free cash

Table 6.1   Distribution of target firms

Type	High liquidity	Low liquidity	Total
Low Q	9	7	16
High Q	10	13	23
Total	19	20	

Table 6.2   Distribution of bidder firms

Type	High liquidity	Low liquidity	Total
Low Q	12	16	28
High Q	9	7	16
Total	21	23	

Table 6.3 Distribution of firms as classified by high free cash flow (HFCF) and low financial slack (LFSF)

Type	HFCF	LFSF	Total
Target	9	13	22
Bidder	12	7	19
Total	21	20	

holdings (HFCF), whereas firms with low liquidity/high growth prospects, i.e., LL and High Q, were considered to have less financial slack (LFSF) to exploit potential investment opportunities. Other firms with low liquidity and low growth opportunities or high liquidity and high growth prospects are deemed by the FCFT to be immune from at least the problems caused by excessive retained earnings. Table 6.3 shows the aggregate number of firms as classified by HFCF and LFSF.

Out of the 39 target firms, 22 fell under this classification and 19 out of 44 bidder firms also fitted these categories. Furthermore, 9 out 22 target firms were HFCF and 13 were LFSF, whereas 12 out of 19 bidder firms were HFCF and 7 were LFSF. The behaviour of these 41 firms during takeover activities is the focus of this model.

To test the effects of takeovers into diversified areas of business on mean target and bidder returns, the same 41 firms which satisfied the previous criteria were considered. The core classification was based on the Industrial Classification Codes for each firm. Sixteen firms were involved in transactions classified as related and the remaining were involved in diversified acquisitive activities. Only the 41 firms from before were selected to develop an efficient step-wise filtering mechanism for predicting abnormal return behaviour. Therefore, since the 41 firms had already been classified in the first instance, this sub-sampling would be the second stage of the screening process.

6.3.5 Results

6.3.5.1 Abnormal returns[7]

Abnormal returns were measured for both bidders and targets using continuously compounded returns over a 100-day period starting 110 days before the initial takeover announcement. Abnormal returns are calculated from the day before the initial announcement until the date of shareholder approval. For target firms, the announcement date is defined as the first day on which a potential bidder expresses an interest in the acquisition of the target firm. Total abnormal returns are

Table 6.4   Target, bidder, and total abnormal returns for high q and low q firms, based on amount of free cash holdings (in percent), i.e., HFCF (high free cash flow) & LFSF (low financial slack firms)

Category	Target returns (p value)*	Bidder returns (p value)	Total returns (p value)
All takeovers	21.31	−1.63	4.29
	(0.03)	(0.01)	(0.00)
Type of bidder firm			
High q firms	23.69	−1.03	3.27
	(0.02)	(0.03)	(0.03)
LFSF	21.39	−1.72	2.72
	(0.00)	(0.02)	(0.00)
Low q firms	21.23	−2.32	2.92
	(0.04)	(0.03)	(0.02)
HFCF	16.62	−2.93	2.03
	(0.01)	(0.00)	(0.00)
Type of Target Firm			
High q firms	20.32	−2.72	2.17
	(0.03)	(0.02)	(0.03)
LFSF	20.05	−2.87	1.94
	(0.00)	(0.01)	(0.00)
Low q firms	22.73	−1.62	3.62
	(0.03)	(0.02)	(0.04)
HFCF	22.26	−1.12	3.79
	(0.02)	(0.00)	(0.00)

*p values or probability values are used to note more exact levels of significance.

calculated as the weighted average abnormal return of targets and bidders. The market values of the share prices of both targets and bidders 10 days before the initial announcement are used as weights. The value of the target firm's equity is reduced by the market value of the target's shares held by the bidder prior to the announcement day.

Table 6.4 provides the returns to targets, bidders, and the weighted average for the entire sample as well as other sub-groups. The table gives results for the entire sample. As indicated, target returns are positive and significant with a mean of 21.31% which is consistent with several other studies. Bidder returns are negative and significant with a mean of −1.63%, and total returns are significant and measure at 4.29%, which is less than the average of 8% reported for only tender offers by Bradley, Desai and Kim and the 11.3% reported by Lang, Stultz and Walkling. However, it is nearer the level of 3.7% reported in Weisbach's study, where he considered both mergers and tender offers during the 1971–82 period (Weisbach, 1990).

The table shows that target returns are about 2 percentage points greater when high q bidders are involved rather than low q bidders. These results are similar to those obtained by Lang, Stultz and Walkling. Furthermore, after further screening, the high q bidder group and selecting only those high q bidders with low financial slack (LFSF), the results are quite revealing. They suggest that these high q bidder firms which have positive investment opportunities but little or no retained cash suffer from lower returns than the average high q bidder by 2.3, 0.69, 0.55 percentage points for target, bidder, and total returns respectively. Similarly, all low q bidder firms were further grouped into those which retained excessive cash (HFCF), and again the results are in accordance with Jensen's hypothesis. In this case, low q bidder firms which retained excessive cash realised lower returns than the average for themselves as well as for their targets. As the table indicates, the target, bidder, and total returns for activities which involved low q HFCF bidder firms was 4.61, 0.61, 0.89 percentage points lower respectively than for average low q bidder firms.

The second half of Table 6.4 analyses transactions from the target firm's perspective. Again, the results indicate that for transactions involving high q target firms with low financial slack (LFSF), target, bidder, and total returns are lower than the average high q target by 0.27, 0.15, 0.23 percentage points respectively. Again, these results suggest – as hypothesised in the FCFT – that even targets with high investment opportunities might consider retaining some cash, in this case to increase their returns during takeover activity. The results for low q target firms – specifically those retaining excess cash (HFCF) – are especially revealing because they suggest that low q target firms should retain excessive cash to increase their returns. The table indicates that bidder and total returns for these HFCF low q target firms were significant and greater than the average returns for low q target firms by 0.5, 0.17 percentage points respectively. These results suggest that Jensen's hypothesis may not be applicable to firms in all categories, i.e., bidder and target, since this is a case where a low q target firm which retains more cash than the average low q target firm actually fares better in abnormal bidder and total returns. However, this finding could be reconciled with the FCFT since the theory implicitly states that by acquiring firms with significant retained earnings or excess cash might actually help bidder firms to finance the leverage needed to acquire the target firm. Subsequently, by increasing leverage, the value of the bidder firm rises due to the benefits of debt, as proposed by the FCFT (Browne and Rosengren, 1987).

Table 6.5   Target, bidder, and total abnormal returns for all takeovers and based on type of acquisition (in percent)

Category	Target returns (p value)	Bidder returns (p value)	Total returns (p value)
All takeovers	21.31 (0.03)	–1.63 (0.01)	4.29 (0.00)
Type of acquisition			
Related	23.89 (0.00)	–0.156 (0.00)	5.62 (0.02)
Unrelated	19.26 (0.00)	–2.37 (0.03)	4.03 (0.02)

The next step in testing our sample is to see if any other type of screening device might help to explain bidder, target, and overall returns. Consequently, Table 6.5 reports the abnormal returns of firms classified by the type of acquisitive activity they were involved in, i.e., related or unrelated area of business. Again, as described in Table 6.5, the target, bidder, and total returns for all takeovers are 21.31%, -1.63%, 4.29% respectively.

Target returns for acquisitions into related types of business are 2.58 percentage points greater than the average and significant. In contrast, target returns for acquisitions into unrelated types of business are 2.05 percentage points lower than the average but remain significant. Bidder returns remain negative for both types of activities but are slightly less negative, i.e., less by 2.21 percentage points, for a firm involved in a related acquisition. Total returns for related firm acquisitions yield 1.59 percentage points greater than in firms with unrelated activities. These results indicate that returns are consistent with the theory of agency costs and Jensen's FCFT. Mean returns are greater for firms with a track record of acquiring only related activity assets. Therefore, firms with diversification programmes into unrelated areas of business do yield lower abnormal returns for both bidders and targets.

6.3.5.2   Cross-section regressions

This section will describe the relation between abnormal returns of target and bidder firms, and their weighted average. The first regression model includes only the q ratios of firms in the takeover activities. The second regression model incorporates other variables using screening devices developed in the previous sections. Firms were classified as

HFCF and LFSF based on similar criteria as before. The following regression models were used:

$$R_i = \beta + \alpha_1 \text{ (bidder } q \text{ dummy)} + \alpha_2 \text{(target } q \text{ dummy)} \qquad (6.1)$$

$$R_i = \beta + \alpha_1 \text{ (bidder } q \text{ LSF/HFCF dummy)} + \alpha_2 \text{(target } q \qquad (6.2)$$
$$\text{LSF/HFCF dummy)} + \alpha_3 \text{(acquisition type dummy)}$$

R_i is the abnormal return from the date of the takeover announcement until the resolution or the delisting, whichever comes first; the q dummy variable for both the bidder and target is equal to 1 if the q ratio is greater than one and 0 if it is less than one. q ratios are considered to be high if they are larger than one or larger than the industry average.[8] In the second regression model, firms are classified as low financial slack (LSF) or high free cash flow firms (HFCF) and are assigned a 1 if they are LSF and a 0 otherwise. Similarly, the dummy variable for the acquisitive activity is assigned a 1 if the acquisitive activity is in a related area of business and 0 otherwise.

Table 6.6 shows the results of the first OLS regression model. The first row describes the base case when both the target and the bidder firms have low q ratios. The target firm earns 29.6% on average and the bidder returns –2.1%. Both coefficients are significant in this model and consistent with previous studies.[9] In the second regression, when the target firm has a high q ratio, target firm returns are 9 percentage points lower. This result is consistent with other studies which indicate that less added value can be created by taking over a well-managed firm. On the whole, bidder returns are negatively related to the target's q value and positively related to bidder q value. However, only the

Table 6.6   Regressions of target, bidder, and total abnormal returns on q characteristics

Variable	Target returns (p value)	Bidder returns (p value)	Total returns (p value)
Constant	0.2962 (0.00)	–0.0213 (0.00)	–0.044 (0.00)
Target firm high q	–0.0931 (0.00)	–0.0436 (0.03)	–0.083 (0.00)
Bidder firm high q	0.0332 (0.20)	0.0621 (0.00)	0.0429 (0.41)
R^2	.08	.04	.02

bidder *q* is significant in the third regression and returns are 6.2 percentage points higher when bidders have a high *q*. Again, this is consistent with previous work which found that bidder firm returns are greater for well-managed bidders. When both targets and bidders have low *q* ratios, total returns are –4.4%. These total returns are 8.3 percentage points lower when the target has a high *q* ratio. Due to the insignificance of total returns in the third regression, the *q* ratio of the bidder is not significant. This model indicates that the *q* ratio of the target firm plays a significant role, whereas the *q* ratio of the bidder firm does not significantly factor into the regression.

The overall explanatory power of the regression is quite low.[10] However, it is not uncommon for the R^2 of regression models which use market model residuals as independent variables to have relatively low explanatory power.[11] In the scope of this study, it is the difference in the explanatory powers between this model and the following which is relevant.

Table 6.7 incorporates other variables of interest using the screening devices discussed earlier. Firms are classified using the HFCF and LFSF criteria. The base case describes low *q* bidder firms with HFCF and low *q* target firms also with HFCF into a take over of an unrelated business. The target and total returns are 22.2% and –5.2% respectively and significant for this base case. Both values are lower than their counterparts in the first model, and perhaps the result of further specification, particularly of the specific type of underperforming, i.e, HFCF, low *q* bidder and target firms, entering into unrelated types of business

Table 6.7   Regressions of target, bidder, and total abnormal returns on *q* characteristics, free cash holdings, and type of target

Variable	Target returns (p value)	Bidder returns (p value)	Total returns (p value)
Constant	0.2217 (0.00)	–0.0184 (0.43)	–0.052 (0.00)
Target firm high *q* LFSF	–0.1263 (0.01)	–0.0182 (0.01)	–0.0434 (0.00)
Bidder firm high *q* LFSF	0.0482 (0.91)	0.0341 (0.00)	0.0632 (0.31)
Related acquisition	0.0362 (0.00)	0.0832 (0.00)	0.0651 (0.00)
R^2	0.16	0.17	0.23

activities. The coefficients for the target firm's q ratio and the type of acquisition seem to be significant in target returns. The bidder's q ratio is not significant for target returns. Target firm returns are 3.6 percentage points higher on average when firms complete a related acquisition. Target returns could increase by upto 12.6 percentage points if the target was not a high q firm.

Bidder firm returns in the second column indicate that the q ratios of both target and bidder firms as well as the type of acquisition are significant. The q ratios of bidder firms and the type of acquisition are positively related to bidder returns and have a combined positive effect of almost 11.7 percentage points. The results also significantly indicate that when a high q target firm is not involved in the acquisition, it could increase bidder returns by 1.82 percentage points. Target and bidder firm returns are significantly and negatively related to target firms with high q ratios. Furthermore, when the target firm has a high q ratio plus low financial slack, there is an even greater negative impact, i.e., target firm returns reduced by a further 3.3 percentage points and bidder firm returns reduced by a further 2.5 percentage points, as indicated by a comparison with Table 6.6.

Lastly, the q ratios of target firms and the type of acquisition are significant in total returns. Total returns are 6.3 percentage points higher when the bidder firms have a high q ratio, and by 6.5 percentage points when the acquisition is in a related area with a combined effect of over 12 percentage points. The q ratio of the bidder firm does not play a significant role in total returns. The regression models can explain about 16% of the cross-sectional variation in abnormal returns of target and bidder firms and 23% of total returns as indicated by their R^2 values. Again, as discussed earlier, although these R^2 values are low in absolute terms they are acceptable and in relative terms higher than their corresponding values from the first model.

6.3.5.3 Evaluation

If q ratios are potential measures of managerial performance, the regression results in this study support the view that more value can be created when poorly managed firms, i.e., low q firms, are taken over. In addition, the benefits are greater when a well-managed bidder (high q bidder) takes over a low q target firm. The study classified both low q and high q firms into HFCF and LFSF firms to test Jensen's hypothesis in different types of bidder and target firms. High q bidder and target firms with LFSF confirmed Jensen's hypothesis and enjoyed less than average returns, e.g., a high q bidder firm with LFSF had lower bidder returns than the average high q bidder firm; a high q target firm with LFSF had lower target returns than the average high q target firm. Similarly, following the FCFT, low q bidder and target firms with HFCF should have performed worse than LFSF bidder and target firms . However, Jensen's predictions hold here only for the low q bidder firms with HFCF. In low q target firms with HFCF, target, bidder and total returns are surprisingly higher. As mentioned before, these results do not confirm Jensen's hypothesis, since low q target firms with HFCF fare better in all returns. That is, greater value is added to all parties when a well-managed firm with cash to spend takes over a poorly managed HFCF rather than a LFSF firm. However, the FCFT also implies that acquiring firms with HFCF helps bidder firms finance the leverage needed for the acquisition. Subsequently, by increasing leverage, the value of the bidder firm rises due to the benefits of debt as proposed by the FCFT. Therefore, acquiring or taking over a low q target firm with HFCF is a value-enhancing opportunity by the market and shareholders as indicated by evidence in India.

This study considered the similarity of firms in acquisitions and takeovers. The market is said to react negatively when a firm diversifies its corporate assets into unrelated business. The results here support the hypothesis since bidder, target, and total returns are positively and significantly related to the type of acquisition. These results are consistent with the theory of agency costs and Jensen's FCFT. Mean returns are greater for firms with a record of acquiring related assets. Therefore, firms diversifying into unrelated areas of business do produce lower abnormal returns for both bidders and targets.

6.3.5.4 Discussion

This study analysed the relationship between bidder, target, and total abnormal returns for different types of firms during takeovers and acquisitions. If q is used as a measure of firm quality, the results indicate that after takeovers, target, bidder, and total returns are greater if the target is a low-quality firm being acquired or taken over by a high-quality firm. However, after classifying firms into HFCF and LFSF, results did not confirm Jensen's FCFT. The results demonstrate that low-quality and high-quality firms which do not abide by the FCFT's implications on retaining cash suffer from less than average returns except for low q target firms with excess cash. Returns are greater for all firms in an acquisition or take over of related lines of business. Diversifying a firm's activities through acquisitions into unrelated lines of business yields lower returns. There is some sense to analysing abnormal returns to firms during acquisitive activities through an FCFT approach. The inclusion of firm quality and the type of acquisitive activity in the regressions enhances the results and the explanatory power of the model.

6.4 Using the financial structure of firms as a signalling mechanism against takeovers

6.4.1 Introduction

The chapter now considers issues affecting smaller firms before being taken over, acquired, or even driven out of the market. Specifically, using the long-purse theory of predation, this section attempts to model an observable contract between small firms and banks or investors which might remove some of the financial constraints applied by bidders against them during takeovers (Tirole, 1988).

6.4.1.1 Background

The MRTP Amendment Act in 1991 encouraged take over activity in the Indian market. But if it will increase efficiency, improve poorly performing firms, or reduce competition as larger incumbent firms become more dominant, still remains a question. The recent regulations introduced by the Indian government, i.e., the Substantial Acquisition of Shares and Takeover Code (1994), have tried to increase the transparency of take over activity so that the threat of takeovers constrains inefficient Indian firms. However, the risk of eliminating small and medium-size firms by reducing the opportunity to compete with their larger rivals remains a counterproductive threat in a market for corporate control. There is much evidence on the scale of entry as well as the decision to enter a market. This section considers how smaller firms can use their financial structures and banks to survive take over attempts.

6.4.2 Theory

6.4.2.1 Predation

Predation occurs when an incumbent firm tries to drive out new entrants to markets. As a deterrent, an incumbent firm could either signal to possible entrants that entry would be unprofitable or take direct actions, often costly to itself, which makes entry unprofitable. This section considers the *long-purse* theory of predation. In this instance, the mechanism which motivates the predation is asymmetric information about the entrant firm's predicted quality (and thus its profitability). The entrant must raise capital to enter the market. This difficulty is exacerbated by the imperfect capital market where investors or financiers cannot know the entrant's true quality. Thus, entrant firms desire to signal information to the capital market which could provide the true type information. This signalling simultaneously alleviates the information problems in the capital market and signals to rival firms in the product market. This signal is also what motivates the incumbent to take over. The informational value of financial structure becomes essential when modelling predation motivated by financial constraints. These informational issues – the asymmetric information regarding entrant quality, the agency cost between firm and investor, and the incumbent's reaction to financial information provided by the entrant – are what allow successful predation in the long-purse story. Most models posit that the entrant could be profitable if it remains in the market beyond the first time period; therefore, predation causes an inefficient allocation of financing – i.e., in a perfect capital market the entrant will always be funded if profitable.

This section considers the possibility of a contract between an entrant and a bank (or investors) which could circumvent the incumbent's strategy to take over or even prey. An observable contract, formed in the capital market, provides information to the incumbent in the market. Such a contract removes the financial constraints on the entrant which the incumbent uses to bankrupt the entrant. In this way, banks serve as mediators who are able to handle asymmetric information and agency costs more efficiently than stock markets alone.

6.4.2.2   Literature review: long-purse predation, signalling and contracting

Long-purse predation models predict that the financially strong firms control the market. Financial constraints impede rivals' competition. Tirole presents a basic model. There is a fixed cost K which must be financed by the entrant each period before its production can commence (Tirole, 1988). Tirole allows the entrant to fund the F partially with equity (E) so that external finance required is $D = K - E$. Rather than model uncertainty about the entrant's quality, uncertainty is due to states of nature. The entrant's profits (π) come from a distribution on $[\pi_a, \pi_b]$. Since the firm must repay the loan with interest, the firm is profitable when $\pi \geq D(1 + r)$; otherwise, the firm goes bankrupt and creditors receive $\pi - B$, where B is the cost of bankruptcy proceedings. Tirole defines the opportunity cost of funds as r_0.[12] Therefore, the entrant will only invest/enter when $\int_{(K-E)(1-r)}^{\pi} [\pi - (K - E)(1 + r)] (f(\pi)$

$\partial \pi - (1 = r_0) E \geq 0$. This means that the firm must expect returns higher than the opportunity costs of the equity which it provides. The predator's strategy is clear: $[E_\pi(\pi) - (1 + r_0)K] - [BF((1 + r)(K - E))] \geq 0$, where $F(\ )$ is the cumulative distribution. If the entrant enters, the incumbent preys or acquires as much E as possible in Period 2 to lower the E available since E is the previous period's profits. The incumbent preys if the benefits of monopoly profits in later periods exceed the predation cost in the initial period. The incumbent needs only to reduce the rival's profits to encourage exit.

This assumes that the creditors do not have the bargaining power and thus earn just breakeven profits. Predation occurs by reducing the expected profits of the firm given the uncertain states of nature. A more realistic model makes predation even more likely by assuming that the breakeven rate of interest of r_0 depends upon the information available about the entrant. A higher r_0 might correspond to a younger and less mature firm or a firm which has a low value of physical capital. In this model the r_0 is constant for any type of entrant and it is the level of external finance (debt), $K - E$, which is essential for predation. One can see that a higher r_0 would also reduce the likelihood of remaining in the market.

The issue of asymmetric information in the capital market opens the possibility of having different interest rates for firm types. There are two main ways to model this uncertainty. The first method is to make the debt premium or interest rate (r_0) higher for low-quality firms. The other is to hold the premium which the creditors require constant, but to reject firms below a specific level of quality. Either method yields that borrowing is costly for a high-quality firm if the creditor cannot discover its true type. The importance of information here suggests that high-quality firms might desire to signal their types via their financial structure. Incumbents do not face information problems, either because they do not need external finance, or by virtue of incumbency they have a history which suggests high-quality. It is the high-quality entrant which seeks a separating mechanism in the capital market. By separating, high-quality firms can guarantee that they receive funds with certainty or that they can borrow at the lowest r_0.

Poitevin models the signalling-predation problem by demonstrating that high-quality firms will take on enough debt to separate themselves from the low-quality firms, and the entrant's financial structure conveys information to the investors (Poitevin, 1989). Predation occurs in a similar way to Tirole's basic framework. The level of debt required in a separating equilibrium is high and debt reduces the probability that an entrant can remain solvent when preyed upon. Poitevin considers two types of entrants, differentiated by their cost of production: C_l (low) and C_h (high). Since there are only two types, he attaches the probabilities m and $1 - m$, respectively, rather than specify a distribution. The incumbent is perfectly valued by the capital market and its marginal cost is known, C_i. Each must finance a fixed cost K to produce. Poitevin captures the idea of states of nature, as in Tirole's model; however, rather than specify the profit as uncertain, he specifies that a random component of fixed cost (and thus profit) is uncertain.

The entrant's profit in this framework becomes: $P(Q)q_e - C_e + a_e$, where $Q = q_o + q_i$, a_e is the random shock, and subscripts e and i denote the entrant and the incumbent, respectively. Since a_e is distributed over $[a_o, a_1]$, one can derive a breakeven state of nature a_E such that: $P(Q)q_e - C_e + a_E + D_e + E_e - K = D_e(1 + r_o)$, where D is debt level and E is equity level. Thus, the probability of bankruptcy for the entrant is $F(a_E)$. Like Tirole, there is an assumption that investors provide capital whenever non-negative returns occur. Firms then choose financial policies, such that $t = (D, r, E, N)$, where r is interest rate on borrowing and N is the number of new shares to be issued if equity is issued to raise capital. The essential information to note is the level D and E which the entrants choose. In this model the incumbent also faces a similar profit scheme. Both entrants and incumbents are posited to choose the financial policy which maximises the original shareholder's equity value.

The interesting feature in this model is the mechanism by which predation occurs. Under instances where only the low-cost entrant is profitable, the low-cost firm, which should receive financing in a perfect capital market, can be denied financing if investors cannot distinguish between the two firm types. Poitevin shows that low-cost firms can signal their type by taking on enough debt (call the level D^*). For this to be an incentive compatible for high-cost firms, debt must be so high that the breakeven $a_E = a_1$. Thus $P(Q)q_e - C_h + a_1 + D_e + E_e - K = D_e(1 + r_o)$, the high-cost firm never profits in any state of nature. Investors know the entrant's type by the level of debt.

Signalling, however, has its costs. By taking on this high level of debt, the entrant opens itself up to predation. The incumbent realises that by driving the entrant away, it can earn monopoly profits in the future. The incumbent also knows the entrant's financial structure. If it is not public, the incumbent at least knows that the debt is at least D^* if entry occurs. The incumbent expands output and reduces both $P(Q)$ and q_e. Moreover, note that the D^* required to separate increases the pressure of bankruptcy. One can simplify the breakeven condition to see: $P(Q)q_e - C_l + a_E + E_e - K - D_e r_o = 0$. The rise in the D_e and the decrease in $P(Q)q_e$ make the required breakeven a_E higher. Therefore, the probability of bankruptcy for the entrant $F(a_E)$ increases. Predation is rational to the incumbent. Poitevin's results are useful in demonstrating a cost of overcoming imperfect capital markets, yet it also shows how a contract between a bank and an entrant, perhaps through profit sharing, may be a better way to overcome the information problems. Signalling through debt is costly.

Ravid and Sarig also find that higher-quality firms signal their quality by increasing their debt (Ravid and Sarig, 1991). The signalling benefits result because firms are committing cash flows to servicing debt.[13] They model the cash flow (x), and therefore profitability, of firms as coming from a distribution $F(x, \theta)$, where q represents the type/quality of the firm. The firm type comes from a family, $\theta \in [\theta_1, \theta_2]$, where a higher subscript denotes higher quality. Ravid and Sarig also define the information structure such that insiders (current shareholders) know the true type and that outsiders (new shareholders) have to infer the type. In brief, they include the tax benefits of debt along with the *distress costs*, or bankruptcy costs of debt, and maximise the value of the firm to insiders. They find that the level of debt employed is positively related to firm quality, in a separating equilibrium. Firms with high debt are expected by investors to have high cash flows. Again financial structure provides information to the capital market. Unlike Poitevin's model, this one suggests that incumbents would keep debt in their capital structure. Poitevin's model predicts that incumbents would hold no debt.

Another useful signalling model to consider was proposed by Gertner, Gibbons and Scharfstein (1988). They devise a two-audience signalling model – any signal by a firm to the capital market is also observed by the rival, which in turn influences the actions taken in the product market competition. Since the rival's actions affect the original firm's profits, the financial decision and the product market outcome are related. The model considers two firms, A and B, both of which need to finance an investment K. Firm A will have either high profit (π_h) or low profits (π_l) with probabilities ϕ and $1 - \phi$, respectively. Firm A presents a contract to the capital market which specifies a debt service level (D) and an equity participation level (α). Implicit in this contract is that firm A can calculate its ex ante expected product market profit. If it is higher when firm B is uninformed, then A chooses a contract so that firm B and the capital market are uninformed regarding the true type. If profits are higher when B is informed, firm A offers a contract that yields a separating equilibrium. The signalling issue is typical as in Poitevin's model and it is the contracting problem which is more useful in this analysis.

The authors formulate the contract as (α, D) such that the firm pays the creditor $min \{D + \alpha(\pi - D), \pi\}$. Here, the firm has the bargaining power, as all creditors will accept a contract as long as the expected return equals the opportunity cost of the K funds. Thus, creditors' strategy is to accept the contract if $E[min\{D + \alpha(\pi - D), \pi\}] \geq (1 + r_o)K$. Firm A knows its true value so it will only offer contracts which – given its decision to separate or not – maximise its return $max\{(1 - \alpha)(\pi - D)\}$. The underlying assumption which allows this profit-sharing arrangement is that ex post returns are verifiable. If these returns are unverifiable, then there are agency costs to monitoring the true profit level. A firm's reported profit π_r might not be the true profit. The tradeoff between these agency costs and eliminating the financial constraints which encourage predation is considered by Bolton and Scharfstein (1990).

Bolton and Scharfstein consider the deep-purse problem and possible solutions that creditors can achieve via contracting. Their work is quite noteworthy in that they tied the information problem and predation into an optimal contract. It is necessary to examine their model in detail to see how they mitigate the principal agent problem. There are two firms, A and B, both of which need to finance a fixed cost F each period to produce. Production is profitable for both firms (positive NPV). Firm A has a *deep pocket* and firm B must get financing from the capital market. Like many other models, there are two states of nature (profits) for B: π_1 and π_2, such that $\pi_1 < \pi_2$, with probabilities θ and $1 - \theta$, respectively. The expected profit (π_o) is such that $\pi_0 = \theta\pi_1 + (1 - \theta)\pi_2 > F$, so that B is always profitable. Bolton and Scharfstein make the realised profit unobservable, thus there is an agency problem – B can report a false profit level. They model a two-period game so that the investor can punish bad reports of profits in the second period by restricting funding in the second period.

The model places the bargaining power in the hands of the investors who make the contract offer to firm B; firm B's strategy is to accept the contract if it provides a positive return. To model the contract, R_i is the payment from firm to investor if state π_i is reported. The investors place into the contract through the variable $\beta_i \in [0,1]$ which is the probability they will get finance in the second period if they report π_i. The contract offered to firm B maximises the investor's expected profit subject to the individual rationality constraint of the firm given that it agrees to the contract, a limited liability constraint, and incentive compatibility constraints such that the firm truthfully reports the true profits.[14] The optimal contract becomes a vector $(\beta_1, \beta_2, R_1, R_2) \in R^4$ such that this optimisation problem is solved. By appropriately adjusting the β_i, the investor can force the firm to report truthfully in the first period.[15] One can see that the agency problem here is solved by contracting rather than requiring the firm to signal its true type.

Since this contract is observable to firm A, the incumbent, the financial structure influences the competition in the product market as reported by Gertner, Gibbons and Scharfstein (1988). Firm A tries to lower B's first period profits to increase the likelihood of exit by increasing the probability of low profit to level= μ, such that $\mu > \theta$. By considering the difference between monopoly profits and duopoly profits , π^m and π^d, they find conditions for preying: when the marginal benefit of preying is greater than its cost = c. The optimal contract is maximised with a no-predation constraint. Observability of contracts is essential for this deterrence effect because the contract credibly signals to firm A that preying is unprofitable.

6.5 Basic model of no-predation contracting

Having reviewed the pertinent literature for firms regarding predation another type of contract which would attempt to get an entrant firm's incentives such that it will reveal its true profit without having to use a termination threat to mitigate the agency problem is considered. The termination threat is what allows and actually encourages firm A to prey. The contract must be observable so that firm A will not prey and must include an incentive structure so that firm B will not cheat its investors.

As in other models, consider a situation with two firm types for the entrant, a low marginal cost (c_L) and a high-cost (c_H). The incumbent's marginal cost is known by all players to be c_I. Both the incumbent and the entrant need to finance a fixed cost K each period in order to produce; the incumbent is assumed to have no financial constraint so its cost can be financed with its equity, whereas the entrant firms must borrow from creditors. To introduce a stochastic element in the model, the market demand is $P(Q) = a - Q$, where $a \in [a_o, a_1]$ where the probability distribution function of a is $f(a)$. The game with both entrant and incumbent in the market is such that the expected profits of each can be determined. It is assumed that both firms in the duopoly are profitable. If the incumbent drives the entrant out of the market then the incumbent gets the monopolist profit.

The main assumption is that both the high and low-cost entrants are expected to be profitable in the duopoly situation; however, only the low-cost firm can be profitable once it gets financial backing. To force this situation to occur one can calculate the expected profits for the high-cost firm. The equilibrium outcome quantity is: $q^*{}_H = \dfrac{a - 2c_H + c_I}{3}$ and the price is $p^* = \dfrac{a + c_H + c_I}{3}$.[16] The expected duopoly profit for the high-cost firm is therefore:

$$E[\pi^d_{C_H}] = \int_{a_0}^{a_1} (\frac{a + c_H + c_I}{3})(\frac{a - 2c_H + c_I}{3})f(a)\partial a - K^*(1 + r_0). \tag{6.3}$$

Since r_o is the risk-free cost of capital, one can set the expected profit equal to zero and solve for K^*. By making the required K level in the model $K^* + \varepsilon$, where $\varepsilon > 0$, the model has the high-cost entrant unprofitable when it must finance and service the fixed cost K each period. The model then has the following assumptions:

$$E[\pi^d_{C_H}] = \int_{a_0}^{a_1} (\frac{a + c_H + c_I}{3})(\frac{a - 2c_H + c_I}{3})f(a)\partial a - K(1 + r_0) < 0 \tag{6.4}$$

$$E[\pi^d_{C_L}] = \int_{a_0}^{a_1} (\frac{a + c_H + c_I}{3})(\frac{a - 2c_H + c_I}{3})f(a)\partial a - K(1 + r_0) \geq 0 \tag{6.5}$$

Therefore, it is profitable for the low-cost producer to enter the market – the problem is to design a contract which could prevent predation. The expected monopoly and duopoly for the incumbent are the following:[17]

$$E[\pi^d_{C_I}] = \int_{a_0}^{a_1} (\frac{a + c_L + c_I}{3})(\frac{a - 2c_I + c_L}{3})f(a)\partial a \text{ and } E[\pi^m_{C_I}] = \int_{a_0}^{a_1} (\frac{a + c_I}{2})(\frac{a - c_I}{2})f(a)\partial a$$

$$\tag{6.6}$$

The expected benefit of driving the entrant out of the market in each future period is the following:

$$E[\pi^m_{C_I}] - E[\pi^d_{C_I}] = \int_{a_0}^{a_1} (\frac{a + c_I}{2})(\frac{a - c_I}{2}) - (\frac{a + 2c_L + c_I}{3})(\frac{a - 2c_I + c_L}{3})f(a)\partial a \geq 0$$

$$\tag{6.7}$$

By the assumptions of the model, the signalling issue has been eliminated. This model implicitly uses Poitevin's separating equilibrium by requiring such a high-financed fixed-cost K that a high-cost entrant is unprofitable. Thus, all firms which can rationally request to borrow K are low-cost firms which are profitable. The issue now is to try to formulate an observable contract which will deter predation while keeping the agency cost problem between the entrant and the creditor minimised. The strategy is to make the firm indifferent between reporting the true profit level (π) and a false profit level ($\underline{\pi}$). The information issue is that profits cannot be verified or the contracting problem would become trivial. If a firm's profits are verifiable, then a profit-sharing contract between the creditor and entrant can ensure that the incumbent will not prey. Since demand is stochastic, the firm knows the true p and the creditor has only an expectation of it, $E[\pi]$. This is the problem that Bolton and Scharfstein deal with in their two stage model – the firm must be threatened with funding termination to get it to report the *truth* (Bolton and Scharfstein, 1990).

Assume that the creditor has the bargaining power because it makes a contract offer to a firm. The creditor makes its decisions based upon its expected return. The creditor will always finance the low-cost entrant because the expected return (if the firm tells the truth) is greater than $K(1 + r_0)$, the opportunity cost of the funds. The contract could be a profit-sharing one as in Gertner, Gibbons and Scharfstein (1988). This specifies $\alpha \in (0,1)$ where the creditor receives an α percentage of the firm's profits. The expected return for the bank is then the following:

$$E[R] = K(1+r_0) + \alpha \int_{a_0}^{a_1} (\frac{a+c_L+c_I}{3})(\frac{a-2c_L+c_I}{3})f(a)\partial a - K(1+r_0) \quad (6.8)$$

By assumption (6.5), this is greater than the opportunity cost of providing finance K. With a profit sharing contract some truth-telling mechanism must be designed.

Consider a strategy in which the creditor adjusts the finance interest cost r_0 to r according to the firm's reported $\underline{\pi}$. Since the creditor knows $E[\pi_{C_L}^d]$ for each period, it can use this as a benchmark for either rewarding or punishing the firm. In any given period if $\underline{\pi} > E[\pi_{C_L}^d]$, then the creditor rewards the firm by adjusting the interest rate down. With r instead of r_0 in equation (6.5), the firm's expected profit changes as r changes. This is the expected profit in each period, so as the required r changes so does the benchmark profit level, $E[\pi_{C_L}^d]$. The problem is to specify a revelation mechanism which will make the firm indifferent between telling the truth and lying. The upper (π^1) and lower bounds (π^0) on the profit are calculated by evaluating the profit at $a = a_1$ and $a = a_0$, respectively. Thus:

$$\pi_t^1 = (\frac{a_1 + c_L + c_I}{3})(\frac{a_1 - 2c_L + c_I}{3}) - K(1+r_t)$$

$$\pi_t^0 = (\frac{a_0 + c_L + c_I}{3})(\frac{a_1 - 2c_L + c_I}{3}) - K(1+r_t) \qquad (6.9)$$

In each period t, the firm's report must be between these bounds.

Since the creditor has been given the bargaining power, the creditor can make the firm indifferent by specifying functions which leave the firm's expected profit equation constant at each time period. Since the contract will specify profit sharing, the firm is left with $(1-\alpha)^*\pi_t$ in each period. Since the model considers different time periods, the subscript t is added to represent time, with initial period denoted as $t = 0$. The equation of interest is the following:

$$(1-\alpha)\int_{a_0}^{a_1} (\frac{a + c_L + c_I}{3})(\frac{a - 2c_L + c_I}{3})f(a)\partial a - K(1+r_0) +$$

$$(1-\alpha)\sum_{t=1}^{T}\partial t \int_{a_0}^{a_1} (\frac{a + c_L + c_I}{3})(\frac{a - 2c_L + c_I}{3})f(a)\partial a - K(1+r_0) =$$

$$(1-\alpha)\pi_0 + (1-\alpha)\sum_{t=1}^{T}\partial t[\int_{a_0}^{a_1} (\frac{a + c_L + c_I}{3})(\frac{a - 2c_L + c_I}{3})f(a)\partial a - K(1+r_t + f_t(\pi_t - 1)$$

$$(6.10)$$

The function $f_t(\pi_t)$ adjusts the interest rate between time periods so that the expected return is equated to the remaining payoffs to the firm. The interest rate required therefore evolves according to $r_t = r_{t-1} + f(\pi_{t-1})$. Equation (6.10) is the ideal contract for the creditor. The left-hand side is the expected profit of the entrant if the game persists for T periods. The right-hand side of the equation is the reported profit of the entrant and how the interest rate would have to evolve over time.

The optimal contract would specify the exact functional forms for $f(\pi_{t-1})$, the adjustment function of the interest rate. Since $E_{t-1}[\pi_{L,t}^d]$ is the benchmark profit for the interest rate adjustment, the function could be $f_t(\pi_{t-1} - E_{t-1}[\pi t])$. The subscript on the t denoted that the function could change as time evolved. The series $\{f_t\}_{t=0}^{T}$ cannot be determined at $t = o$ because the reported $\{\pi_t\}_{t=0}^{T}$ are not all known at $t = o$. If such a series can be determined, then there is no incentive for the entrant to misreport the true profit. It might be instructive to consider how the first two periods could be revealed. The remaining periods after the first two must be captured in a function which equates their values. In the first period, the firm reports π_o, therefore, the investor's choice of $r_1 = r_o + f_o(\underline{\pi}_{t-1})$. The function $f_t : [\pi_t^0, \pi_t^I] \to \underline{\pi}_t$ must be designed to make the firm indifferent. Thus the following:

$$(1-\alpha)\int_{a_0}^{a_1}(\frac{a+c_L+c_I}{3})(\frac{a-2c_L+c_I}{3})f(a)\partial a - K(1+r_0) +$$

$$(1-\alpha)\partial\int_{a_0}^{a_1}(\frac{a+c_L+c_I}{3})(\frac{a-2c_L+c_I}{3})f(a)\partial a - K(1+r_0)) + V =$$

$$(1-\alpha)\underline{\pi}_0 + (1-\alpha)\partial\int_{a_0}^{a_1}(\frac{a+c_L+c_I}{3})(\frac{a-2c_L+c_I}{3})f(a)\partial a - K(1+r_0+f_0(\underline{\pi}_0)) + V$$

(6.11)

For simplicity, it is assumed that the profits after the third period are equated by proper adjustment of the function (aggregated in V). If the adjusting function is chosen appropriately, the firm should be indifferent between any report it makes. Since the firm is indifferent, the creditor can require it to report the true profit.

The problem with this interest rate adjustment function is that when a contract is written between the entrant and the creditor, the creditor will have to make the function state contingent. The exact function used to make the firm indifferent during different time periods depends upon the history of reported profits. The contract must be observable, credible, and satisfy each party's incentive compatibility constraints in order to prevent the incumbent from preying. Since the function used depends upon the entrant's reports, a contract $(\alpha, K, f_t\{\pi_t\}_{t=0}^T)$ cannot be written with f_t explicitly given for every time period. The contract must specify an exact contingency for every possible historically reported profit. With a continuous distribution of possible reports, this problem is extremely difficult.

6.6 Further issues

If such a contract can be created and the *truth-telling* mechanism does work, predation will not occur because the incumbent realises that the contract between the entrant and creditor guarantees each an expected profit. The incumbent would not prey only because the contract between the entrant firm and the bank is known to be designed so that the entrant does not gain from cheating. The contract lasts for T periods of competition. If the incumbent increases its output to make the profit of the entrant decline, the losses for the entrant in the future periods are absorbed by the bank who will by contract still finance the firm. There is no termination threat of funding so the entrant has a *deep pocket* and can always get K finance in every period. The contract reveals to the incumbent that a monopoly will never occur because the entrant will always be in the market.

Perhaps the incumbent could prey for several periods consecutively, lowering the entrant's profits, forcing the interest rate up, which causes a cycle of expected low profits or losses. The incumbent would likely have to prey for several periods for this to occur. The early lost profit must be less than the discounted benefit of the monopoly for this to occur. The only hopes that the incumbent could have with this strategy is that the creditor would attempt to renegotiate the contract. If one considers contract renegotiation as possible, predation might still be possible if the incumbent causes serious losses to the creditors. This would depend upon the relative assets of the incumbent and those of the creditors.

As stated earlier, assumption (6.4) suppresses the signalling problem by modelling the possibility that a high-cost entrant might want to seek entry. The model does not need such a high fixed cost K, but then the low-cost firm would have to signal its quality somehow. It would have to take on more debt than needed to finance the fixed cost; it dissipates some of its duopoly profit by wastefully holding excess cash. By holding more debt than necessary, the low-cost firm can still separate from the high-cost firm. The level of debt must be enough for the high-cost firm to have a negative expected profit – it would not even seek funds if it expected losses every period (individually rationality constraint).

6.7   Conclusion and policy implications

This chapter examines the informational value of a firm's financial structure for its performance during acquisitive activities. It also considers the benefits and costs of a more active market for corporate control in India. The FCFT is used to examine signalling effects of earnings retention as well as diversification on bidder and target returns. For the latter, it hypothesised that an active market for corporate control might crowd out smaller firms and create industrial concentration in a market already dominated by large conglomerates. At a microeconomic level, it considered whether the financial structure of some firms may reveal too much information often to their own detriment. In this regard, a model is presented based on the Long-Purse theory of predation which attempts to develop an observable contract between firms and banks to reduce informational asymmetries and agency costs in firms during take over attempts. Banks would serve as better mediators in this market as they can handle informational asymmetries and agency costs more efficiently than stock markets alone.

Recent take over legislation abolished the 1969 MRTP Act requiring government approval of all takeovers. This fostered the development of an active Anglo-Saxon type market for corporate control. However, is such a market in India's best interest at this point in its liberalisation process? Evidence from the UK and US suggests disadvantages, including short-termism, an exacerbation of agency costs between shareholders and managers, and an increase in the concentration of industry. There is to some degree an incentive for firms to operate inefficiently, i.e., low q firms retaining excessive earnings, in order to maximise their short-term returns during takeovers. Another important consideration in India is lack of efficient corporate governance mechanisms. Singh lists some deficiencies, including: conflicts of interest and lack of cohesion among many controlling families; the adverse effects of large inter-group investments on small shareholders in conglomerate companies; the exclusion of ordinary shareholders from corporate decisions including restructuring, mergers, divestment (Singh, 1998). Ideally, takeovers and mergers are the market mechanisms which are intolerant of inefficiencies and intend to create greater value in the end. However, as mentioned before, the costs of weeding out inefficiencies in the Indian market may be too high at this stage in development, especially with the little *acquisition appraisal* experience they have so far. The exclusion of small and medium-sized firms by predatory behaviour is one cost of promoting an active market for corporate control. As suggested above, Japanese and German bank based systems of corporate governance seem to provide useful examples for India. Banks have lower transaction costs and are able to deal more efficiently with the problems of asymmetric information, agency costs, and short-termism. Clearly, takeovers can reduce inefficiencies within the market, but at some costs to the economy as a whole. Therefore, before encouraging an active market for corporate control, it is important for India to consider the context within which it already operates.

7
Conclusions

7.1 Conclusion

The positive relationship between excess cash flow and investment is well known, but the decision environment which determines cash flow theory remains unresolved. This study tried to fill this gap by considering if decisions to use internal finance stem from the managerial/principal agent (MPAA) or the more commonly accepted asymmetric information (AIA) considerations. Evidence here supports the agency model of MPAA behaviour rather than information asymmetry which assumes perfect capital markets. This study is a fundamental departure from the evidence in the literature which rarely distinguishes between the MPAA and AIA.

The MPAA assumes that managers are more interested in objectives like sales maximisation, size of the firm, and perquisites, rather than the market value of the firm. Since the evidence supports the MPAA rather than the AIA, overinvestment by old, more mature firms 'crowds out' investment by young, dynamic firms at or above the market discount rate. Consequently, the allocation of resources in the economy implied by the MPAA practice of investment is inefficient from a welfare point of view. This study began by developing a very basic model based on firm characteristics which affect the choice of best policy for shareholders. The chapters that followed considered the benefits and disadvantages accruing to shareholders in particular in different situations including the choice and level of leveraging, bankruptcy, and mergers and acquisitions. These events were examined within the context of the informational consequences of managerial financing choices on shareholder value. The technical findings from this study are discussed below including some of the policy implications. The study concludes by discussing some of its limitations and then by suggesting how to improve India's capital markets based on firm-level evidence.

7.2 Summary of findings

7.2.1 Internal finance as a source for investment

Chapter 2 began by introducing and discussing the two distinct approaches to the cash flow theories of investment: namely, the MPAA and the AIA. The AIA suggests that managers try to maximise shareholder value while the MPAA believes that managers are primarily interested in the growth of the firm. These differences remain crucial throughout this study, for differing behaviour of managers in their approach to internal finance alters firm behaviour. Consequently, the efficient allocation of resources by firms is often determined by the approach the manager chooses. Evidence in India suggested that most managers opted for the MPAA rather than the AIA.

7.2.2 An examination of cash retention strategies

Chapter 3 attempted to demonstrate that in a dynamic situation, paying no dividends can be an optimal strategy for some firms. Jensen's FCFT is less useful with imperfect capital markets. Some firms which ought to disburse funds as dividends as per the FCFT can justify holding cash to add value based on the difference between the costs of internal and external finance. This finance premium varies according to individual firm characteristics and thus undermines the FCFT in certain instances.

The chapter showed how cash retention can be good, given uncertainty and two choices: retaining cash or paying dividends. The expected values of the two alternatives depend on the external finance premium and the underlying economic conditions reflected in the probability of a good investment (P). The resulting breakeven curve between the two strategies suggests a set of solutions from paying all dividends to retaining all cash depending on ϕ, P, q_0, q_1, q_2. The model reveals that a high enough external finance premium justifies retaining excess cash.

The empirical analysis examined optimal mixed strategies. Since firms' total excess cash often exceeds their excess cash in the current year, it implies a cash retention strategy. This finding suggests that firms are either ideally retaining excess cash as a buffer against negative economic conditions or that shareholders are risking managerial abuse as the FCFT predicts. It appears that by separating good and bad firms, there is a difference in treatment of retained cash and dividends. Investment in high q firms appears positively related to dividend payment and cash flow whereas the low q firms' investment is negatively related to dividend payment and cash flow. The difference in the determinants of investment suggests that firms should follow different finance strategies.

Calculating optimal retained earnings implies that firms are behaving close to the optimal during the time period examined. The results of regressions appear significant and suggest that high q firms and firms with high growth rates should retain more cash. The positive coefficient for retained earnings suggests that it might be optimal for some firms who do not presently retain cash to withhold future cash flow. Sometimes firms would have benefited from retaining excess cash from previous periods. The assumption that firms use their optimal cash strategies becomes central to these findings. The critical determinant of optimal cash retention is the external finance premium. Low q firms have less reason to retain excess cash unless they expect to use it for investment soon; only small, low q firms which would face higher external finance premia should retain cash. If the primary determinant of the external finance premium is firm size, then large firms – even high q firms – would benefit less from retaining cash. Small, high q firms need to retain cash. Public information can make the high q firm appear to have very low-quality investments so that the capital market underestimates the firm's potential. These firms maximise their expected future value by relying on internal funds.

Firms find valid reasons to justify the retention of cash flow. Sometimes retained cash will be misused, but sometimes retention benefits the firms' shareholders. The explanation depends on firm characteristics. No firm which can obtain external finance at low-cost can justify retaining excess cash as a buffer unless a large economic downturn is expected. Only firms which face stiff external finance premia can benefit from cash retention. Excess cash allocation must consider asymmetric information or remain incomplete. Excess cash is not always misinvested and Chapter 3 developed a framework to examine possible abuses.

7.2.3   Effects and determinants of debt

Chapter 4 began by considering how Indian firms arrive at a given debt/equity mix and how different sources of capital affect firm performance in India. The first model looked at the more general determinants of leverage, and the following model incorporated Jensen's FCFT to test the effects of leverage on firm performance. The results of the first model suggest that the dominant factor in determining leverage between firms is firm size. The results indicate that larger firms have considerable advantages over smaller firms in credit markets. Macroeconomic factors, cash flow, real tangible assets, and growth in the real size of firms also play important roles in explaining the variation in leverage across firms. Further, although deregulation was not included in this model due to data limitations, it would have had a significant influence on the financial structure of firms. The second model examines the FCFT's hypotheses regarding the significance and the type of relationship for leverage in Indian firms. Contrary to the FCFT, results indicate that not only are there negative effects of debt on firm performance, but also that chosen levels of liquidity and other factors depend more on a firm's financial structure than on its growth opportunities. Liquidity has played a more significant role in affecting performance in firms with excess retained earnings than in firms with excess debt. These differences mark a critical departure from the fundamental predictions of the FCFT, specifically the positive influence of debt on firm value. These results imply that the FCFT's predictions are inapplicable in weak capital markets such as India's, and that the underlying assumptions need to be reassessed given the misaligned incentive structure of India's state-managed banking system.

From a policy point of view, there is one critical implication for India's reform process. India is liberalising many of its closed markets within the financial sector and privatising commercial and industrial Indian state-owned financial enterprises, albeit at a very slow rate. Although a number of foreign and domestic financial institutions have entered the capital market, they have entered as portfolio investors in equity and only recently were allowed to become debt suppliers. If the norms of corporate governance as seen in developed capital markets are to be applied in India, banks and financial institutions need to be privatised. Perhaps then the presence and size of debt in the financial structure of firms might have a disciplinary impact on firm managers. Besides the agency problem, the evidence suggests that the capabilities of Indian banks and financial institutions do not meet the minimum standards since a high debt/equity ratio is associated with low performance. By no means are these problems unique to India as apparent from the experiences of other countries. Banking systems only work if they are allowed to suffer the costs of their bad decisions, i.e., bankruptcy.

7.2.4   The use of earnings retention in predicting corporate bankruptcy models

Chapter 5 tried to decipher the role of a firm's capital structure during and before possible bankruptcy. In doing so, it first looked at a firm's financial structure as a possible predictor of bankruptcy, and it then examined how a firm's treatment differed after bankruptcy, based on its leveraging ratios, equity ownership, etc. The chapter began by considering the definition of corporate bankruptcy and then explaining the role of the state in liquidation and debt renegotiation. It then described Indian bankruptcy restructuring procedures under the SICA Act of 1985 and its legal body, the BIFR. An analysis of these legal and administrative procedures revealed that India's definition of corporate sickness is too narrow and consequently any assistance entitled to these sick firms often arrives too late. Further complications are added by delays caused by inefficient bankruptcy reorganisation procedures which only hinder and lessen the likelihood of a possible recovery.

The following section examined the theoretical factors involved in the interaction between the capital structure of a firm and possible restructuring schemes. It provided proof of how bargaining power can shift away from banks to firms as the leveraging ratio increases, leading to a possible overinvestment problem. In the latter part of this section, empirical evidence using corporate data was tested against the aforementioned theory. It considered the effects of subsidies, sacrifices, and irregular accounting practices within the Indian context. A detailed description of several violations under the auspices of restructuring and refinancing in the public interest was presented. In the fifth section a logistic model for better bankruptcy prediction was developed using earnings retention as a specification mechanism. It used results from the previous chapter, specifically the potential quality of investments for firms to further classify firms before any such analysis. This specific model was tested against previous work using the same Indian data set, and its classification techniques do improve prediction rates to a certain degree. The chapter concluded by first mentioning the various reforms which have occurred since 1992. It then specifically addressed certain policy changes which might fit within a market-driven framework and better align the incentives of both sick firms and their potential rescuers.

7.2.5   Factors affecting the market for corporate control

Chapter 6 examined the informational value of a firm's financial structure for its performance during acquisitive activities. It also considered the benefits and costs of a more active market for corporate control in India. The FCFT is used to examine signalling effects of earnings retention as well as diversification on bidder and target returns. For the latter, it hypothesised that an active market for corporate control might crowd out smaller firms and create industrial concentration in a market already dominated by large conglomerates. At a microeconomic level, it considered whether the financial structure of some firms may reveal too much information, often to their own detriment. In this regard, a model was presented based on the Long-Purse theory of predation which attempts to develop an observable contract between firms and banks to reduce informational asymmetries and agency costs in firms during take over attempts. Banks would serve as better mediators in this market as they can handle informational asymmetries and agency costs more efficiently than stock markets alone.

Takeovers and mergers are the market mechanisms which are intolerant of inefficiencies and intend to create greater value in the end. However, as mentioned before, the costs of weeding out inefficiencies in the Indian market may be too high at this stage in development, especially with the little *acquisition appraisal* experience they have so far. The exclusion of small and medium-sized firms by predatory behaviour is one cost of promoting an active market for corporate control. As suggested above, Japanese and German bank based systems of corporate governance seem to provide useful examples for India. Banks have lower transaction costs and are able to deal more efficiently with the problems of asymmetric information, agency costs, and short-termism. Clearly, takeovers can reduce inefficiencies within the market, but at some costs to the economy as a whole. Therefore, before encouraging an active market for corporate control, it is important for India to consider the context within which it already operates.

7.3 Limitations of study and future work

It is important to note some of the limitations of this study. The collection of corporate data can be difficult for a country like India, especially where limited accountability standards exist so far. For firm-level data, heterogeneity in accounting definitions and limited time series information presented the most obvious difficulties. Consequently, as pointed out throughout this study, much of the data collection required gathering information from different sources including the Reserve Bank of India Bulletins, the Mumbai Stock Exchange Directory, and individual firm balance sheets. Therefore, allowing for slight inconsistencies in the data set might suggest that the empirical results need to be interpreted with some caution. Also, throughout this study, various determinants of firm behaviour are considered, but clearly there are many more factors which could be considered. The analytical framework could be extended to include determinants such as government intervention, technical innovation, and other macroeconomic shocks as well as intangible factors including discrete government subsidies through special relations. It is likely that the inclusion of some of these explanatory variables in this study might improve the results.

Clearly, an important step in improving the accountability of firms is the standardisation and timely dissemination of the accounts of all listed firms. Such steps would not only help research endeavours similar to this one, but it would also lead to greater transparency and accountability. Specifically, the availability of firm data before and after India began its financial sector liberalisation in 1991 would perhaps lead to greater insights. Further research might consider the effects of the liberalisation programme by examining each of the cases in this study before and after 1991. Since this study aimed to examine firm-level performance within the context of the overall Indian capital market, it tried to set out the basis and direction of such corporate behaviour research in general. Further work in assessing a single theoretical problem such as testing the effects of certain fiscal policy measures may represent an important area of research.

This study should be regarded as a pilot attempt to examine the choice of financial structures at a firm level in India. Some of the issues could be addressed through more sophisticated modelling and others by obtaining more relevant time series data. To this point, there has not been – until this study – an attempt to model the financial behaviour of Indian firms within a managerial or asymmetric information framework. The results in this study do not claim to be conclusive by any means, but at least suggest a useful framework by which future research in data collection, theoretical analysis, and empirical testing may be undertaken.

7.4   Further policy implications

The evidence presented in this study also offers an interesting perspective on the more general issue of stock market activity and its implications for the resource allocation process in the economy. The results here suggest that the stock market is an important but by no means the sole mechanism for efficient resource allocation. In other words, although the complaints about the misallocation of resources in the economy due to stock market activity are valid, they may be exaggerated. There is a view in the literature that stock market activity encourages speculation, excessive volatility of share prices, short-termism, etc. and channels resources into socially non-productive activities; consequently, stock market development may not be a beneficial endeavour for a country like India. The results in this study offer a powerful counter-argument. Given that managerial perceptions are more important than market perceptions for various firm-level decisions and given that the stock market plays a limited role as a source of finance, it is unlikely that stock market activity has detrimental implications for the resource allocation process in the economy as has been suggested.

This conclusion raises questions about the other implications of stock market activity for firms over and above its financing and signalling functions. Clearly, the stock market plays many other roles in a market economy, including: a market for corporate control; a catalyst for corporate governance; means for transferring risks among various economic agents; managers may be concerned about stock market activity because of the link between managerial compensation and stock prices by way of stock options; managers are concerned about share prices if their job security is linked to the performance of the share price; stock market developments influence the debt capacity of the firm. All of these considerations are relevant for India especially as it is actively reforming its financial sector and capital markets. They are also important in view of the current global interest in emerging markets and the proliferation of investors from around the world. Much needs to be done by way of market microstructure reforms.

As mentioned throughout this study, mismanagement is a widespread phenomenon in corporate India due to the unchallenged controlling power of state-managed promoters. The degree of India's economic 'illiberalism' was recently highlighted in a joint report put forward by the World Bank and Confederation of Indian Industry. Their study concluded that many Indian firms continue to be hamstrung by huge competitive disadvantages – the direct result of 'decades of dysfunctional policies and regulations and poor financial infrastructure' (World Bank, 2002). The study found that excessive red tape had tied Indian business in knots so that on average Indian managers spent about 16% of their time dealing with various government officials compared to 5.8% in other developed countries. Furthermore, the high occurrence of non-performing assets of public sector banks, the large number of bankruptcy cases falling under the BIFR, and the high proportion of non-dividend-paying firms among listed firms reflect the extent of this mismanagement. In the interests of investors and from the perspective of improving India's international competitiveness, the Indian authorities need to concentrate on matters of corporate governance. Certainly, one solution would be to empower shareholders themselves by limiting the ownership rights of state-managed promoters. Furthermore, Indian regulatory authorities need to pay more attention to the improvement of the market's function of evaluating securities more efficiently so that the market's price signals do not misguide investors.

These considerations are also relevant to the debate on the costs and benefits of stock market dominated economic systems versus bank dominated economic systems and their implications for corporate governance and overall efficiency of the resource allocation process. As previously discussed, in some circumstances, banks are better suited for allocating certain resources. Specifically, as examined in previous chapters, banks are more efficient in financing the market for corporate control by lowering transaction costs and dealing more efficiently with the problems of asymmetric information, agency costs, and short-termism. It is believed that banks would serve as better mediators in this market as they are able to handle these problems more efficiently than stock markets alone. Therefore, as important as the development of stock markets and banks is for India, their particular choice depends to a large extent on their stage of development. As suggested in this study, in some cases it may be more efficient for them to develop and strengthen a bank-based financial system at the beginning of the liberalisation process. The evidence in this study also indicates that managerial perceptions are more important than market perceptions with regard to many capital market decisions at the firm level. Lastly, the evidence offers rationale and supports the financial sector reforms and capital market development initiatives undertaken in India. For, as long as the Indian institutional framework continues to be characterised by moral hazard, high transaction costs, and incentive problems, India's growth will remain below its potential.

Appendix 1: Derivation of Model Constraints

Case 1: Assume that each investment possibility occurs with a probability of 1/3. Assume that $q_2 > q_1$ and that $x(q_1 - 1) > f$.

Expected Value of Cash Retention $\geq$ Expected Value of Cash Disbursement

$$\frac{1}{3}q_2x + \frac{1}{3}q_1x + \frac{1}{3}q_0x \geq \frac{1}{3}[\max(q_2x - x - \phi; 0) + x] + \frac{1}{3}[\max(q_1x - x - \phi; 0) + x] + \frac{1}{3}x$$

By the assumption the $x(q_1 - 1) > \phi$ (1A)

$$\frac{1}{3}q_2x + \frac{1}{3}q_1x + \frac{1}{3}q_0x \geq \frac{1}{3}[q_2x - x - \phi + x] + \frac{1}{3}[(q_1x - x - \phi + x] + \frac{1}{3}x$$

$$q_2x + q_1x + q_0x \geq [q_2x - \phi] + [q_1x - x - \phi + x] + x$$

$$q_0x \geq -2\phi + x$$

$$q_0x - x \geq -2\phi \text{ becomes } -q_0x + x \leq 2\phi \text{ or } x(1 - q_0) \leq 2\phi$$

$$\frac{x(1 - q_0)}{2} \leq \phi \qquad\qquad (1B)$$

It is clear that the requirements which favour a policy of cash retention depend upon the values of q_0, q_1, and ϕ. Condition (1A) depends upon q_1 and condition 2 (1B) depends upon q_0.

Case 2: Assume that each investment possibility occurs with a probability of 1/3. Assume that $q_2 > q_1$ and that $x(q_1 - 1) < \phi$ and $x(q_2 - 1) > \phi$.

Expected Value of Cash Retention $\geq$ Expected Value of Cash Disbursement

$$\frac{1}{3}q_2x + \frac{1}{3}q_1x + \frac{1}{3}q_0x \geq \frac{1}{3}[\max(q_2x - x - \phi; 0) + x] + \frac{1}{3}[\max(q_1x - x - \phi; 0 + x] + \frac{1}{3}x$$

By the assumption the $x(q_1 - 1) < \phi, \ x(q_2 - 1) > \phi.$ (2A)

$$\frac{1}{3}q_2x + \frac{1}{3}q_1x + \frac{1}{3}q_0x \geq \frac{1}{3}[q_2x - x - \phi + x] + \frac{1}{3}[0 + x] + \frac{1}{3}x$$

$$q_2x + q_1x + q_0x \geq [q_2x - \phi] + [x + x]$$

$$q_1x + q_0x \geq 2x - \phi$$

$$q_1x + q_0x - 2x \geq -\phi \text{ becomes } -q_1x - q_0x + 2x \leq \phi$$

$$x(2 - q_1 - q_0) \leq \phi \qquad\qquad (2B)$$

As in Case 1, predictions from this model will rely upon the values of q_0, q_1, and ϕ. In this case the q_1 value is necessary in both conditions (**2A** and **2B**).

Case 3: Assume that each investment possibility occurs with a probability of 1/3. Assume that $q_2 > q_1$ and that $x(q_1 - 1) < \phi$. In this case, the expected value of disbursing cash reaches its minimum. According to the model, the constraint B should become less stringent given the initial assumptions.

Expected Value of Cash Retention $\geq$ Expected Value of Cash Disbursement

$$\frac{1}{3}q_2x + \frac{1}{3}q_1x + \frac{1}{3}q_0x \geq \frac{1}{3}[\max(q_2x - x - \phi; 0) + x] + \frac{1}{3}[\max(q_1x - x - \phi; 0) + x] + \frac{1}{3}x$$

By the assumption the $x(q_1 - 1) < \phi$ and $x(q_2 - 1) < \phi$, $\qquad\qquad$ (3A)

$$\frac{1}{3}q_2x + \frac{1}{3}q_1x + \frac{1}{3} + q_0x \geq \frac{1}{3}x + \frac{1}{3}x + \frac{1}{3}x$$

$$q_2x + q_1x + q_0x \geq x + x + x \text{ becomes } x(q_2 + q_1 + q_0) \geq 3x$$

$$(q_2 + q_1 + q_0) \geq 3 \qquad\qquad\qquad (3B)$$

Clearly, condition 2 (**3B**) depends purely on upon the quality of the investment opportunities; therefore, condition 2 is less stringent in this case than in the previous two cases. In Case 3, the restricitive constraint is 3A which requires that the fee, ϕ be large in order to satisfy its requirements. Another way to interpret the constraint is that the quality of the investments must be low which contradicts constraint 3B. The only way it appears possible for Case 3 to hold is if the fee f is prohibitively large.

Appendix 2: Deriving the Relationship between Investment Probability and ϕ

Case 1: Re-examining constraint (1B) without the assumption that $P = 1/3$. $q_0 = 0$ is still the assumption used in examining this case.

$$\frac{P}{2}q_2x + \frac{P}{2}q_1x + (1-P)q_0x \ge \frac{P}{2}[q_2x - x - \phi + x] + \frac{P}{2}[q_1x - x - \phi + x] + (1-P)x$$

$$P(q_2x) + (q_1x) + (2 - 2P)(q_0x) \ge P[q_2x - \phi] + P[q_1x - \phi] + (2 - 2P)x$$

$$Pq_2x + Pq_1x + 2q_0x - 2Pq_0x \ge Pq_2x - P\phi + Pq_1x - P\phi + 2x - 2Px$$

$$2q_0x \ge 2x - 2Px - 2P\phi + 2Pq_0x$$

By assuming that $q_0 = 0$, this simplifies to :

$$2P\phi \ge 2x - 2Px$$

$$\phi \ge \frac{2x(1-P)}{2P} \quad \text{In order to solve for } P:$$

$$\phi \ge \frac{x}{P} - x \quad \text{this can be rearranged so that}$$

$$P \ge \frac{x}{\phi + x} \tag{1B}$$

This is the new constraint (1B) used to analyse the solutions favouring a cash retention policy. Clearly, the relationship between P and ϕ can be determined given various values for x.

Case 2: Finding the breakeven level of x, given constraint (2A).
From Appendix 1, Case 2, we know that constraint (2B) is $x(2 - q_1 - q_0) \le \phi$. By substituting the values assumed for the study ($q_0 = 0$; $q_1 = 1.1$; $\phi = 50,000$) we can easily find the breakeven level of x.
$x(2 - 1.1 - 0) \le 50,000$ which is obviously $.9x \le 50,000$.

Given the assumptions the breakeven level of x is clearly $x = \dfrac{50,000}{.9}$ or

55,555. As discussed earlier, for Case 2 to meet constraint (2B) realistically, the assumption of $\phi = 50,000$ and $q_1 = 1.1$ may need to be altered.

Re–calculating constraint **(2B)** to find the relationship between probability and premium ϕ.

$$\frac{P}{2}q_2x + \frac{P}{2}q_1x + (1-P)q_0x \geq \frac{P}{2}[q_2x - x - \phi + x] + \frac{P}{2}[0+x] + (1-P)x$$

$$P(q_2x) + P(q_1x) + (2-2P)(q_0x) \geq P[q_2x - \phi] + P[x] + (2-2P)x$$

$$Pq_2x + Pq_1x + 2q_0x - 2Pq_0x \geq Pq_2x - P\phi + Px + 2x - 2Px$$

$$Pq_1x + 2q_0x - 2Pq_0x \geq -P\phi + Px + 2x - 2Px$$

$$Pq_1x \geq -P\phi - Px + 2x \quad \text{by assuming that} \quad q_0 = 0.$$

$$Pq_1x + Px - 2x \geq -P\phi \quad \text{or equivalently,} \quad -\left(\frac{Pq_1x + Px - 2x}{P}\right) \leq \phi$$

This can be written $as \frac{2x}{P} \leq \phi + q_1x + x$ which is rearranged:

$$P \geq \frac{2x}{\phi + q_1x + x} \tag{2B}$$

Case 3: Finding the relationship between probability of a good investment and the premium value, ϕ.

$$\frac{P}{2}q_2x + \frac{P}{2}q_1x + (1-P)q_0x \geq \frac{P}{2}[x] + \frac{P}{2}[x] + (1-P)x$$

$$P(q_2x) + P(q_1x) + (2-2P)(q_0x) \geq P[x] + P[x] + (2-2P)x$$

$$Pq_2x + Pq_1x + 2q_0x - 2Pq_0x \geq Px + Px + 2x - 2Px$$

$$Pq_2x + Pq_1x + 2q_0x - 2Pq_0x \geq 2Px + 2x - 2Px$$

$$x(Pq_2 + Pq_1 - 2Pq_0) \geq 2x - 2q_0x \quad \text{this is equivalent to}$$

$$x(Pq_2 + Pq_1 - 2Pq_0) \geq x(2 - 2q_0)$$

From $Pq_2 + Pq_1 - 2Pq_0 \geq 2 - 2q_0$ it is straightforward to see that the new constraint:

$$P \geq \frac{2 - 2q_0}{q_2 + q_1 - 2q_0} \tag{3B}$$

Clearly, this is not really a relationship between P and ϕ, for f never plays a role in expected values of either strategy. The required probabilities for a dominant strategy of cash retention will depend on the actual q values of the investments.

Notes

1 Introduction

1. Corbett and Jenkinson (1994) compare these differences and discuss the adjustments needed for flow-of-funds and company accounts.
2. See Allen (1993) and Stiglitz (1992) for detailed discussions.
3. There are three all India development banks: Industrial Development Bank of India (IDBI), Industrial Finance Corporation of India (IFCI), Industrial Credit and Investment Corporation of India (ICICI). At the state level each state has a State Financial Corporation (SFC) and an Industrial Development Corporation (SIDC).
4. *Reserve Bank of India Bulletin*, 1993.
5. See Harris *et al.* (1994) for similar evidence in Indonesia, Jaramillo *et al.* (1993) for Ecuador, Nabi (1989) for Pakistan, and Tybout (1983) for Colombia.

2 Internal Finance as a Source of Investment

1. The neoclassical theory of investment is due to Jorgenson *et al.* (1963, 1966, 1967, 1971), primarily based on the neoclassical theory of optimal capital accumulation. The liquidity theory is based on the work of Meyer and Kuh (1957), Duesenberry (1958), Kuh (1963) and others. The accelerator theory, the oldest of the investment models, is based on the work of Clark (1917), Chenery (1952), Koyck (1954), Eisner (1964) and others. The managerial and asymmetric information approaches to investment can be considered versions of the liquidity theory and therefore fall under the rubric of cash flow theory of investment. Some explanations exist for the liquidity theory: (a) realised profits measure expected profits and investment is determined by profit expectations (Tinbergen, 1938), and (b) investment may be constrained by the supply of funds (Meyer and Kuh, 1957; Meyer and Glauber, 1964; Kuh, 1963; Duesenberry, 1958; Meyer and Strong, 1990). In the strong version of the liquidity theory, the financial constraint operates at all times; the cost of funds schedule becomes inelastic when internal funds are exhausted. In the weaker version, financial constraint operates at low rates of capacity utilisation while extreme pressure on capacity may result in the use of outside sources of finance.
2. Financing hierarchy may also be based on transactions costs, tax advantages, costs of financial distress, etc.; however, these are likely to be less important than agency and asymmetric information problems.
3. Baumol (1959,1967), Marris (1963, 1964), Grabowski and Mueller (1972) and others are examples of the managerial capitalism approach. The agency cost approach focuses on contracting aspects within the overall framework of the

principal agent model and is associated with Jensen and Meckling (1976) and others.

4. Stultz (1990) presents a model in which managerial discretion and information asymmetries exist simultaneously.

5. *Financial slack* is defined as the difference between internal finance and capital expenditures and shows how far the firm can avoid external finance while undertaking capital expenditures. *Financial slack* will be used and discussed in greater depth in the following chapters.

3   Cash Retention Strategies

1. Point C in Figure 3.1 is depicted at the same level of r as A, but depending on the lending multiplier, the new r level of point C will vary. More often, it is higher than point A during a credit crunch.

2. Asymmetric information in its simplest form creates a situation in capital markets characterised by Akerlof's *Lemons Problem* as discussed earlier.

3. Tobin's q is calculated as (market value of common equity + value of long-term debt)/ gross assets. Gross assets are used as replacement costs since it incorporates both the assets and liabilities of a firm as well as its holdings of other firms (Summers, 1981).

   Under certain conditions marginal and average q are equal (Hayashi, 1982). However, there are several instances when the average q and the marginal q can differ. These include the following: private managerial information, speculative bubbles in the stock market, or market fads where values differ from their fundamentals (Blanchard, Rhee and Summers, 1993, 116).

4. The variation in investment quality does not have to be finite since there could be an infinite number of investments which differ in quality. Estimations of an investment's quality will differ according to different analyses. The model simplifies this issue by considering three discrete investments; however, the q parameter of these projects could be altered. The probability can be varied to capture both managerial choices and underlying economic conditions.

5. Figures 3.4 and 3.5 will depict the set of solutions for Case 1 and Case 2 respectively. These graphs will be discussed when benchmark cases of the model are examined, i.e., an external finance premium and a cash flow x are assumed.

6. In determining the breakeven level of $x = 100,000$ used in the figure, ϕ was assumed at 50,000; therefore, to accurately depict the situation, the plot should be truncated at $\phi = 50,000$ (and appropriately at the corresponding probability P).

7. By requiring that $x(q_1 - 1) \leq \phi$, there is another constraint which will cut through the region above the breakeven curve. If x and q_1 are fixed at a certain *benchmark* then this constraint becomes a vertical line at the value ϕ determined by the constraint.

8. A banking relationship could reduce the importance of net worth (the partial $\frac{\partial \phi}{\partial w}$ declines) and causes the effect of maturity or size to be non linear. In this case, $\frac{\partial^2 \phi}{\partial w^2} > 0$; therefore, as a firm matured or grew bigger,

the φ would drop substantially. Clearly, different sources of external finance would have different effects, not all of which would reduce external finance premium.

9. Many firms were acquired by others or became bankrupt during the period under examination. These were removed to keep the yearly data consistent regarding which firms remained in the sample.

10. Both Tobin's q and the market to book ratio were used as quality measures. Since all Tobin's q values appeared to be less than unity, this suggested that no firms had good investments. This is not necessarily a bad finding for many studies have revealed that Tobin's q for the aggregate economy was lower than unity during this period in India. By using the mean as a dividing point, the empirical work which follows seeks to determine if relative investment quality reveals that firms are following optimal earnings retention strategies.

4 The Cost of Capital

1. The financial statements for the largest 100 publicly traded firms were gathered. There has been some debate as to the weighting and the choice of firms used in this survey since small firms as a group face very different constraints in financial markets compared to their larger counterparts, as indicated in the previous chapter. Therefore, these comparative statistics are used a general guide and not as specific measures.

2. The Re-finance Corporation for Industry Ltd (RCI) was established for this purpose in 1958 and was subsequently merged with the Industrial Development Bank of India (IDBI) which was set up in 1964.

3. The first of these was the Industrial Finance Corporation (IFC), established in 1948. This was followed in 1951 with the setting up of regional institutions – the State Financial Corporation (SFC). Subsequently, the National Industrial Development Corporation (NIDC) was set up in 1954 and the Industrial Credit and Investment Corporation of India (ICICI) was floated in 1955. In 1964 the Industrial Development Bank of India (IDBI) was established as an institution for long and medium term finance.

4. Commercial banks are committed to providing 40% of their finances to 'priority sectors' which in addition to agriculture and other non-industrial activities, includes small-scale industry as well. Approximately 30% of this is at concessional rates of interest.

5. Other financial institutions including life insurance companies had been nationalised earlier. All property insurance companies were taken over by the central government in 1971.

6. Since 1988, there has been some simplification in the structure of administered rates.

7. A more detailed examination and discussion of leverage-induced bankruptcy costs will follow in the next chapter.

8. 'Moderate ranges' excludes firms such as holding companies whose main purpose might be to assume significant levels of debt and then used as a proxy firms during takeovers, mergers, etc.

9. Based on calculations in Titman and Wessels (1988) and DeAngelo and Masulis (1980).

10. See Maddala (1992) under modified zero regression method.
11. Gupta (1984) devised a measure for the real cost of equity. It is the sum of the average earnings yield and the ten year average growth rate in real non-farm domestic product. This is an approximate measure of the expected earning prospects of firms after taking into account firms' current yields and the past growth of the economy excluding the farm sector.
12. However, a problem may arise with this estimator if the unobservable effects which have been included in the error term are correlated with some of the regressor variables. For example, managers' risk aversion may cause them to invest in fewer positive net present value projects and thus slow the growth of their firm. This would imply that the omitted variable measuring risk is correlated with both leverage and growth. This simultaneity would render the 'random effects' estimators inconsistent. However, the estimation approach known as 'fixed effects' yields consistent estimates regardless of the correlation between firm-specific error components and the regressors.
13. A cross-comparison of common ratios amongst firms with different levels of debt will lead to significant discrepancies, as shown by Platt (1990). Therefore, one solution to this problem is to limit the sample to firms with similar levels of leverage in their financial structure (Platt and Platt, 1990).
14. Excess implies greater than the average for this particular data set which had already been pre-selected based on their 35%–40% levels of debt in their financial structures. Therefore, firms with excessive debt are those with greater than average debt within this pre-selected set. The same holds true for excessive retained earnings.
15. Bhagwati notes: 'the Indian embrace of bureaucratic controls was also encouraged by additional objectives, none of them served well by the control system in practice. One was the prevention of concentration of economic power by licensing the creation and expansion of capacity. But, if monopoly power was to be reduced, the virtual elimination of domestic and foreign competition, i.e., the elimination of the contestability of the market, was hardly the way to do it' (Bhagwati, 1993).

5 Earnings Retention as a Specification Mechanism in Predicting Corporate Bankruptcy

1. Government of India, BIFR (1995).
2. This might lead to a problem of *moral hazard* by having the same bank or financial institution as creditor as well as designer of the restructuring scheme.
3. These figures are the result of two sets of data. The first is a list of decisions taken by the BIFR in its first five years between July 1987 and July 1992 entitled *Review of Disposals* (*September 1992*). The second data set is taken from a set of reports describing sanctioned schemes under Section 18(4) of the SICA. This data has been used in several reports and studies including one by the Government of India, 1993.
4. The following is an excerpt from a Board member's report arguing how liquidation instead of rehabilitation 'would destroy all possibilities of

salvaging productive facilities, choke off the chance of debt recovery, finish the prospect of protecting a large proportion of employment' (Mahfooz, 1993).

5. Government of India, Ministry of Finance, Department of Economic Affairs (1993).

6. Government of India, Ministry of Finance, Department of Economic Affairs (1993).

7. Based on marginal gains model in Ponssard (1981).

8. For six of these firms, projections were based on 350 working days, and for another one 356. These figures are from actual data presented in annual BIFR reports.

9. In Ananth, Gangopadhyay and Chaudhari, (1994) a restructuring proposal was discovered where capacity figures were almost 33% than actual capacity. Even with such blatant overestimation, the project was labelled viable.

10. The DSCR is a ratio of the amount of income left for covering debt repayment in each year to the debt (interest and principal) that has to be repaid to term lenders.

11. Based on an examination in Ananth, Chaudhari and Gangopadhyay (1994) of 120 rehabilitation schemes over a three year period.

12. Tobin's q is calculated as (market value of common equity + value of long-term debt)/gross assets. Gross assets are used as replacement costs since it incorporates both the assets and liabilities of a firm as well as its holdings of other firms (Summers, 1981).

13. $Z = 1.2X_1 + 1.4X_2 + 3.3X_3 + 0.6X_4 + 1.0X_5$ where Z= overall index; X_1 = Working Capital/Total assets; X_2 = Retained Earnings/Total Assets; X_3 = Earnings Before Taxes and Interest/Total assets; X_4 = Market Value of Equity/Book Value of Total Debt; X_5 = Sales/Total Assets. Due to the original computer format arrangement, variables X_1 through X_4 must be calculated as absolute%age values. Only variable X_5 should be expressed in a different manner; that is, a Sales/Total Assets ratio of 200% should be included as 2.0.
For private companies, Altman based his model on a 1969–75 mixture of 61 manufacturing and 50 retailing organisations. Thus, the model for private companies is the following:
$$Z = 0.717X_1 + 0.847X_2 + 3.107X_3 + 0.420X_4 + 0.998X_5$$
where X_4 becomes Book Value of Equity/Book Value of Total Liabilities and the Cut-off Points are the following: $Z \geq 2.90$ Æ Healthy; $2.90 \geq Z \geq 1.23 \geq$ Gray Area; $Z \leq 2.90 \geq$ Distress.

14. Wilcox Model: $x > 0$ = Healthy; $x < 0$ = Distress;
P (Failure) $= 1$ if $x < 0$
$= [(1 - x) / (1 + x)]^N$ if $x > 0$
N = Adjusted Cash Position / a
Adjusted Cash Position = [Adjusted Cash Position + 0.7(Current Assets other than Cash) + 0.5(Long-term Assets – Liabilities]
a = [Mean Adjusted Cash Flow]^2 + Variance of Adjusted Cash Flow]$^{0.5}$
x = [Mean Adjusted Cash Flow / A]
Adjusted Cash Flow = [Net Income – Dividend – 0.3 (period-to-period increase in Non-Cash Assets – 0.5(period-to-period increase in long-term assets + Stock Issued in Merger or Acquisition]

15. $(X_{i,E}) = \text{Mean}\ (X_{i,\ F})$

    X = financial ratio, i = ratio 1,....,n; E = estimation period; F = forecast period

    'Industry relative ratios for a given industry are more stable than unadjusted ratios since there is a zero difference in their means between the estimation and forecast periods as compared to some difference for the unadjusted ratios. Thus, industry relative ratios are relatively more stable over time and hence should lead to more accurate forecasts' (Platt and Platt, 1990).

16. This derivative shows that the rate of change in probability with respect to X involves both B and the level of probability from which the change is measured. This value is greatest when $P = .5$.

17. The list of textile companies was prepared from the following:

    a. sick cotton textile companies coming under the National Textile Corporation Ltd.

    b. companies listed as sick by the Industrial Credit & Investment Corporation of India Ltd.

    c. companies explicitly taken over by the government for bankruptcy reasons.

    d. companies being assisted by the Industrial Reconstruction Corporation of India Ltd.

18. High technology industries might use higher gearing ratios so that they have greater leverage, whereas low technology industries might not use as much debt. A cross-comparison of common ratios amongst the different industries will lead to significant discrepancies, as shown by the Platts' study (Platt and Platt, 1990).

19. As it is difficult to quantify the specific number of cases, it occurred with greater frequency between 1990 and 1992, the latter portion of the period under study.

6 Factors Affecting the Market for Corporate Control

1. Other regulations pertaining to take over activity in India:

   (a) Indian Companies Act (1956) – any scheme of arrangement or settlement by shareholders/creditors of the firm, if and when approved by not less than 3/4 of the creditors and members, also requires the sanction of the courts. Companies in India are not allowed to invest more than 30% of their net worth in the shares of other companies without government approval (Section 372 of the Act).

   (b) Monopolies and Restrictive Trade Practices Act (1969) [MRTP] – To ensure that companies controlling 25% or more of the market for any product shall not become anti-competitive and are therefore prohibited from acquiring more than 10% stakes in any other company (Section 108A to 108I of the Act).

   (c) Foreign Exchange Regulations Act (1973) [FERA] – Regulates the dealings in foreign exchange and as such becomes relevant if and when shares in Indian firms are allotted to non-resident individuals.

   (d) Sick Industrial Companies Act (1985) [SICA] – SICA is a special statute to remove bottlenecks contained in various laws in the way of revival and rehabilitation of sick firms.

2. See Bradley, Desai and Kim (1988); Asquith, Bruner and Mullins (1987); Lang, Stultz and Walkling (1989).
3. See Rumelt (1974). He provides evidence that conglomerate firms underperform other firms . Sicherman and Pettway (1987) also provide evidence that prediction errors of contracting inefficiency is significantly higher from real asset diversification than real asset concentration.
4. Nearly identical to *financial flexibility*.
5. The minimum requirements for the sample set included the following:
   (a) Daily stock returns must be available in for the 100-day period starting 110 days before the initial take over announcement.
   (b) Public announcement of take over.
   (c) Balance sheet availability.
6. Liquidity is defined as the ratio of Current Assets/Current Liabilities.
7. Abnormal returns for targets and bidders are computed as the cumulative market model prediction error from the announcement date of the take over until the effective date. Cumulative market model prediction errors are measured around the announcement of all financing events. The cumulative prediction error for the common stock of firm j on day t is defined as the following:

$$\sum_{t=1}^{T} PE = R_{jt} - (\alpha_j + \beta_j R_{mt})$$

R_{jt} = continuously compounded rate of return for the common stock of firm j on day t.

R_{mt} = continuously compounded rate of return for the BSE equally weighted index on day t.

α_j, β_j = OLS estimates of firm j's market model parameters. (Doukas, 1995)

8. Other classification procedures have been tested including cut-offs at one, the industry average, and the industry median. For the purposes of the testing conducted in this paper, a relative rather than an absolute measure was needed and therefore a simple dummy variable method is used.
9. See Bradley, Desai and Kim (1988); Asquith, Bruner and Mullins (1987); Lang, Stultz and Walkling (1989).
10. This might be due to noise, mispecification, and the inclusion of further omitted variables might help.
11. See Lang, Stultz and Walkling (1989) and Bradley Desai, and Kim (1988).
12. Tirole requires banks to be competitive, thus earning zero profits. By equating the expected return from giving the loan D with the opportunity cost of D, or $(1 + r_o)D$, r_o is implicitly defined.
13. In this model, dividends also signal high firm quality because they also restrict cash flows.
14. The exact details are suppressed here to get to the issue of contract design under the threat of predation.
15. With the two-period problem, the exact result of this model is that: $R1^* = \pi_1$, $\beta_1^* = 1$, $R2^* = \pi_o$.
16. Derived from Poitevin's model of two or greater player games.
17. Poitevin's signalling equilibrium.

Bibliography

Akerlof, G. (1970) *The Market for Lemons: Quality Uncertainty and the Market Mechanism. Quarterly Journal of Economics*, 84: 488–500.

Allen, D. (1991) 'The Determinants of the Capital Structure of Listed Companies: The Financial Manager's Perspective', *Journal of Management*, 16: 103–23.

Allen, S. (1993) *Post-retirement Increases in Pensions in the 1980s: Did Plan Finances Matter?* NBER Working Paper, No. 4413.

Altman, E. (1968) 'Financial Ratios, Discriminant Analysis and the Prediction of Corporate Bankruptcy', *Journal of Finance*, 23: 589–609.

Altman, E (1983) *Corporate Financial Distress: A Complete Guide to Predicting, Avoiding, and Dealing with Bankruptcies*, New York: John Wiley & Sons.

Altman, E. and Izan, H. (1984) *Identifying Corporate Distress in Australia: An Industry Relative Analysis*, Working Paper, New York University.

Ananth, S., Gangopadhyay, P. and Goswami, O. (1992a) *Industrial Sickness in India: Initial Findings*, Government of India, Ministry of Industry, March.

Ananth, S., Gangopadhyay, P. and Goswami, O. (1992b) *Industrial Sickness in India: Characteristics, Determinants and History, 1970–1990*, Government of India, Ministry of Industry, October.

Ananth, S., Chaudhuri, S. and Gangopadhyay, P. (1994) 'Price Uncertainty and Credit Product Linkage', *Journal of International Trade and Economic Development*, 4: 93–113.

Ananth, S., Chaudhari, S., Gangopadhyay, P. and Goswami, O. (1994), *Industrial Sickness in India: Institutional Responses and Issues in Restructuring*, Indian Statistical Institute, April.

Ang, J., Chua, J. and McConell, J. (1982) 'The Administrative Costs of Corporate Bankruptcy: A Note', *Journal of Finance*, 37: 219–26.

Arrow, K. (1962) 'Economic Welfare and the Allocation of Resources for Invention', in (ed.) J. Schmookler *The Rate and Direction of Inventive Activity: Economic and Social Factors*, Princeton: Princeton University Press for the NBER.

Asquith, P. and Mullins, D. (1986) 'Equity Issues and Stock Price Dilution', *Journal of Financial Economics*, 15: 61–89.

Asquith, P., Mullins, D. and Bruner, R. (1987) *Merger Returns and the Form of Financing*, Working Paper, MIT.

Athey, M. and Laumas, P. (1994) 'Internal Funds and Corporate Investment in India', *Journal of Development Economics*, 45: 287–303.

Atje, R. and Jovanovic, B. (1993) 'Stock Markets and Development', *European Economic Review*, 32: 1167–89.

Barclay, M. and Smith, C. (1995) 'The Maturity Structure of Corporate Debt', *Journal of Finance*, 45: 342–67.

Bardhan, P. (1984) *The Political Economy of Development in India*, Oxford: Basil Blackwell.

Barnes, P. (1987) 'The Analysis and Use of Financial Ratios', *Journal of Business, Finance, and Accounting* (Winter 1987): 449–61.

Baumol, W. (1959) (1965) (1967) *Business Behavior, Value and Growth*, New York: Macmillan.

Baumol, W. (1965) *Economic Theory and Operations Analysis*, Englewood Cliffs, NJ: Prentice–Hall.

Berle, A. and Means, G. (1932) *The Modern Corporation and Private Property*, New York: Macmillan.

Beaver, W. (1966) 'Financial Ratios as Predictors of Failures', *Journal of Accounting Research*, 4: 71–102.

Berle, A. and Means G. (1989) 'Agency Costs, Net Worth, and Business Fluctuations', *American Economic Review*, 79: 14–31.

Bernanke, B. and Gertler, M. (1990) 'Financial Fragility and Economic Performance', *Quarterly Journal of Economics*. February: 87–114.

Bernanke, B., Gertler, M., and Gilchrist, S. (1993) 'Role of Credit Market Imperfections in the Monetary Transmission Mechanism: Arguments and Evidence,' *Scandinavian Journal of Economics*, 95: 43–64.

Betts, J. and Belhoul, D. (1987) 'The Effectiveness of Incorporating Stability Measures in Company Failure Models', *Journal of Business, Finance and Accounting* (Autumn): 323–34.

Bhaduri, S. (1999) 'A Critical Appraisal of the Effects of Financial Liberalization on Corporate Investment: India 1990–1995,' *International Journal of Development Banking (India)*, 1:3–11.

Bhaduri, S. (2000) 'Liberalisation and Firms' Choice of Financial Structure in an Emerging Economy: The Indian Corporate Sector', *Development Policy Review*, 18: 413–54.

Bhagwati, J. (1993) *India in Transition: Freeing the Economy*, Oxford: Oxford University Press.

Bhattacharya, S. and Ritter, J. (1983) 'Innovation and Communication: Signalling with Partial Disclosure', *Review of Economic Studies*, 50: 331–46.

Blanchard, O., Rhee, C. and Summers, L. (1993) *The Stock Market, Profit, and Investment*, NBER Working Paper, No. 3370.

Blanchard, O., de-Silanes, L. and Shleifer, A. (1994) 'What Do Firms Do with Cash Windfalls?', *Journal of Financial Economics*, 36: 337–60.

Bolton, P. and Scharfstein, D. (1990) 'Theory based on Agency Problems in Financial Contracting', *American Economic Review*, 80: 93–106.

Bradley, J., Jarell, L. and Kim, O. (1985) '*Tax Reform, Interest Rates, and Capital Allocation*,' NBER Working Paper, No. 1708.

Bradley, M., Desai, A. and Kim, E. (1988) 'Synergistic Gains from Corporate Acquisitions and their Division between the Stockholders of Target and Acquiring Firms', *Journal of Financial Economics*, 21: 3–40.

Brainard, W., Shoven, J. and Weiss, L. (1980) 'The Financial Valuation and the Returns to Capital', *Brookings Papers on Economic Activity*, 2: 453–511.

Browne, L. and Rosengren, E. (1987) *The Merger Boom: Proceedings*, Federal Reserve Bank of Boston.

Calomiris, Charles and Hubbard, Glenn. (1990) 'Firm Heterogeneity, Internal Finance, and Credit Rationing', *Economic Journal* 100: 90–104.

Carlin, W. and Mayer, C. (1999) *Finance, Investment and Growth*, CEPR Discussion paper, 2233.

Caruthers, J., Pinches, G., Mingo, K. (1973) 'The Stability of Financial Patterns in Industrial Organizations,' *Journal of Finance*, 28: 389–96.

Castanias, R. (1983) 'Bankruptcy Risk and Optimal Capital Structure', *Journal of Finance*, 38: 1617–35.

Castanias, R. and Chaplinsky, H. (1990) 'Managerial and Windfall Rents in the Market for Corporate Control,' *Journal of Economic Behaviour and Organization*, 18: 153–84.

Chaplinsky, S. and Niehaus, G. (1990) *The Determinants of Inside Ownership and Leverage*, University of Michigan Working Paper.

Chari, V. and Jaganathan R. (1988) 'Seasonalities in Security Returns: The Case of Earnings Announcements', *Journal of Financial Economics*, 21: 101–21.

Chauvin, K. and Hirschey, M. (1993) 'Advertising, R&D Expenditures and the Market Value of the Firm', *Financial Management*, 22: 128–40.

Chenery, H. (1952) *Turkish Investment and Economic Development Ankara*, United States Operations Mission to Turkey, Foreign Operations Administration.

Cherian, S. (1996) *The Stock market as a Source of Finance : a Comparison of U.S. and Indian Firms*, World Bank Working Paper, No. 1592.

Chirinko, R. (1993) 'Business Acceleration and the Law of Demand: A Technical Factor in Economic Cycles', *Journal of Economic Literature*, 31: 1875–911.

Chirinko, R. and Schaller, H. (1995) 'Why Does Liquidity Matter in Investment Equations?', *Journal of Money, Credit and Banking*, 27: 527–48.

Clark, J. (1917) *The Distribution of Wealth : A Theory of Wages, Interest and Profits*, New York: Macmillan.

Clark, P. (1979) 'Investment in the 1970's: Theory Performance and Prediction', *Brookings Papers on Economic Activity*, 1: 73–113.

Cobham, D. and Subramaniam, R. (1995) *Corporate Finance in Developing Countries: New Evidence for India*, University of St. Andrews, Discussion Paper 9512.

Corbett, J. and Jenkinson, T. (1994) *The Financing of Industry, 1970–1989: An International Comparison*, CEPR Discussion Paper, No. 958.

Cowling, K. and Waterson, M. (1976) 'Price Cost Margins and Market Structure', *Economica*, 43: 267–74.

DeAngelo, H. and Masulis, R. (1980) 'Optimal Capital Structure under Corporate and Personal Taxation', *Journal of Financial Economics*, 8: 3–29.

Dellariccia, L. and Marquez, R. (2000) *Flight to Quality or Captivity: Information and Credit Allocation*, IMF Working Paper.

Demirguc-Kunt, A. and Maksimovic, V. (1994a) *Capital Structures in Developing Countries*, World Bank Working Paper (1320).

Demirguc-Kunt, A. and Maksimovic, V. (1994b) *Stock Market Development and Firm Financing Choices*, World Bank Working Paper (1461).

Demirguc-Kunt, A. and Maksimovic, V. (1999), 'Institutions, Financial Markets and Firm Debt Maturity', *Journal of Financial Economics*, 54: 295–336.

Dhumale, R. (1997) *The Case for Earnings Retention in the Development of Corporate Bankruptcy Models*, Cambridge Discussion Papers, No. 93.

Diamond, D. (1991) 'Monitoring and Reputation: The Choice between Bank Loans and Directly Placed Debt', *Journal of Political Economy*, 99.

Donaldson, G. (1961) *Corporate Debt Capacity: A Study of Corporate Debt Policy and the Determinants of Corporate Debt Capacity*, Boston: Harvard Business School Research Division.

Doukas, J. (1995) 'Overinvestment, Tobin's q and Gains from Foreign Acquisitions', *Journal of Banking and Finance*, 19: 1285–303.

Downe, E., and Pan, W. (1992) 'Why does Business Invest'? An Analysis of Industry Accounting Data,' *Journal of Post Keynesian Economics*, 15: 51–61.

Duesenberry, J. (1958) *Business Cycles and Economic Growth*, New York: McGraw Hill.

Easterbrook, F. (1984) 'Two Agency Cost Explanations of Dividends', *American Economic Review*. 74: 650–9.

Eisner, R. (1964) 'Factors in Business Investment,' NBER General Series, No. 102.

Fama, E. (1985) 'What's Different About Banks?', *Journal of Monetary Economics*, 15: 29–39.

Fazzari, S., Hubbard G. and Petersen., B. (1988) 'Financing Constraints and Corporate Investment', *Brookings Paper on Economic Activity*, 1: 142–206.

Friedman, B. and Laibson, D. (1989) 'Economic Implications of Extraordinary Movements in Stock Prices', *Brookings Papers on Economic Activity*, 2: 137–189.

Frydl, E. (1987) *Changes in the Organisation and Regulation of Capital Markets*, BIS Monetary and Economics Department.

Fundenberg, D. and Tirole, J. (1986) 'Signal Jamming Theory of Predation', *RAND Journal of Economics*, 17: 366–76.

Gale, D. and Hellwig, M. (1985) 'Incentive Compatible Debt Contracts: The One Period Problem', *Review of Economic Studies*, 52: 647–63.

Gertler, M. (1988) 'Financial Structure and Aggregate Economic Activity: An Overview', *Journal of Money, Credit and Banking*, 20: 559–96.

Gertner, R., Gibbons, R. and Scharfstein, D. (1988) 'Simultaneous Signalling to the Capital and Product Markets', *RAND Journal of Economics*, 19: 173–190.

Gilson, S. (1989) 'Management Turnover and Financial Distress', *Journal of Financial Economics*, 25: 345–67.

Glen, J. K., Miller, R. and Shah, S. (1995) *Dividend Policy and Behaviour in Emerging Markets*, Washington, DC; International Finance Corporation.

Government of India, Bajaj Committee (1992) *Report of the Inter-Ministerial Working Group on Industrial Restructuring*, March 1992.

Government of India, BIFR (1992) *Review of Disposals*, September 1992.

Government of India, BIFR (1995) *A Review as on 31st December 1994*, January 1995.

Government of India, Ministry of Finance, Department of Economic Affairs (1993) *Public Sector Banks and Financial Sector Reform: Rebuilding for a Better Future*, December 1993.

Government of India, Narasimham Committee (1991) *Report of The Committee on the Financial System*, December 1991.

Grabowski, H. and Mueller D. (1972) 'Managerial and Stockholder Welfare Models of Firm Expenditures', *Review of Economics and Statistics*, 54: 9–24.

Greenwald, B., Stiglitz, J. and Weiss, A. (1984) 'Informational Imperfections in Capital Markets and Macroeconomic Fluctuations', *American Economic Review*, 74: 194–199.

Grossman, S. and Hart, O. (1982) 'Takeover Bids, the Free Rider Problem and the Theory of the Corporation', *Bell Journal of Economics*, 11: 42–64.

Grossman S. and Hart, O. (1986) 'The Costs and Benefits of Ownership: A Theory of Vertical and Lateral Integration', *Journal of Political Economy*, 94: 691–719.

Gupta, L. (1969) *The Changing Structure of Industrial Finance in India: The Impact of Institutional Finance*, New Delhi: Oxford University Press.

Gupta, R.. (1984) 'Simultaneous Comparison of Scale Estimators,' *Sankhya: Indian Journal of Statistics*, 46: 275–80.

Hadlock, C. (1998) 'Ownership, Liquidity and Investment', *RAND Journal of Economics*, 29: 487–508.

Harris, M. and Raviv, A. (1990) 'Capital Structure and the Informational Role of Debt', *Journal of Finance*, 45: 321–49.

Harris, M. and Raviv, A. (1991) 'Theory of Capital Structure,' *Journal of Finance*, 46: 297–355.

Harris, M. *et al.* (1996) 'The Capital Budgeting Process: Incentives and Information,' *Journal of Finance*, 51:1139–74.

Hayashi, F. (1982) *Effect of Liquidity Constraints on Consumption: a Cross Sectional Analysis*, NBER Working Paper, No. 882.

Himmelberg, C. and Petersen, M. (1994) 'Commercial Paper, Corporate Finance and the Business Cycle: A Microeconomic Perspective', NBER Working Paper 4848.

Hoshi, T., Kashyap, A. and Scharfstein, D. (1990) 'Bank Monitoring and Investment: Evidence from the Changing Structure of Japanese Corporate Banking Relationships', in *Asymmetric Information , Corporate Finance and Investment*, ed. R. Glenn Hubbard, pp. 105–26, Chicago and London: The University of Chicago Press.

Hoshi, T., Kashyap, A. and Scharfstein, A. (1991) 'Corporate Structure, L:iquidity and Investment: Evidence from Japanese Industrial Groups', *Quarterly Journal of Economics*, 106: 33–60.

Howe, J. (1990) 'Insider Trading in the OTC Market', *Journal of Finance*, 45: 1273–95.

Hsiao, C. (1989) *Analysis of Panel Data.*, New York: Cambridge University Press.

Hubbard Glenn (1990) 'Introduction', in *Asymmetric Information, Corporate Finance and Finance*, Chicago: University of Chicago Press: 1–14.

Izan, H. (1984) 'Corporate Distress in Australia,' *Journal of Banking and Finance*, 8: 303–20.

Jaramillo, F., Schiantarelli, F. and Weiss, A. (1993) *The Effect of Financial Liberalisation on the Allocation of Credit: Panel Data Evidence for Ecuador*, Policy Research Working Paper, World Bank.

Jensen, M. (1986) 'Agency Costs of Free Cash Flow, Corporate Finance and Takeovers', *AER Papers and Proceedings*, 76 (2): 323–9.

Jensen, M. (1987) 'Symposium on Investment Banking and the Capital Acquisition Process,' *Journal of Financial Economics*, 15: 1–281.

Jensen, M. (1993) 'The Modern Industrial Revolution, Exit and the Failure of Internal Control Systems', *Journal of Finance*, 48: 831–80.

Jensen, M. and Meckling, W. (1976) 'Theory of the Firm: Managerial Behaviour, Agency Costs and Capital Structure', *Journal of Financial Economics*, 3: 305–60.

Jorgenson, D. (1963) 'Capital Theory and Investment Behaviour', *American Economic Review*, 53: 247–59.

Jorgenson, D. *et al.* (1963) *A Comparison of Alternative Econometric Models of Quarterly Investment Behavior*, Working Papers in Economic Theory and Econometrics / Berkeley, No. 55.

Jorgenson, D. *et al.* (1966) *The Predictive Performance of Econometric Models of Quarterly Investment Behavior*, Working Papers in Economic Theory and Econometrics / Berkeley, No. 111.

Jorgenson, D. *et al.* (1967) *Tax Policy and Investment Behavior: Further Results,* Working Papers in Economic Theory and Econometrics,Berkeley, No. 146.

Jorgenson, D. *et al.* (1971) *U.S. Income, Saving, and Wealth, 1929–1969',* Discussion Paper Harvard Institute of Economic Research, No. 266.

Kashyap, A., Stein, J., and Wilcox, D. (1993) *Monetary Policy and Bank Lending',* NBER Working Paper, No. 4317.

Kashyap, A. and Stein, J. (1992) 'Monetary Policy and Bank Lending', Paper prepared for NBER Conference on Monetary Policy: 1–54.

Kester, W. (1986) 'Capital and Ownership Structure: A Comparison of Japanese and United States Manufacturing Corporations', *Financial Management,* 5: 5–16.

Koch, A. (1943) *The Financing of Large Corporations, 1920–1939,* New York: NBER.

Koyck, L. (1954) *Distributed Lags and Investment Analysis,* Amsterdam: Elsevier.

Kuh, E. (1963) *Capital Stock Growth: A Micro-Econometric Approach,* Amsterdam: North-Holland Publishing Co.

Lang, L. and Litzenberger, R. (1989) 'What Information is Contained in the Dividend Announcement?' *Journal of Financial Economics,* 24:181–191.

Lang, L., Stultz, R. and Walkling R. (1989) 'Managerial Performance, Tobin's *q* and the gains from successful tender offers', *Journal of Financial Economics,* 24: 137–154.

Lang, L., Stulz, R. and Walkling, R. (1991) 'A Test of the Free Cash Flow Hypothesis: The Case of Bidder Returns', *Journal of Financial Economics* 14: 399–422.

Lang, L., Otek, E. and Stultz, R. (1996) 'Leverage, Investment and Firm Growth', *Journal of Financial Economics,* 40: 3–29.

La Porta, R., Lopez-de-Silanes, F., Shleifer, A. and Vishny, R. (1998) 'Law and Finance', *Journal of Political Economy,* 106.

Leibenstein, H. (1976) *Beyond Economic Man,* Cambridge, Mass.: Harvard University Press.

Lo, A. (1986) 'Logit versus Discriminant Analysis: A Specification Test and Application to Corporate Bankruptcy', *Journal of Econometrics,* 31: 151–78.

Lowe, P. and Rohling, T. (1993) 'Agency Costs, Balance Sheets and the Business Cycle', *Journal of Financial Management,* 14: 538–553.

MacKie-Mason, Jeffrey K. (1990) 'Do Firms Really Care Who Provides Their Financing?' in *Asymmetric Information, Corporate Finance and Finance,* Chicago: University of Chicago Press.

Maddala, G. (1992) *Introduction to Econometrics,* New York: Macmillan.

Mahfooz, A. (1993) *A Critique of the Goswami Report,* September.

Malitz, I. (1985) 'The Investment Financing Nexus: Some Empirical Evidence', *Midland Corporate Finance Journal,* 3: 53–9.

Marris, R. (1963) (1964) *The Economic Theory of 'Managerial' Capitalism,* London: Macmillan.

Marris, R. (1964) *The Economic Theory of Managerial Capitalism,* Glencoe: Free Press.

Masulis, R. and Korwar, A. (1986) 'Seasoned Equity Offerings: An Empirical Investigation', *Journal of Financial Economics,* 15: 91–118.

Mayer, C. (1988) 'New Issues in Corporate Finance', *European Economic Review,* 32: 1167–89.

Mayer, C. (1990) 'Financial Systems, Corporate Finance and Economic Development', in *Asymmetric Information, Corporate Finance and Investment*, ed., R. Hubbard, Cambridge: NBER.

McConnell, J. and Muscarella, C. (1985) 'Corporate Capital Expenditure Decisions and the Market Value of the Firm,' *Journal of Financial Economics*, 14: 399–422.

McConnell, J. and Servaes, H. (1995) 'Equity Ownership and the Two Faces of Debt', *Journal of Financial Economics*, 39: 131–57.

McFadden, D. (1973) 'Conditional Logit Analysis of Qualitative Choice Behavior,' in P. Zarembka (ed.) *Frontiers in Econometrics*, New York: Academic Press.

Meyer, J. and Glauber, R. (1964) *Investment Decisions, Economic Forecasting, and Public Policy'*, Division of Research, Graduate School of Business Administration, Harvard University.

Meyer, J. and Kuh, E. (1957) *The Investment Decision*, Cambridge, Mass.: Harvard University Press.

Meyer, J. and Strong, J. (1990) 'Valuation Effects of Holding Gains on Long Term Debt,' *Journal of Accounting and Economics*, 13: 267–83.

Mikkelson, W. H. and Parch, M. (1985) 'Stock Price Effects and Costs of Secondary Distributions', *Journal of Financial Economics*, 14: 165–94.

Miller, M. (1977) 'Debt and Taxes', *Journal of Finance*, 32: 261–76.

Miller, M. (1988) 'The Modigliani–Miller Propositions after Thirty Years', *Journal of Economic Perspectives*, 2: 99–120.

Mitchell, M., McCormick, R. and Maloney, M. (1993) 'Managerial Decision Making and Capital Structure', *Journal of Business*, 66: 189–217.

Modigliani, F. and Miller, M. (1958) 'The Cost of Capital, Corporation Finance and the Theory of Investment', *American Economic Review*, 48: 261–97.

Modigliani, F. and Miller, M. (1963) 'Corporate Income Taxes and the Cost of Capital: A Correction', *American Economic Review*, 53: 433–43.

Morck, R., Shleifer, A. and Vishny, R. (1990) 'Do Managerial Objectives Drive Bad Acquisitions?' *Journal of Finance*, 45: 31–48.

Mueller, D. (1972) 'A Life Cycle Theory of the Firm', *Journal of Industrial Economics*, 20: 199–219.

Mueller, D. and Reardon, E. (1993) 'Rates of Return on Corporate Investment', *Southern Economic Journal*, 60: 430–53.

Myers, K. (1984) *Growth, External Financing, and the Bank*, Country Policy Dept., World Bank.

Myers, S. (1977) 'Determinants of Corporate Borrowing', *Journal of Financial Economics*, 5: 14–175.

Myers, S. (1984) 'Corporate and Financing and Investment Decisions When Firms Have Information that Investors Do Not Have', *Journal of Financial Economics*, 13: 187–221.

Myers, S. and Majluf, N. (1984) 'Corporate Financing and Investment Decisions When Firms Have Information That Investors Do Not Have', *Journal of Financial Economics*, 13: 187–221.

Nabi, I. (1989) 'Investment in Segmented Capital Markets,' *Quarterly Journal of Economics*, 104: 453–62.

Nachman, D. and John, K. (1985) 'Risky Debt, Investment Incentives and Reputation in Sequential Equilibrium', *Journal of Finance*, 40: 863–78.

Niehaus, G. (1983) 'Leveraged ESOP Financing and Risk,' *Financial Analysts Journal*, 46: 10–13.

Oliner, S. and Rudebusch, G. (1993) 'Sources of the Financing Hierarchy for Business Investment', *Review of Economics and Statistics*, 74: 643–54.

Pantalone, C. and Platt, M. (1987) 'Predicting Failure of Savings and Loan Associations', *Real Estate and Urban Economics Association Journal*, 15: 46–64.

Penrose, E. (1959) *The Theory of the Growth of the Firm*, Oxford: Basil Blackwell.

Petersen, M. and Rajan, R. (1994) 'Benefits of Lending Relationships: Evidence from Small Business Data,' *Journal of Finance*, 49: 3–37.

Pettit, R. (1972) 'Dividend Announcements, Security Performance and Capital Market Efficiency', *Journal of Finance*, 27 (5):993–1007.

Pettway, R. and Radcliffe, R. (1985) 'Impacts of New Equity Sales upon Electric Utility Share Prices', *Financial Management*, 14: 16–25.

Pinches, G., Mingo, K. and Caruthers, J. (1973) 'The Stability of Financial Patterns in Industrial Organisations', *Journal of Finance*, 28: 389–96.

Pinegar M. and Wilbricht, L. (1989) 'What Managers Think of Capital Structure Theory: A Survey', *Financial Management*, 18: 82–9.

Platt, H. (1990) 'Business Cycle Effects on State Corporate Failure Rates,' *Journal of Economics and Business*, 46: 113–27.

Platt, M. (1990) 'Bankruptcy Discriminant with Real Variables', *Journal of Business Finance–Accounting*, 18: 491–510.

Platt, H. and Platt, M. (1990) 'Development of a Class of Stable Predictive Variables: The Case of Bankruptcy Prediction', *Journal of Business, Finance and Accounting*, 17: 31–51.

Poitevin, M. (1989) 'Financial Signalling and the 'Deep Pocket' Argument', *RAND Journal of Economics*, 20: 26–40.

Ponssard, J. (1981) *Competitive Strategies: An Advanced Textbook in Game Theory*, New York: North Holland.

Prais, S. (1976) *The Evolution of Giant Firms in Britain: A Study of the Growth of Concentration in Manufacturing Industry in Britain, 1909–70*, Cambridge: Cambridge University Press.

Radelet, S. and Sachs, J. (1998) 'The Onset of the East Asian Financial Crisis', *Harvard Institute for International Development*, 4, no. 2.

Rajan, R. (1992) 'Insiders and Outsiders: The Choice between Informed and Arm's-Length Debt', *Journal of Finance*, 47: 1367–400.

Rajan, R. (1994) 'Why Bank Credit Policies Fluctuate: A Theory and Some Evidence', *Quarterly Journal of Economics*, 109: 339–441.

Rajan, R. and Zingales, L. (1995) 'What Do We Know About Capital Structure?' *Journal of Finance*, 50: 1521–60.

Rajan, R. and Zingales, L. (1998) *The Cost of Diversity: the Diversification Discount and Inefficient Investment*', NBER Working Paper, No. 6368.

Rangarajan, C. and Jadhav, N. (1992) 'Issues in Financial Sector Reform', in B. Jalan, (ed.), *The Indian Economy Problems and Prospects*, New Delhi: Penguin Viking Ltd.

Ravid, S. and Oded, S. (1991) 'Financial Signalling by Committing Cash Outflows', *Journal of Financial and Quantitative Analysis*, 26: 165–80.

Ravid, S. and Sarig, O. (1991) 'Dividend Surprises Inferred from Option and Stock Prices,' *Journal of Finance*, 47: 1623–40.

Reserve Bank of India (various issues) *Reserve Bank of India Bulletin*, Bombay: Reserve Bank of India.

Ross, S. (1977) 'The Determinants of Financial Structure: The Incentive Signalling Approach', *Bell Journal of Economics*, 8: 23–40.

Ross, T. (1991) 'On the Relative Efficiency of Cash Transfers and Subsidies,' *Economic Inquiry*, 29: 485–96.

Rozeff, M. (1982) 'Growth, Beta and Agency Costs as Determinants of Dividend Payout Ratios', *Journal of Financial Research*, 5: 249–59.

Rumelt, R. (1974) *Strategy, Structure and Economic Performance*, Cambridge, Mass.: Harvard University Press.

Samuel, C. (1996) *The Stock Market as a Source of Finance: A Comparison of U.S. and Indian Firms*, World Bank, Policy Working Paper (1592).

Shleifer, A. and Vishny, R. (1993), 'Liquidation Values and Debt Capacity: A Market Equilibrium Approach', *Journal of Finance*, 47: 252–75.

Sicherman, N. and Pettway, R. (1987) 'Acquisition of Divested Assets and Shareholder Wealth', *Journal of Finance*, 42: 1261—73.

Singh, A. (1998) *How Competitive are the Emerging Markets? An Analysis of Corporate Rates of Return from Nine Emerging Markets,'* IMF Seminar Series.

Singh, A. and Hamid, J. (1992) *Corporate Financial Structures in Developing Countries*, Washington DC: International Finance Corporation.

Smith, C. and Watts, R. (1992) 'The Investment Opportunity Set and Corporate Financing, Dividend and Compensation Policies', *Journal of Financial Economics*, 32: 263–92.

Stewart, G. (1991) *The Quest for Value*, New York: HarperCollins Inc.

Stiglitz, J. (1974) 'Incentives and Risk Sharing in Sharecropping', *Review of Economic Studies*, 41(2): 27–59.

Stiglitz, J. (1992) 'Capital Markets and Economic Fluctuations in Capitalist Economies', *European Economic Review*, 36: 269–306.

Stiglitz, J. and Weiss, A. (1981) 'Credit Rationing in Markets with Imperfect Information', *American Economic Review*, 71: 393–410.

Stoh, M. and Mauer, D. (1996) 'The Determinants of Corporate Debt Maturity Structure', *Journal of Business*, 69: 279–311.

Stultz, R. (1990) 'Forward Exchange Rate and Macroeconomics,' *Journal of International Economics*: 12: 285–99.

Summers, L. (1981) 'Taxation and corporate investment: A *q* Theory Approach', *Brookings Papers on Economic Activity*: 67–127.

Tinbergen, J. (1938) *Business Cycles in the United States of America, 1919–1937*, Geneva: League of Nations.

Titman, S. and Wessels R. (1988) 'The Determinants of Capital Structure Choice', *Journal of Finance*, 43: 1–19.

Tirole, J. (1988) *The Theory of Industrial Organisation*, Cambridge, Mass: MIT Press.

Travlos, N. (1987) 'Corporate Takeover Bids, Methods of Payment and Bidding Firm Stock Returns', *Journal of Finance*, 42: 943–63.

Tybout, J. (1983) 'Credit Rationing and Investment Behavior in a Developing Country,' *Review of Economics and Statistics*, 65:598–607.

Vishny, R. (1988) 'Alternative Mechanisms for Corporate Control,' *American Economic Review*: 79:842–52.

Vogt, S. (1994) 'Cash Flow/Investment Relationship: Evidence from U.S. Manufacturing Firms', *Financial Management*, 23: 3–20.

Wade, R. and Veneroso, F. (1998) 'The Asian Crisis: The High Debt Model vs. the Wall Street–Treasury–IMF Complex', *New Left Review*, 228: 3–23.

Weisbach, M. (1990) 'An Agency Perspective on Franchising,' *Financial Management*, Spring, 27–35.

Weisbach, M. and Kaplan, S. (1990) Acquisitions and Diversification: What is Divested and How Much Does the Market Anticipate?', Working Paper, University of Chicago.

Weiss, L. (1990) 'Bankruptcy Resolution: Direct Cost and Violation of Priority Claims', *Journal of Financial Economics*, 27: 1–26.

Wilcox, J. (1976) 'The Gambler's Ruin Approach to Business Risk', *Sloane Management Review*, Fall 1976: 33–46.

Williamson, O. (1964) *The Economics of Discretionary Behaviour: Managerial Objectives in a Theory of the Firm*, New Jersey: Prentice-Hall.

World Bank and Confederation of Indian Industry (2002) *Investment Climate in India: Impact on Competitiveness of Manufacturing Firms*, Joint Report presented in New Delhi, India.

Wruck, K. (1990) 'Financial Distress, Reorganisation and Organisational Efficiency', *Journal of Financial Economics*, 27: 437–65.

Zavgren, C. (1985) 'Assessing the Vulnerability of Failure of American Industrial Firms: A Logistic Analysis', *Journal of Business, Finance and Accounting*, 12: 19–45.

Zmijewski, M. (1984) 'Methodological Issues Related to the Estimation of Financial Distress Prediction Models', *Journal of Accounting Research* (Supplement), 22: 59–82.

Index